MILTON STUDIES

XVI

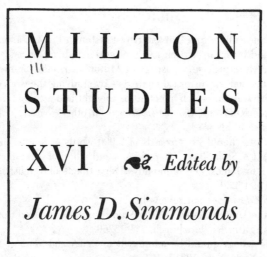

MILTON
STUDIES
XVI ❧ *Edited by*

James D. Simmonds

UNIVERSITY OF PITTSBURGH PRESS

MILTON STUDIES

is published annually by the University of Pittsburgh Press as a forum for Milton scholarship and criticism. Articles submitted for publication may be biographical; they may interpret some aspect of Milton's writings; or they may define literary, intellectual, or historical contexts—by studying the work of his contemporaries, the traditions which affected his thought and art, contemporary political and religious movements, his influence on other writers, or the history of critical response to his work.

Manuscripts should be upwards of 3,000 words in length and should conform to the MLA *Style Sheet*. Manuscripts and editorial correspondence should be addressed to James D. Simmonds. Department of English. University of Pittsburgh, Pa. 15260.

Milton Studies does not review books.

Within the United States, *Milton Studies* may be ordered from the University of Pittsburgh Press, Pittsburgh, Pa. 15260.

Overseas orders should be addressed to Feffer and Simons, Inc., 100 Park Avenue, New York, N.Y. 10017, U.S.A.

Library of Congress Catalog Card Number 69-12335

ISBN 0-8229-3174-5 (Volume I) (out of print)

ISBN 0-8229-3194-X (Volume II)

ISBN 0-8229-3218-0 (Volume III)

ISBN 0-8229-3244-X (Volume IV)

ISBN 0-8229-3272-5 (Volume V)

ISBN 0-8229-3288-1 (Volume VI)

ISBN 0-8229-3305-5 (Volume VII)

ISBN 0-8229-3310-1 (Volume VIII)

ISBN 0-8229-3329-2 (Volume IX)

ISBN 0-8229-3356-X (Volume X)

ISBN 0-8229-3373-X (Volume XI)

ISBN 0-8229-3376-4 (Volume XII)

ISBN 0-8229-3404-3 (Volume XIII)

ISBN 0-8229-3429-9 (Volume XIV)

ISBN 0-8229-3449-7 (Volume XV)

ISBN 0-8229-3465-5 (Volume XVI)

US ISSN 0076-8820

Published by the University of Pittsburgh Press. Pittsburgh. Pa. 15260

CONTENTS

CONTENTS

MILTON STUDIES

XVI

EVE, THE SEPARATION SCENE, AND THE RENAISSANCE IDEA OF ANDROGYNY

Marilyn R. Farwell

IN THE last ten years, as scholars of Milton have felt the influence of the women's movement on the academic world, Milton's attitudes toward women have been alternately defamed and praised.[1] Despite some premature indications of weariness with the debate, as if the argument over Milton's feminism or antifeminism only deterred us from the more serious matters of punctuation and cosmology, this question is now one of the most vigorous and interesting in Milton scholarship.[2] Not only has this discussion provided us with insights concerning Milton's attitude toward women, knowledge necessary for understanding Milton's life and art, it has also introduced us to matters which previously have been ignored or considered tangential. One such matter is androgyny. This ancient mythic ideal of the unity of male and female principles in God and in the first human being has furnished substance for the argument which maintains that Milton's inclusion of the female principle in his descriptions of God and humanity affirms his respect for women. Although aspects of this mythic pattern have been part of Milton scholarship for years, the concentration on the term androgyny and the use of this idea to defend Milton's opinion of women, particularly of Eve, are new.[3] However, the idea is fraught with problems from both historical and feminist points of view, and, I believe, a thorough analysis is necessary to determine the viability of this term for Milton.

The exploration of androgyny in Milton's poetry and in other areas of literature owes much to interest in this idea created by feminist scholars and theoreticians over the last fifteen years. Initially, many students of androgyny embraced the idea as a panacea; later, after theoretical probing, many dismissed it as hypocritical. These positions have been held at different times by the same writer.[4] If we are to use this idea to describe Milton's attitude toward women, we must take advantage of these insights; as we are quick to demand of Milton's feminist assailants that they learn the historical and ideological context in which he wrote, so we must be alert to feminist analyses which have brought androgyny into question. By applying these insights to the historical

3

ideas of androgyny available to Milton, we will, I believe, begin to clarify the limits of this idea for analysis of Milton's female characters. To encompass this material in a short essay, I have chosen to limit my application of these ideas to Eve and to the crucial separation scene in *Paradise Lost*, for, as some argue, it is in Book IX that the androgynous couple becomes, symbolically as well as literally, separate and fallen.[5] I hope to prove that androgyny is inadequate and inaccurate as a description of the complex character of Eve and as a tool for the interpretation of the separation scene.

The separation is a scene not only crucial to our understanding of Milton's use of androgyny, but also most problematic to our reading of Milton's long and problem-filled poem. Not long ago, A. E. Barker claimed that Eve's insistence on working alone at the beginning of Book of IX "currently presents us with one of the most serious cruxes confronting our interpretive endeavors."[6] The commentary on this section of *Paradise Lost* divides into two vigorously opposing camps. On the one hand, critics believe that, in practical terms, the separation constitutes the Fall itself, or that, less drastically, it forges one more link in the chain of Adam's and Eve's spiritual deterioration. Because, they argue, Eve insists upon her own will and therefore fails in her wifely duty of obedience, and because Adam neglects to assert his natural authority, the separation scene becomes the penultimate instance of an imperfection which they exhibit throughout the poem.[7] So influential has been this view that one critic remarked that to believe Adam fell before the Fall "is the conclusion of all the respectable critics; or to be considered a respectable critic of Milton, one must at least hold that view."[8] On the other hand is a strong group of critics who refuse to acknowledge that the separation scene is permeated with fatalism. These scholars mitigate the fatalism of the first approach by arguing that Adam's and Eve's reason and freedom remain intact throughout their temptations and even through their errors of judgment.[9] The mistake of separation does not negate their sufficiency to encounter Satan.

An essential part of this last argument must center on the nature of Eve, for if she is incapable of the liberty to decide and act alone, she and Adam are indeed fated at the moment they separate for the first time. A number of scholars, primarily women interested in forging a characterization of a substantial Eve to counter descriptions of her "mental triviality,"[10] have focused our attention on an Eve who, with Adam, inherits the freedom for which Milton adamantly argues in *Areopagitica*. Thus Stella Revard asserts that the radical nature of Miltonic freedom "would die were Adam the 'prince' to tyrannize the will of the 'subject'

Eve, and the repercussions of that death would be felt all the way to the throne of God where originated the principle of government sustained by the willing and loving service of inferiors to their lord."[11] Diane McColley, whose extensive reparation of Eve's character constitutes the major defense of her leave-taking in Book IX, argues that to deny Eve's sufficiency is also to deny "Milton's libertarian principles."[12] While critics who wish to reject this position must argue with James Holly Hanford that the logic of *Areopagitica* "does not apply to the immature and weak,"[13] the defense of Eve's right to free choice at the beginning of Book IX has led not only to a cautious respect for what at most can be termed an error of judgment, but also to McColley's bold assertion that Eve may have a right to tend her garden alone.[14]

Eve's sufficiency cannot, however, be maintained only on the basis of Milton's concept of freedom. Eve's ontological status must be considered a predeterminant of her right to freedom. If the description of her relationship with Adam is such that she constitutes only part of a whole, this scene does embody the Fall; if, on the other hand, the relationship is such that she and Adam can sustain separation without destroying individual wholeness and sufficiency, then this scene provides a temptation, perhaps a temptation to growth. Although critics disagree on the specific nature of their relationship, most cluster around the vague belief that Adam and Eve are inseparably one, bound in an ontological whole, for which several critics have rescued the term androgyny. In these approaches, Adam and Eve represent two aspects of human existence united in paradisal harmony. Individuality, in these cases, is a postlapsarian experience. Although the biblical description of husband and wife as one flesh provides a foundation for such a belief, more influential are the Renaissance Platonic, mystical, and allegorical interpretations of which, as we shall see, androgyny is a part. Frank Huntley describes a pattern of Western thought, prominent in *Paradise Lost,* which relies on the image of the marriage of male and female in these Platonic and Hegelian terms: "there is a division into two universal terms; these terms are opposites; at the outset one of them is usually given a higher value than the other; and they must be of such a kind as to allow their combination to produce an ideal, a *tertium quid* which is greater than the mere sum of the two parts."[15] The allegorical fusion of Adam and Eve in a static ontological whole has been described variously as the union of soul and body, soul and intellect, reason and senses. As Michael Lieb notes, the result is a relationship in which "two halves complement each other in one whole union."[16]

Other descriptions of the androgyny of Adam and Eve amplify this point of view. Don Parry Norford finds in the ancient androgynous myths of world parents, of yin and yang, metaphors for the relationship of Adam and Eve; thus he must conclude that "because of her rebellion and fall, man and woman, *yang* and *yin*, formerly united in fruitful interchange, become opposites."[17] Virginia Mollenkott suggests a feminist tendency in Milton's androgynous images, which she claims have "egalitarian implications." She also depicts the Fall as that time at which "the masculine and feminine principles were parted from each other."[18] Joan Webber applies androgyny to her account of both God and humanity, but at the same time, she recognizes the ambivalent implications of this approach for a reading of *Paradise Lost*. "Male and female," she states, "are aspects of Creation, like light and dark, which grow more distinct the farther they are removed from heaven"; thus Adam and Eve are *both* an inseparable whole and two separate individuals.[19] In demanding both, she is not forced, as are the others, to read the separation scene as fatal. I will return to Webber's important observation of the tension between the couple as a whole and as separate individuals. At this point, however, it is important to note the current use of androgyny to describe the relationship between Adam and Eve, the deduction by some that this fact proves Milton's egalitarian impulses, and, finally, the implications of fatalism for this interpretation of the separation scene.

These numerous androgynous and allegorical definitions of Adam and Eve necessitate a more thorough analysis of Milton's use of Renaissance theories of androgyny. The seventeenth-century equivalents of the ontological inseparability of Adam and Eve can be found in Philonic allegorical tradition, in Hermeticism, cabalism, alchemy, and the mystical tradition of Jacob Boehme. Milton certainly knew these philosophies, although scholars disagree about the extent of his knowledge and its application to his poetry. Sister Mary Irma Corcoran, Joseph Duncan, Arnold Stein, and John Halkett all note the importance of Philonic and Platonic traditions, but dismiss their ultimate importance to Milton's depiction of Adam and Eve.[20] Many critics contend that Hermeticism and alchemy as well as the philosophy of Boehme influenced *Paradise Lost*; Christopher Hill, for example, underscores Milton's close connection with Hermetic ideas.[21] While scholars argue the extent of Milton's knowledge of the *Zohar*, the primary source of the Jewish cabala, none disputes the probability of his acquaintance with this area of religious thought.[22] These arguments and Milton's overt references to Hermeticism in early poems such as *Il Penseroso* and *De Idea Platonica*, as well as his expressed admiration for Philo in *Pro Populo Anglicano Defensio*[23] establish his knowledge of systems of thought which define the first human as androgynous. Yet in *Tetrachordon,* Milton argues against this idea explicitly, for, he maintains, the first parent could not be both male and female, "however the Jewes fable, and please themselves with the accidentall concurrence of *Plato's* wit, as if man at first had bin created *Hermaphrodite*" (YP, II, p. 589). Only a close analysis of these theories will determine the nature of Milton's commitment to them.

Although each of the occult and mystical Renaissance philosophies offers a unique account of the creation and the fall, their points of agreement narrate a coherent story of first androgynous being. The story of the first human being who is both male and female is as old as Plato's *Symposium* and Philo's allegorical treatment. A number of theologians found this myth appealing, and Judeo-Christian traditions included it as a minority report on the early chapters of Genesis. The first human, Adam, is made in the image of God, who is pure reason and pure spirit. Thus Adam, too, is reason and spirit; he is basically masculine reason which has controlled and subsumed that female element most often defined as the emotions. The most interesting and perhaps heretical aspect of this account is that at first Adam is incorporeal because he is the pure image of God. Philo separates the man made from clay and the man first formed in the image of God. It is the latter man who is bisexual.[24] The *Hermetica* describes this being in the following manner: "And the first Mind,—that Mind which is Life and Light,—being bisexual . . . gave birth to Man, a Being like to Himself. And He took delight in Man, as being His own offspring; for Man was very goodly to look on, bearing the likeness of his Father."[25] In their desire to unite Christian and pagan philosophies, Renaissance thinkers such as Pico della Mirandola, Marsilio Ficino, and Leone Ebreo considered cabalism directly related to Christian Platonism and compatible with Hermeticism. Cabalistic thought of the Renaissance offers the incorporeal, archetypal man in which the male is the mental and the female the "animastic."[26] Jacob Boehme insists upon a similar spiritual nature for his androgyne:

Seeing then, that *Adam* did bear the image of the kingdom of God (which was eternal and incorruptible, and stood in paradise) therefore we can with no ground say, that he did bear the image of the kingdom of this world. For this world is transitory and corruptible: But the image in *Adam* was not transitory, or corruptible. Also if we will say, that *Adam* (before his fall) lived in the source [or property] of the four elements, then we can no way maintain that *Adam* was not a corruptible image. For at the end, the four elements must pass away, and go into the eternal element.[27]

Aside from the incorporeal nature of Adam, the most striking feature of this first human is his identity with maleness, for the male is both a part and the whole of the androgyne. The female element, on the other hand, is a subsumed part of Adam and represents different qualities for different thinkers. In general, she symbolizes the lower side of the human being, that which relates to the passions and the material world. Adam as male is enjoined to control the female side of himself, and as long as control is maintained, Adam remains free and perfect. The part which the female principle plays in this union can be pinpointed in Gerrard Winstanley's description of the sins he finds in his contemporaries: "they have been led by the powers of the curse in flesh, which is the *Feminine* part; not by the power of the righteous Spirit which is Christ, the *Masculine* power."[28] The cabalists made this distinction, a distinction mirrored in the Hermetic notion of the female element as Nature. In each case, the female is neither a separable and unique entity nor a worthy one.

However, if we leave our analysis of the androgyne's female side at this point, we will have simplified the account of the way in which the female was viewed. A few of these thinkers also gave her the powers of creation and wisdom, but ultimately both of these images were subsumed by the male principle. Because one of the most exclusive functions of the female in society is creation and reproduction, androgyny can be seen as a male attempt to appropriate the power of creation for himself. In an analysis of alchemical ideas, Sally Allen and Joanna Hubbs conclude that in the seventeenth-century document *Atalanta fugiens*, by Michael Maier, the union of male and female was "achieved by denying the independent status of the feminine and by containing and arrogating her creative powers."[29] In one version of the cabala, the ten sephiroths, the ten names or emanations of God, are represented by various male and female qualities, the most important of which are the first sephiroth, which is the father, the mind, and the third, which is the female who forms, who creates.[30] The notion of Adam partaking in the act of creation is familiar to many of these philosophies and is an example of the appropriation of the female principle for the purposes of creation. Perhaps the most positive description of the female element is to be found in Boehme's account of Sophia, for she who is a part of the spiritual man is "the chaste, high, noble, and blessed virgin (the divine wisdom)."[31] Like Spenser's use of Venus as the androgyne, this definition is inviting, but Boehme soon counters the positive with the negative. When Adam loses Sophia, he is given Eve, a very different creature, as a consolation:

Yet as concerning *Eve*, we must acknowledge that she was created to this corruptible life, for she is the woman of this world; and at this time it could not be otherwise. For the spirit of this world, with its tincture, had overcome and possessed *Adam*, so that he fell down into a sleep, and could not generate out of himself the image of the virgin according to the discovery of the noble and chaste virgin (the wisdom of God), which was the matrix in him, which was joined [or espoused] to him out of the heavenly *limbus;* where according to which (in his being overcome) the elementary woman was given to him, vis. *Eve,* who (in the spirit of the world's overcoming) was figured after a bestial form.[32]

We must then conclude, with some minor qualifications, that the female principle is described in these accounts as negative and, perhaps more important for this study, as merely part of a static whole.

The implications of the prelapsarian relationship of male and female are important as a basis for the description of the Fall. Because the relationship fuses two parts in a single, static entity, the Fall will occur if the female element should wander off, or, more likely for this ontological structure, if the male should lose control of the female side of himself. These accounts describe the Fall as separation of the prelapsarian and transcendental unity of male and female. Thus, in another departure from the book of Genesis, these philosophers are forced either to identify two falls or to single out a fall occurring at a time different from that described in the Bible. The theological focal point is the descent from a spiritual, paradisal harmony to a material world. For example, the *Hermetica* describes the Fall as man falling to (falling in love with) Nature:

And having learnt to know the being of the Administrators, and received a share of their nature, he [man] willed to break through the bounding circle of their orbits; and he looked down through the structure of the heavens, having broken through the sphere, and showed to downward-tending Nature the beautiful form of God. And Nature, seeing the beauty of the form of God, smiled with insatiate love of Man, showing the reflection of that most beautiful form in the water, and its shadow on the earth. And he, seeing this form, a form like to his own, in earth and water, loved it, and willed to dwell there. And the deed followed close on the design; and he took up his abode in matter devoid of reason. And Nature, when she had got him with whom she was in love, wrapped him in her clasp, and they were mingled in one; for they were in love with one another.[33]

In her study of Giordano Bruno and the Hermetic tradition, Frances Yates summarizes this philosophy's account of the Fall: "it is true that this is a Fall which involves loss, that Man in coming down to Nature and taking on a mortal body puts this mortal body, puts his mortal part, under the dominion of the stars, and it is perhaps punished by the separation into two sexes."[34] Boehme specifically defines two falls, one from spirituality into corporeality and another at the eating of the apple: "Thou canst not better comprehend, apprehend or undstand this [the twofold birth], than in and by thy *own body*, which, through the first fall of *Adam* with all its (the body's) birth or geniture, fitness, faculties and will, is become just such a house as the place of this world is come to be."[35] In Boehme's unique account of Adam's fall, archetypal man loses Sophia, his muse, refuge, and redeemer. He is rewarded with Eve, over whom he has no control and in whom he finds not wisdom, but antagonism.

This condensed account of Paradise and the Fall in Renaissance theologies of androgyny does not support a positive view of the female principle or encourage a notion of equality between men and women. For these reasons, contemporary feminist theorists have strongly criticized this mythical ideal as it appears historically and currently. The primary objection is that androgyny does not solve the dilemma that at first sight it appears to remedy. Originally intended to furnish an image to overcome sex-role stereotypes in language, thought, and practice, androgyny both maintains the traditional identification of male with the higher spiritual world and female with the lower material world and employs theories of dominance and subservience. Such writers as Mary Daly and Adrienne Rich first espoused this idea, then foreswore any allegiance to it because androgyny actually reinforced stereotypical thinking. In an earlier essay I, too, criticized this notion, and, in the process, identified two paradigms for the analysis of androgyny: fusion and balance. In the dominant and traditional theories of fusion, the male principle is given control of the female principle, in part to absorb her powers of creativity and in part to subdue the lower, chaotic elements; in the less prominent theories of balance, an attempt is made, rarely successful, to establish a fluid interchange of equally valid principles.[36] Like all Platonic and mystical theories of androgyny, Renaissance theories are clearly examples of fusion. These approaches maintain the stereotypical identification of male and female principles and suggest— indeed demand—the male's dominance of the female. The ontological and transcendental entity which is androgynous is a static, fused whole in which the male element is both part of the whole and the whole itself. This account of androgyny cannot easily be adopted to defend Milton's attitude toward women; in fact, it would more readily prove his misogyny. I believe, however, that Milton did not adopt this theory for *Paradise Lost*.

At first glance, Milton appears to use traditional androgynous imagery when he describes Adam primarily as reason and Eve as emotion and nature. Adam is that reasonable creature, the image of the Creator, who is made for contemplation; his large front, or forehead, indicates the centrality of his mind (IV, 300).[37] Adam's obviously superior mind allows him to be Eve's tutor, and, in one significant incident, to dispel her anxiety over her dream with his knowledgeable analysis of fancy. When, during Raphael's visit, Adam presumes to take flight into "studious thoughts abstruse" (VIII, 40), Eve, who has been listening intently and presumably learning along with Adam, leaves to await a less abstract discourse. Milton seems never to tire of telling his reader of Adam's superior mind and of his reflection of God's truth and wisdom.

On the other hand, Eve is the image of Adam, which must include reason, but not, presumably, to the same degree. Although we assume that Eve is a reasonable creature, many early images align her with the material world of passion, the senses, and the body. Northrop Frye argues that Eve must be seen as the creature to Adam's creator: "We think of God as male primarily because he is the creator: we think of Nature as female, not merely as a mother from whose body we are born, but as a creature of God."[38] This questionable image of creation, based on Aristotelian biology, is reflected in the imagery that Milton devises, as Marcia Landy notes when she points to the terms associated with male and female: "the male is the creator, the actor, the active principle, the authority. Mother Nature is distinguished as creation, and is mainly acted upon."[39] Eve is introduced to us in physical terms, terms which underscore her close relationship to nature. She is made for softness, Adam for contemplation; as a result, she exists for Adam. Milton often compares Eve and Mother Nature through parallel imagery: both are fruitful and "all-bearing" (V, 338); both are "wanton" and therefore lack the restraint of pure reason. Milton's early description of Eve includes her hair in "wanton ringlets" (IV, 306), which is later echoed when he characterizes the nature through which Raphael walks as "Wanton'd as in her prime" (V, 295). Just as the garden in which Adam and Eve live needs constant pruning and control, so Eve's mind needs Adam's control to allay her fears, anxieties, and misconceptions. Befitting her alliance with the world of the senses, Milton describes an Eve fearful after her dream, "With Tresses discompos'd, and glowing Cheek" (V, 10); when Adam and Raphael move to their abstruse thoughts, Eve retires because she prefers to mingle abstract thoughts with "conjugal Caresses" (VII, 56).

If these images were both constant and overwhelming throughout the poem, we might at this point take leave of further analysis and acknowledge the primarily androgynous nature of their ontological relationship. Such a step would also necessitate our acknowledgment of the fatalism in the separation scene. Yet this scene and Milton's description of Eve are, I believe, more complex. Inviting us to view this couple both as an ontological unit and as two separate individuals, Joan Webber's approach suggests that we oversimplify the text when we prefer one interpretation to the other; we must, Webber contends, see these two interpretations in constant, dynamic interchange. Another way to describe this paradox is through the tension Milton creates between imagery and drama. When we allow the drama to exist in fruitful tension with the imagery, we no longer have a statically fused couple incapable of individual growth or action, but two people in a dynamic, growing balance, in which each has a separate existence as well as a purpose in their union. This tension as well as some important ideological considerations provide context for the discussion of Adam and Eve in the separation scene. In *Paradise Lost*, then, Milton qualifies the purely allegorical and androgynous Adam and Eve by three means: by his dynamic ontology, by the importance allowed to Eve's rational side, and, finally, by Eve's growth throughout the poem.

In the first context, Raphael, the main proponent of Milton's dynamic ontology, argues that existence cannot be defined by static ontological categories, but must be viewed as potentiality, as almost unlimited growth by which body can work up to spirit (V, 478). Every creature found obedient can gradually move up the scale of perfection, as Raphael's organic image indicates:

> So from the root
> Springs lighter the green stalk, from thence the leaves
> More aery, last the bright consummate flow'r
> Spirits odorous breathes: flow'rs and thir fruit
> Man's nourishment, by gradual scale sublim'd
> To vital spirits aspire, to animal,
> To intellectual, give both life and sense,
> Fancy and understanding, whence the Soul
> Reason receives, and reason is her being.   (V, 479–87)

Each creature, moving from the one first matter, ascends the scale from the physical to the spiritual, from the body to reason in proportion to its specific potential. This theory establishes two important principles. In the first, the difference among various creatures, primarily those in related categories, is one of degree, not kind; for, as Raphael states, humans can work up to the level of the angels: "time may come when men / With Angels may participate . . . Your bodies may at last turn all to spirit, / Improv'd by tract of time, and wing'd ascend / Ethereal, as wee" (V, 493–94, 497–500). The second important assumption is that the physical self is not a static category, but an incipient spirit. Thus, anyone who at one point represents the natural and material world is not bound to remain at that level. Theoretically, then, Eve has the potential to grow into more wisdom and spirituality. Dramatically, this ontology is mirrored in an Eden which demands individual growth and choice. As Barbara Lewalski notes, "Milton's vision of the prelapsarian life admits no dichotomy between the states of Innocence and Experience."[40] Milton sets the stage, then, for an Eve who is not confined to a static ontological definition.

Growth is contingent on obedience, obedience on knowledge, and, since the potential for knowledge resides in the reason, Eve's growth depends upon her rational capacity. Eve's reason undercuts a simple identification of woman with nature or emotion. Milton's concept of marriage demands not only that woman be accorded a rational capacity, but also that the difference between the husband and wife's reasoning abilities be one of degree, not kind. Milton informs us, in many of his prose writings, that the basis of holy wedlock is mental communion. As Adam claims in his argument with God, "Of fellowship I speak / Such as I seek, fit to participate / All rational delight" (VIII, 389–91). Although John Halkett argues that Milton's "meet and happy conversation" rests not on intellectual communication, but on companionship and society,[41] other critics emphasize the importance of the rational powers. Merritt Hughes, in a footnote, links Adam's request for another self in Book VIII to the classical idea of friendship, Cicero's *alter idem;* in an essay defending Eve, Allan Gilbert claims that she has distinct reasoning powers.[42] The intellectual conversation to which Halkett refers could well be analogous to "studious thoughts abstruse," which hardly determine rational capability. Conversation and fellowship demand rational ability, and Milton's insistence on these goals in marriage requires that Eve's reason be, as Dorothy Durke Miller has argued, of "near equality."[43] Paul Siegel notes that Puritan emphasis on fellowship and partnership was influenced by those Renaissance humanists who, like Thomas More, believed women to have rational souls that could be educated.[44] Milton's Eve, therefore, is not ontologically distinct from Adam; she is his copartner. In Book VIII, Adam describes the kind of human being necessary to complete him, not an opposite who will fill a gap in his own being, not someone with whom he can be fused for perfection, but rather someone who, although admittedly not an exact equal, will provide balance and interchange. This being will not complete him ontologically, but complement him existentially in a relationship of responsibility.

Milton's emphasis on Eve's rational abilities and potential for growth sets the stage for the final context—the dramatic context in which Eve is, like Adam and the Son, given the opportunity to grow through adversity. Although less dramatic than Adam's, her growth takes place throughout the poem. Eve begins her life looking downward, worshiping her own image in the lake; but, unlike Vaughan's sinners in "The World," who keep their eyes on the earth and its wealth, Eve turns from her kneeling position to consider loftier things. As Eve herself states, she praised her own reflection in the pool with "unexperienc't thought" (IV, 457). With the major exception of Diane McColley, most critics ignore Eve's growth from inexperienced thought to independent decisions based on experienced thought. Thus, the images of emotion, fancy, wantonness, and nature are clustered in the earlier books in which she appears; the images are mitigated with increasing tension as we approach Book IX. As the poem progresses, Eve begins to test her judgment and thought. At first, in the passage concerning her dream, Adam takes over the hortatory function, in his customary way, and carefully explains the function of fancy. But Eve does not always defer to Adam; gradually she ventures her own ideas, making Book IX not a surprise, but a logical step in her growth. When Raphael is still at a distance and Adam, seeing him approach, orders Eve to bring in the abundance of their harvest, Eve agrees, but obeys only after she corrects his notion of the abundant storage of their goods:

> *Adam*, earth's hallow'd mould,
> Of God inspir'd, small store will serve, where store,
> All seasons, ripe for use hangs on the stalk;
> Save what by frugal storing firmness gains
> To nourish, and superfluous moist consumes.   (V, 321–25)

Here she asserts her rightful knowledge and mastery of the household she manages. Later, Eve's decision to leave the two boys to their abstract thinking can be interpreted as an independent choice. She is not a passive creature who leaves or moves only when bidden, for as Milton makes clear, she leaves "as not with such discourse / Delighted, or not capable her ear / Of what was high: such pleasure she reserv'd / *Adam* relating, she sole Auditress" (VIII, 48–51).

Milton, then, consciously mitigates the simple view that Eve represents only emotion or nature; he prepares us for an Eve who has rational abilities, an Eve who has moved, according to dramatic juxtapositions and implications, from an unthinking response to her own image to an educated capability for independent judgments. She is not ontologically allegorical, but a dynamic and growing individual; for in *Paradise Lost* individuality, life experience, and pain are not foreign to paradisal harmony. Her relationship with Adam cannot be described as either static or fused. The balance by which Milton characterizes their union assumes a separate as well as a related existence.

Approaching the separation scene free from an ontological structure which would necessitate fatalism allows us a more open response to the first argument between Adam and Eve. While it is true that they are stronger together, their strength is based on existential support and responsibility rather than androgynous, ontological fusion. Because they both have grown, the strength of their relationship does not preclude individual strength or sufficiency. They encounter each other in Book IX as two people who have learned much through education and experience; they are not the same people we found in Book IV. The Eve who once said to Adam that "what thou bidd' st / Unargu'd I obey" (IV, 635–36) now feels confident enough to initiate her first independent suggestion for their welfare. Like all their decisions in the pre- and postlapsarian states, her suggestion rests not on absolute knowledge, but on growing awareness of herself and her strength and on an insight into the possible legitimacy of her claim. Her judgment cannot be assumed to be right or wrong, but only to be legitimate within the context that she— and we—have been given. Her initial request sounds so reasonable and well considered, so much like Adam's own argument with God, that Adam, the image of God's wisdom, must acknowledge that "Well hast thou motion'd, well thy thoughts imploy'd" (IX, 229). It is an argument that sounds reasonable, and, it seems, one that Adam finds difficult to answer. Significantly, Adam does not dismiss Eve with the attitude that she has no right to this kind of freedom or that obedience to him precludes separation. In fact, Adam does not make obedience a major issue; instead, the encounter is a drama in which two growing individuals attempt to discover and work out the most viable answer to their immediate problem. The answer, as always, is not simple.

In their argument, then, both exhibit weakness and strength. Neither is simply right or wrong. Adam seems unable to deny the legitimacy of Eve's suggestion, although he rightly points to the great dangers involved. Adam counters Eve's first argument, for the garden does not need the attention that Eve at first thinks it must demand; but, responding to the underlying assumption that Eve has the ability and right to work alone, Adam can only warn her that this proposed action would involve great hazards. Adam also rightly argues that they are stronger together, but in his mistaken notion—one on which Raphael has already spoken—that "I from the influence of thy looks receive / Access in every Virtue" (IX, 309–10), he reflects a perversion of the truth that they are stronger together. When Adam claims that temptation should not be sought, he does so in a Miltonic context which argues against cloistered virtue. Because confronting and responding to temptation have been the way to knowledge in Eden, Adam once again is slightly off target. Finally, he appeals weakly to obedience, but that, too, is quickly qualified by a recognition that trial unsought may be a source of virtue and that Eve must choose—she must not be forced to stay. Adam, thus, has some important insights into this situation, but he is not sure of the right answer; nor can he positively claim anything but the danger inherent in separation.

Eve's argument also demonstrates specific insights as well as serious problems. Eve's request—or, more importantly, the assumption of freedom on which it is based—is legitimate in the context that Milton has created. Although Adam cannot deny this legitimacy, he is not able to convince Eve of the real dangers that exist beyond their limited realm. While her knowledge of the foe is real—she overheard the angel warn Adam (IX, 275–78)—Eve does not exhibit the kind of caution which is necessary to avoid being surprised by sin. She also becomes entangled in a you-don't-trust-me argument which is unnecessary for her position. Finally, the inconclusiveness of their arguments, their inability to reach a simple right or wrong answer, demonstrates that the principles of strength together and freedom to grow as individuals exist side by side; one does not preclude the other. Any decision as to which is more important must be made at each specific moment. Nor does the fact that the Fall happens soon after destroy the legitimacy of Eve's action, although it may bring her wisdom into question. She leaves surrounded by danger, but in Milton's Eden that is business as usual.

Can this analysis determine whether or not Milton's attitude toward women was positive or ahead of his time? If androgyny is central to his description of the first parents, I believe that we must conclude, with others, that misogyny is a key to Milton's thinking about women. If, however, he mitigates this androgynous and allegorical interpretation of Adam and Eve in the manner suggested above, then his picture of Eve— and by implication, of womankind—allows her the positive possibilities of individuality, separateness, and, at times, independence. Such a position is, I believe, reflected in *Paradise Lost*, but it alone cannot prove any egalitarian views on Milton's part. At most, this position negates a simple accusation of misogyny and points to Milton's complex, albeit at times ambivalent, view of women. Eve's ontological uniqueness in *Paradise Lost*, particularly in the separation scene, supports the contention that Milton values the complexity of human nature—male and female.

University of Oregon

NOTES

1. See David Aers and Bob Hodge, " 'Rational Burning': Milton on Sex and Marriage," in *Milton Studies*, XIII, ed. James D. Simmonds (Pittsburgh, 1979), pp. 3–34; S. A. Demetrakopoulos, "Eve as a Circean and Courtly Fatal Woman," *Milton Quarterly*, IX (1975), 99–106; Cheryl H. Fresch, "The Hebraic Influence Upon the Creation of Eve in *Paradise Lost*," in *Milton Studies*, XIII, ed. James D. Simmonds (Pittsburgh, 1979), pp. 181–99; Diana Hume George, "The Miltonic Ideal: A Paradigm for the Structure of Relations Between Men and Women in Academia," *CE XL* (1979), 864–73; Sandra M. Gilbert, "Patriarchal Poetry and Women Readers: Reflections on Milton's Bogey," *PMLA*, XCIII (1978), 368–82; Marcia Landy, "Kinship and the Role of Women in *Paradise Lost*, " in *Milton Studies*, IV, ed. James D. Simmonds (Pittsburgh, 1972), pp. 3–18, and "Milton and the Modern Reader," in *Milton Studies*, IX, ed. James D. Simmonds (Pittsburgh, 1976), pp. 3–36; Barbara Kiefer Lewalski, "Milton on Women—Yet Once More," in *Milton Studies*, VI, ed. James D. Simmonds (Pittsburgh, 1974), pp. 3–20; Diane Kelsey McColley, "Free Will and Obedience in the Separation Scene of *Paradise Lost*," *SEL*, XII (1972), 103–20, " 'Daughter of God and Man': The Subordination of Milton's Eve," in *Familiar Colloquy: Essays Presented to Arthur Edward Barker*, ed. Patricia Bruckmann (Ottawa, 1978), pp. 196–205, and "Eve's Dream," in *Milton Studies*, XII, ed. James D. Simmonds (Pittsburgh, 1978), pp. 25–45; Virginia R. Mollenkott, "Milton and Women's Liberation: A Note on Teaching Method," *Milton Quarterly*, VII (1973), 99–103; Stella P. Revard, "Eve and the Doctrine of Responsibility in *Paradise Lost*," *PMLA*, LXXXVIII (1973), 69–78; Elaine B. Safer, " 'Sufficient to Have Stood': Eve's Responsibility in Book IX," *Milton Quarterly*, VI, (1972), 10–14; Kathleen M. Swaim, " 'Hee for God only, Shee for God in Him': Structural Parallelism in *Paradise Lost*," in *Milton Studies*, IX, ed. James D. Simmonds (Pittsburgh, 1976), pp. 121–49; and Joan Malory Webber, "The Politics of Poetry: Feminism and *Paradise Lost*," in *Milton Studies*, XIV, ed. James D. Simmonds (Pittsburgh, 1980), pp. 3–24.

2. A graceful reference to this situation can be found in Barbara Lewalski's title, "Milton on Women—Yet Once More."

3. Discussion of the mythical unity of male and female principles can be found in Joseph E. Duncan, "Archetypes in Milton's Earthly Paradise," in *Milton Studies*, XIV, ed. James D. Simmonds (Pittsburgh, 1980); Virginia R. Mollenkott, "Some Implications of Milton's Androgynous Muse," *Bucknell Review: Women, Literature, Criticism*, ed. Harry R. Garvin (Lewisburg, Pa., 1978), pp. 27–36; Don Parry Norford, " 'My Other Half': The Coincidence of Opposites in *Paradise Lost*," *MLQ*, XXXVI (1975), 21–53, and "The Separation of the World Parents," in *Milton Studies*, XII, ed. James D. Simmonds (Pittsburgh,

1978), pp. 3–24; John T. Shawcross, "The Metaphor of Inspiration in *Paradise Lost*," in *Th' Upright Heart and Pure: Essays on John Milton Commemorating the Tercentenary of the Publication of "Paradise Lost*," ed. Amadeus P. Fiore, Duquesne Studies/Philological Series, X (Pittsburgh, 1967), 75–85; and Webber, "The Politics of Poetry." Mollenkott is most direct in her use of this idea to defend Milton's attitude toward women. Ultimately, any study of the mythic dimensions of Milton's poetry is indebted to Northrop Frye. Central to this study is "The Revelation to Eve," in *"Paradise Lost": A Tercentenary Tribute*, ed. Balachandra Rajan (Toronto, 1969), pp. 18–47.

   4. The first to popularize androgyny as a critical term was Carolyn G. Heilbrun, *Toward a Recognition of Androgyny* (New York, 1973). *Women's Studies*, II (1974), devoted this issue to the debate over androgyny. Adrienne Rich and Mary Daly both espoused, then rejected the idea. Rich, "Diving into the Wreck," *Diving into the Wreck: Poems 1971–72* (New York, 1973), and "Kingdom of the Fathers," *Partisan Review*, XLIII, no. 1 (1976), 30 n.; Daly, *Beyond God the Father: Toward a Philosophy of Women's Liberation* (Boston, 1973), and *Gyn/Ecology: The Metaethics of Radical Feminism* (Boston, 1978), pp. 387–88.

   5. Norford, "The Separation of the World Parents," p. 5; Mollenkott, "Some Implications of Milton's Androgynous Muse," p. 34.

   6. " 'PARADISE LOST': The Relevance of Regeneration," in *"Paradise Lost": A Tercentenary Tribute*, p. 63.

   7. See Millicent Bell, "The Fallacy of the Fall in *Paradise Lost*," *PMLA*, LXVIII (1953), 863–83; Dennis H. Burden, *The Logical Epic: A Study of the Argument of "Paradise Lost"* (Cambridge, Mass., 1967), p. 91; and E. M. W. Tillyard, "The Crisis of *Paradise Lost*," in *Studies in Milton* (1951; rpt. London, 1960), pp. 8–52.

   8. A. G. George, *Milton and the Nature of Man: A Descriptive Study of "Paradise Lost" in Terms of the Concept of Man as the Image of God* (Bombay, 1974), p. 75.

   9. Michael Lieb, *The Dialectics of Creation: Patterns of Birth and Regeneration in "Paradise Lost"* (Amherst, Mass., 1970), p. 191; John C. Ulreich, " 'Sufficient to Have Stood': Adam's Responsibility in Book IX," *Milton Quarterly*, V (1971), 39; and Stanley Fish, *Surprised by Sin: The Reader in "Paradise Lost"* (New York, 1967), p. 231. At times these qualifications are small, but important. Lieb claims, for example, that Eve's desire to work alone is one part of a chain of events "that activate the process by which the Fall may be effected" (p. 191). Arnold Stein's perceptive analysis of the argument at the beginning of Book IX similarly concludes that Adam remains innocent, although he "moves toward the threshold of the fallen world"; see *The Art of Presence: The Poet and "Paradise Lost"* (Berkeley, 1977), p. 114.

   10. E. M. W. Tillyard, *Milton*, rev. ed. (1930; rpt. New York, 1967), p. 221 n.

   11. "Eve and the Doctrine of Responsibility," p. 74.

   12. " 'Daughter of God and Man,' " p. 197.

   13. *A Milton Handbook*, 4th ed. (New York, 1954), p. 211. John S. Diekhoff makes a similar point in "Eve, the Devil and *Areopagitica*," *MLQ*, V (1944), 429–34; Burden also adopts this view in *The Logical Epic*, p. 88.

   14. "Free Will and Obedience in the Separation Scene," p. 115.

   15. "Before and After the Fall: Some Miltonic Patterns of Stasis," in *Approaches to "Paradise Lost": The York Tercentenary Lectures*, ed. C. A. Patrides (Toronto, 1968), p. 2.

   16. *The Dialectics of Creation*, p. 191. See also A. B. Chambers, "The Falls of Adam and Eve in *Paradise Lost*," in *New Essays on "Paradise Lost*," ed. Thomas Kranidas (Berkeley, 1969), p. 128, and Arnold Stein, *Answerable Style: Essays on "Paradise Lost"* (Minneapolis, 1953), p. 79.

17. "The Separation of the World Parents," p. 5.

18. "Some Implications of Milton's Androgynous Muse," p. 34.

19. "The Politics of Poetry," pp. 9 and 14.

20. Corcoran, *Milton's Paradise with Reference to the Hexameral Background* (1945; rpt. Washington, D. C., 1967), pp. 62–71; Duncan, *Milton's Earthly Paradise: A Historical Study of Eden* (Minneapolis, 1972), pp. 42–43; Halkett, *Milton and the Idea of Matrimony: A Study of the Divorce Tracts and "Paradise Lost"* (New Haven, 1970), p. 113. In *Answerable Style*, Stein analyzes the philosophical problem involved in the idea of sameness (pp. 77–84).

21. *Milton and the English Revolution* (London, 1977). See also Irene Samuel, *Plato and Milton* (Ithaca, N.Y., 1947), pp. 35–39; Lieb, *The Dialectics of Creation*, pp. 229–44; J. H. Adamson, "The Creation," in *Bright Essence: Studies in Milton's Theology*, ed. W. B. Hunter, C. A. Patrides, J. H. Adamson (Salt Lake City, 1971), p. 86; and Margaret Lewis Bailey, *Milton and Jacob Boehme: A Study of German Mysticism in Seventeenth-Century England* (New York, 1914).

22. In *Milton's Rabbinical Readings* (Urbana, Ill. 1930), Harris Francis Fletcher has summarized the general assumption of Milton's knowledge of the *Zohar*: although there is no direct connection, "the *Zohar* belongs with a whole library of Jewish works in print and accessible to the seventeenth century scholar who could read them" (p. 76).

23. Trans. Donald C. MacKenzie, in *Complete Prose Works of John Milton*, ed. Don M. Wolfe et al. (New Haven, 1953–), IV, Part 1, pp. 344–45. All references to Milton's prose cite the volumes of this edition as YP.

24. *Philo*, trans. F. H. Colson and G. H. Whitaker, Loeb Classical Library (New York, 1929), 107.

25. Trans. and ed. Walter Scott, (Oxford, 1924), I, pp. 119 and 121.

26. Joseph Leon Blau, *The Christian Interpretation of the Cabala in the Renaissance* (New York, 1944), p. 70. This particular vocabulary derives from the sixteenth-century Christian cabalist, Paul Ricci.

27. *Concerning the Three Principles of the Divine Essence of the Eternal, Dark, Light, and Temporary World* (1648), trans. John Sparrow (London, 1910), p. 370.

28. "The New Law of Righteousness," in *The Works of Gerrard Winstanley*, ed. George H. Sabine (Ithaca, N. Y., 1941), p. 157.

29. "Outrunning Atalanta: Feminine Destiny in Alchemical Transmutation," *Signs*, VI (1980), 215.

30. Blau, *The Christian Interpretation*, p. 71.

31. *Concerning the Three Principles*, p. 374.

32. Ibid., pp. 372–73.

33. See pp. 121 and 123.

34. *Giordano Bruno and the Hermetic Tradition* (Chicago, 1964), p. 28.

35. *The Aurora*, trans. John Sparrow, ed. C. J. Barker and D. S. Hehner (London, 1914), p. 446.

36. Marilyn R. Farwell, "Virginia Woolf and Androgyny," *Contemporary Literature*, XVI (1975), 433–42.

37. All citations of *Paradise Lost* refer to *John Milton: Complete Poems and Major Prose*, ed. Merritt Y. Hughes (Indianapolis, 1957).

38. "The Revelation to Eve," p. 20.

39. "Kinship and the Role of Women," p. 7.

40. "Innocence and Experience in Milton's Eden," in *New Essays on "Paradise Lost*," p. 116. See also Thomas H. Blackburn, " 'Uncloistered Virtue': Adam and Eve in

Milton's Paradise," in *Milton Studies*, III, ed. James D. Simmonds, III (Pittsburgh, 1971), pp. 119–137.

41. *Milton and the Idea of Matrimony*, p. 58.

42. *John Milton: Complete Poems and Major Prose*, p. 373 n; Gilbert, "Milton on the Position of Women," *MLR*, XV (1920), 250.

43. "Eve," *JEGP*, LXI (1962), 544.

44. "Milton and the Humanist Attitude Toward Women," *JHI*, II (1950), 42–53.

"AND BROUGHT HER UNTO THE MAN": THE WEDDING IN *PARADISE LOST*

Cheryl H. Fresch

ALTHOUGH NOT replete with historical-literal details, verses 18 through 24 of Genesis ii necessarily serve as a cornerstone in all Jewish and Christian considerations of the original marriage. Only the conclusion of verse 22, however, directly bears upon the initial meeting of Adam and Eve: "And the rib, which the Lord God had taken from man, made he a woman, and brought her unto the man" (King James Version). Even such Catholic Fathers as Irenaeus and Augustine, who most carefully explain that the marriage was not physically consummated until after the Fall, agree with other theologicans, both Jewish and Christian, that God's bringing Eve to Adam constituted the beginning of the first marriage.[1] Developing their readings of Genesis ii, 22, those Jewish and Christian divines, as well as various narrative and dramatic poets seemed to settle upon one or more of three basic responses to "brought." While Milton's elaboration of the wedding in *Paradise Lost* certainly reveals no incontrovertible influence from any of the handful of poets or theologians whose readings of Genesis we shall survey, his presentation of the wedding and the wooing in Books IV and VIII acquires a sharper identity when viewed against a sampling of other treatments.[2]

None but the heretical could argue against the divine sanction marriage received in Paradise. Because God "brought" the woman, he joined her to the man and thus divinely established marriage. Officiating, therefore, at the first wedding, God was easily understood to have been "the priest" in the Edenic nuptials: "But now thy God hath perfect made thy state, / Linck't thee in marriage with so choyce a mate, / Himselfe the Priest which brought her to thy hand."[3] Behind this popularization lay abundant theological authority, headed by Jesus' own interpretation of Genesis ii, 22: "What therefore God has joined together, let not man put asunder" (Matthew XIX, 6). Leaders among the early Catholic Fathers vigorously defended marriage on the basis of its having been instituted by God himself. Men like Clement, Tertullian, and Chrysostom[4] expressed sentiments very similar to those found, for example, in Origen's *Commen-*

tary on Matthew: "And it is God who has joined together the two in one so that they are no more twain, from the time that the woman is married to the man." In a footnote, Origen offers this alternative reading: "Or, by God the woman is married to the man." The text of his commentary concludes: "And, since God has joined them together, on this account in the case of those who are joined by God, there is a 'gift.' "[5] In one of his several comments on Genesis ii, 22, Cornelius à Lapide reveals that this understanding of "brought," *adduxit,* remained a commonplace of Catholic exegesis: "deinde expergefacto Adamo, Evam ad eum, quasi ad sponsum, adduxerit, ut matrimonio indissolubili illos, id est unum et unam copularet" ("then after Adam awakened, he brought Eve to him, as to a bridegroom, in order that he might join them together, that is one and the other, in indissoluble marriage").[6]

Reformation and Renaissance Protestants also turned to the "brought" of Genesis ii, 22, to establish the sacred origin of the institution of marriage. Donne, for example, voiced this argument at the marriage of Sir Francis Nethersole: "God left not them to goe to one another, but *God brought the woman to the man;* and so this conjunction . . . is limited by God . . . to be . . . between such persons, as God hath brought together in marriage, according to his Institution, and Ordinance."[7] Lecturing on marriage, Henry Smith had presented a similar interpretation approximately thirty years earlier: "Whereas all other ordinaunces were appoynted of GOD by the hands of men, or the hands of Angells, Marriage was ordained by God himselfe, which cannot erre. No man nor Angell brought the Wife to the Husband but GOD himself: so Marriage hath more honour of God."[8] Furthermore, behind Protestant voices like those of Donne and Smith may be heard the authority of Luther and Calvin. Lecturing on Genesis ii, 22, Luther adamantly argues "that marriage is a divine kind of life because it was established by God Himself."[9] And, in Calvin's *Commentaries on Genesis,* the note explaining the "brought" of the same verse concludes, "But if no other reason influenced us, yet this alone ought to be abundantly sufficient, that unless we think and speak honourably of marriage, reproach is attached to its Author and Patron, for such God is here described as being by Moses."[10]

In other readings of Genesis ii, 22, exegetes perhaps somewhat more sensitive to the psychological state of prospective brides and grooms take "brought" to suggest or convey something besides proof of the divine sanction given marriage because God joined Adam and Eve. In *De Genesi contra Manichaeos,* for example, Augustine brings several rather unusual touches to his recitatio of chapter ii, the opening of his treatise's second book. Carrying over the sense of God's rationale when he brought the animals to Adam for naming, Augustine writes of God's bringing Eve to Adam: "Et adduxit illam ad Adam, ut videret quid eam vocaret" ("And he led her to Adam, in order that he could see what he [Adam] called her"). Adam then not only makes the standard "os-ex-ossi-bus-meis" speech, but goes on to resound God's own earlier phrase: "et haec erit mihi adjutorium" ("and this woman will be a helper to me").[11] Although this tract does not offer detailed analysis of the actual meeting and marriage of Adam and Eve, Augustine's purpose in departing from the standard Vulgate reading becomes clearer in *De Genesi ad litteram,* where he suggests that one crucial reason that God brought to Adam first the animals, and then Eve, was perhaps to stimulate Adam's own recognition of his need for a mate like unto himself:

Deinde, numquid ignorabat Deus, nihil tale se creasse in naturis animalium, quod simile adjutorium posset esse homini? An opus erat ut hoc etiam ipse homo cognosceret, et eo commendatiorem haberet uxorem suam, quod in omni carne creata sub coelo, et de hoc aere sicut ipse vivente, nihil ejus simile invenerit? Mirum si hoc scire non posset, nisi omnibus ad se adductis atque perspectis. Si enim Deo credebat, posset hoc illi eo modo dicere, quomodo et praeceptum dedit, quomodo et peccantem interrogavit, atque judicavit. Si autem non credebat, profecto neque hoc scire poterat, utrum ad eum omnia ille, cui non credebat, adduxerit; an forte in aliquibus ab illo remotioribus terrae partibus aliqua ei similia, quae non demonstrasset, absconderit.[12]

[Then was there anything else God was ignorant of, nothing that arose in the natures of living beings in such a manner that could be a helper like to man? Or had this work also been so that the man might get to know himself, and thereby to regard her as his own excellent wife, because in all the flesh created under heaven just as from all that living in this air, he himself had come upon nothing similar to him? It is extraordinary if he was not able to understand this unless all the animals had been led to him and observed. For if he trusted in God, God would have been able to say this to him in the same manner he gave the command, questioned him on the sin, and judged him. If however he did not trust God he truly was not able to understand this, whether he led all the animals to him, and he did not trust him, or by chance he concealed from that man in some far-off parts of the earth some others similar to him which he had not clearly shown.]

Early Protestants also often considered more literal readings of "brought," discovering in the word not just evidence of a divine and mysterious sanction for marriage, but also very practical information about human behavior. Many believed that God's bringing Eve to Adam made a statement about human reason. The marriage manuals of the Spanish humanist John Vives were very popular with sixteenth-century

English Protestants. Vives explains that God brought Eve to Adam—he did not force her upon the man—to allow Adam and Eve to choose to love, free of divine imperatives; "Adam did not ravish Eve, but receaved her, delivered unto him by god the father. He gave her not unto him perforce, but that they shuld mutually love one another." "The judgement of the mynde is the governoure of mans lyfe, the whiche if it go not before all our dedes, we shall slyde and fall into such greate jeoperdies, as we do se daylye chaunce & happen amonge men."[13] Nevertheless, Vives soon announces that, since a young man can be so racked by "the agitations and motions of all affections," he should literally follow Adam's example by allowing his parents to choose and deliver a wife to him, as God did when he brought Eve to Adam: "Therefore the yonge man shuld leave the care of this election to his parentes, whiche have better judgements."[14] God's bringing of Eve, which Vives first interprets as evidence of God's awareness that "The judgement of the mynde is the governoure of mans lyfe," finally, therefore, also becomes evidence of mankind's inability to choose, elect, and judge for itself in the business of marriage.

A number of Protestants apparently leaned toward the second of Vives' interpretations, although they usually suggested or explained that Adam's passivity was virtue, not inadequacy. In a section of his *Common Places* devoted to deciding "Whether it be lawful for children to marrie without the consent of their parents," Peter Martyr supports his view with the "brought" of Genesis ii, 22:

Now shall it be verie well to see, whether it be lawfull for children to contract matrimonie without consent of their parents. Certeinlie Samson would not. And it is a matter of much honestie, and of thankfulness towards the parents, if matrimonie be not contracted without their knowledge and consent. At the beginning, Adam did not choose himselfe a wife: God was his father, and brought Eve unto him.[15]

Obviously, this understanding of "brought" complicates God's role in the first nuptials, for as he now appears to be the father of the groom, rather than the priest conducting the ceremony. Gervase Babington's marginal note on Genesis ii, 22, continues this reading, but also widens it a bit to include the parents of the bride:

It is if you marke it, not onely sayde, that God made Woman, but that hee brought her to Man, and thereby we are taught, that marriage is not every meeting of man and woman together upon theyr owne heads, but when God bringeth not together, except in his feare they meet with consent of Parents, and such as are interested in them, and all due circumstances and order appointed by God, and used by his Church wherein they live.[16]

In Henry Smith's taking Genesis ii, 22, as his text for preaching the importance of parental consent, we see God cast more firmly as father of the bride than as father of the groom or officiating priest: "Againe, in the first institution of Mariage, when there was no Father to give consent, then our heavenly Father gave his consent: God supplied the place of the Father, & brought his Daughter unto her Husband, and ever since, the Father after the same manner, hath offred hys Daughter unto the Husband."[17]

Calvin and Luther, not unexpectedly, had anticipated the remarks of these later Protestants so pragmatically concerned with the behavior of parents and children. While voicing the divine-sanction reading of "brought," Calvin, for example, explains that "Adam did not take a wife to himself at his own will, but received her as offered and appropriated to him by God."[18] More colorfully expressing the same point—that Adam's patient waiting upon the Father was praiseworthy—Luther states that "Adam does not snatch Eve of his own will after she has been created, but he waits for God to bring her to him." Apparently opposed to Augustine's literal interpretation of Adam's naming the woman, Luther goes on: " 'He brought,' he [Moses] says. Who? No doubt . . . the entire Divinity. These say to Adam: 'Behold, this is your bride, with whom you shall dwell, with whom you shall beget children.' "[19] Andreini's *L'Adamo*, incidentally, dramatizes this interpretation of Genesis ii, 22–23, so that the Eternal Father must not only draw Adam's attention to Eve, but then also formally introduce her.[20]

Milton, of course, boldly moves away from the notion of an Adam passively receptive or virtuously patient in receiving from his Father, and from her Father, an equally passive and patient Eve. Few besides Vives seem to anticipate the remarkable treatment Milton gives this sense of "brought" in *Paradise Lost*. John Diodati, for one, notes the following of "brought her": "as a mediator, to cause her voluntarily to espouse her self to Adam." He then concludes his remark with the divine-sanction interpretation: "and to confirm and sanctifie that conjunction."[21] Jacob Cats' *The Original Marriage, A Description of the First Wedding Held in Paradise Between Adam and Eve*, gives much attention to the very extended wooing of Eve, but, in the Dutch diplomat's poem, the divine bringer of Eve is absent, and, when Eve finally yields, she seems not so much to have been convinced by Adam's reasons as exhausted by his persistence.[22] Finally, one of Cornelius à Lapide's glosses on Genesis ii, 22, may coincide in spirit with the first wooing in *Paradise Lost*, the wooing of Eve by which God persuades her to leave her reflection in the lake. Lapide writes that Eve was created away from the sleeping Adam—"in alium locum ab Adamo dormiente" ("in another place away from the sleeping Adam")—and in that other place, before he actually brought her to Adam, God talked with Eve, thereby filling her with knowledge as well as grace: "eamque scientia et gratia repleverit, sicuti repleverat Adamum, ibique cum Eva collocutus sit" ("and there he talked with Eve and filled her with knowledge and agreeableness, just as he had filled Adam").[23]

After surveying the traditional, if somewhat fluid, associations drawn between human behavior and the Father's bringing Eve to be married to Adam, we are perhaps better prepared to note some remarkable details in Milton's presentation of the wooing and the wedding in Eden. While Milton's Adam does not "snatch Eve of his will" any more than Luther's Adam does, neither does he choose patiently to "wait . . . for God to bring her to him." God does, of course, bring her—"On she came, / Led by her Heav'nly Maker" (VIII, 484–85)—but Adam had willed, immediately upon waking, "To find her" (VIII, 479). Of course, Milton's Adam has already seen and come to love Eve in the vision sent to him while he slept. Milton's Adam also enthusiastically and whole-heartedly demonstrates that love "hath his seat / In reason" (VIII, 590–91) when he decides to woo Eve after she, "though divinely brought" (VIII, 500), turns back. As Dennis Burden explains, Adam's wooing and Eve's yielding demonstrate that "their marriage was based on consent. . . . Even though there was only one man and one woman, there was still freedom and choice in their coming together. God is not compelling them to each other."[24] Choosing to follow her and woo her, Milton's Adam manages, on his own, to persuade her to marry him. And if, when she was first brought, she was "Led by her Heav'nly Maker" (VIII, 485), she is brought back, when she returns, by Adam: "To the Nuptial Bow'r / I led her blushing like the Morn" (VIII, 510–11).

Throughout the interlaced wooing and wedding episodes, the sensitive attention Milton brings to the humanization of Eve appears even more impressive than his attention to Adam, especially after we realize how few of Milton's predecessors ever offered insight into Eve's intellectual or emotional response as she was brought to the marriage of Genesis ii, 22. That *Paradise Lost* leaves no doubt of Eve's deciding her own destiny, including her marriage to Adam, is, as Barbara Lewalski insists, Milton's remarkable achievement:

Milton of course accepted the categories of hierarchy and the natural inferiority of women, but his reworking of the Adam and Eve myth has explored with remarkable incisiveness and profundity a basic human predicament. Each character is shown to bear full individual responsibility for his or her own choices, his or her own growth (or lack of it), his or her own contribution to the preservation and perfecting of the human environment; but at the same time, each experiences to the depths of his soul the need for the other, the inescapable bonds of human interdependence. And the truly surprising thing about Milton's portrayal of Eve is that he has examined this dilemma as carefully in regard to the woman as to the man.[25]

Most certainly, Milton's God the Father does not bring a flatly obedient daughter to be joined to Adam; God woos her, wins her, until she chooses to "follow straight" (IV, 476). Furthermore, God persuades her to follow by appealing to her intellect, explaining the reflection in the lake, and telling her the nature of her future relationship with Adam. Adam underlines this last point as he tells Raphael that when Eve first approached him, "Led by her Heavn'ly Maker," she was not "uninform'd / Of nuptial Sanctity and marriage Rites" (VIII, 485, 486–87). When Milton's Eve recounts her experience at the lake, she concludes, "what could I do, / But follow straight?" (IV, 475–76) The question is rhetorical, but Eve could have chosen not to follow. Later, she makes just this choice when she finally sees Adam, stops following her Father and Maker, and turns from the imminent wedding to go back to the lake.

Her turning back requires Adam to woo her to marriage. Part of her behavior in this second wooing sequence must be understood as evidence of her female insight into part of the alluring, but innocent and natural mystery of courtship. Indeed, even Adam recognizes this:

> Yet innocence and Virgin Modesty,
> Her virtue and the conscience of her worth,
> That would be woo'd, and not unsought be won,
> Not obvious, not obtrusive, but retir'd.
> The more desirable, or to say all,
> Nature herself, though pure of sinful thought,
> Wrought in her so, that seeing me, she turn'd.   (VIII, 501–07)

When she agrees to marry, however, to return and follow Adam to the nuptial bower, she yields, as she did at the lake, to the voice of wisdom. She is nevertheless not simply overwhelmed by a superior mind. She knows what "Honor" is, and only after she "*approv[es]*" Adam's "pleaded reason" does she follow him (VIII, 508–10; emphasis mine).

Elaborating his wooing sequence, which, though split into two segments by the flight of the bride, brings Eve finally to embrace the love of her husband, Milton shifts the setting several times. After Eve awakens to life, "Under a shade on flow'rs" (IV, 451) and apparently out of view of the sleeping Adam, she moves off to the lake. She then leaves the lake, following the voice of her Maker, and sees "Under a Platan" (IV, 478) the man to whom she is to be joined. Again the scene changes, however, when she breaks away from marriage and Adam, and the chase, the second wooing segment, develops. Finally, this wooing succeeds, and Adam brings Eve to the "Nuptial Bow'r" (VIII, 510). This two-part procession bringing Eve to the marriage in *Paradise Lost* therefore vividly expresses the most literal sense of "brought," leading Eve, in two phases, from the lake to the final nuptial goal where "the amorous Bird of Night / S[ings] Spousal" (VIII, 518–19).

As we have noted, Cornelius à Lapide also maintained that if God literally "brought" Eve to Adam, he necessarily had to bring her from some place other than where Adam met her. Unlike the Protestant poet, who has Adam's "internal sight" (VIII, 461) envision God standing near him while forming Eve, the French commentator believed that Eve was actually built in that removed spot from which God then brought her to Adam: "videtur colligi, quod Deus costam hanc in alium locum, ab Adamo dormiente parum separatum tulerit ibique ex ea Evam aedificaverit . . . ; deinde expergefacto Adamo, Evam ad eum, quasi ad sponsum, adduxerit" ("it seems to be assumed, that God took this rib to another place, a little apart from the sleeping Adam, and there he built Eve from it . . . then after Adam awakened, he brought Eve to him, as to a bridegroom").[26] Although a sense of physical movement is obviously implicit in "brought," *adduxerit*, few other theologians or poets commenting on Genesis ii, 22, endeavored to make it explicit or to develop it as the wedding procession by which the bride is actually and formally brought to her husband. Andrew Willet even moved to deny such a reading: "Shee is said to bee brought to man, not as though she were made in some other place; but God doth present her and offer her to man, and as it were, married and ioyeth them together."[27]

That the major dramatists and poets treating the Genesis story neglect or minimize this most theatrically adaptable sense of "brought" is especially surprising. As a member of the wedding—as priest, as the father of the groom, or as the father giving away the bride—God is absent from both Loredano's *L'Adamo* (1640) and Vondel's *Adam in Ballingschap* (1664). Indeed, although the setting of Vondel's play is the highly elaborate wedding celebration, God has no actual place in it. The initial meeting and courtship of Adam and Eve has apparently occurred before the play begins, for when the young lovers first come in, they are thoroughly acquainted. Officiating at the nuptials and crowning the newlyweds are Gabriel and Raphael, not God, and since the bride and groom enter together to the ceremony, no one seems required to give away, or bring, the woman to her husband.[28] Narrating *L'Adamo*, Loredano presents no such formal ceremony. Although God is said to have taken "a ribb of *Adam* in the making of Woman," the Father and Maker is not described as bringing the woman to Adam. Adam simply awakes and there she is, while God seems to have vanished: "Scarce was *Adam* released from the power of sleep, when he fixt his eye on the beauty of the woman." The two are immediately quite taken with each other, and Adam soon pronounces them man and wife. God's voice then speaks to prohibit them the fruit of the forbidden tree, to bless them, and to order them to *"Encrease and multiply."*[29] DuBartas also chooses to forego a wedding ceremony and a ritual presentation of Eve. All such formality is mising as Adam awakens to instant love and instant wife. Only an odd reminder of "brought" remains in the adjective "now-come":

> Now, after this profound and pleasing Transe,
> No sooner *Adam's* ravisht eyes did glance
> On the rare beauties of his now-come Half,
> But in his heart he 'gan to leap and laugh,
> Kissing her kindly, calling her his Life,
> His Love, his Stay, his Rest, his Weal, his Wife.[30]

God does, of course, figure more prominently in Andreini's *L'Adamo*, as we have noted. He introduces Adam to his bride: "Embrace now with the arm of thy affection / The virtuous bosom of thy fair companion / Who is called Woman and whose name is Eve."[31] But God does not actually bring her to Adam. Assembling all three for Adam's awakening from sleep, Andreini forfeits the formal entrance of the bride. Finally, although Geoffrey Bullough has shown that Cats' treatment of prelapsarian sex in *The Original Marriage* compares with Milton's attention to it in *Paradise Lost,* and although the wooing of Eve establishes an additional link between the two, the Dutch poem does not show God actually and formally bringing Eve to Adam.

Milton is not, however, unique in setting forth a formal entrance or procession in which the Father brings a bride to Adam. Anyone caring to push at the literal sense of "brought" can understand the same. The word's literal sense receives such elaboration in the accounts of rabbis voicing the traditional Jewish interpretation. In the commentary on Genesis, the *Bereshith Rabbah* contained in the *Midrash Rabbah,* an immensely popular collection which covers the Pentateuch as well as the Song of Songs, Ecclesiastes, Esther, Ruth, and Lamentations, we find the following debate among the various midrashim, or comments, on Genesis ii, 22:

R[abbi] Aibu—others state the following in R[abbi] Bannayah's name, and it was also taught in the name of R[abbi] Simeon b. Yohai—said: He [God] adorned her like a bride and brought her to him; for there are places where coiffure is called building. [Footnote: "Coiffure" stands here for adornment in general. Thus he translates: and the Lord God made the rib into a woman adorned.] R[abbi] Hama b. R[abbi] Hanina said: What think you, that He brought her to him from under a carob tree or a sycamore tree! [Footnote: As though she were an uncared-for foundling.] Surely He first decked her out with twenty-four pieces of finery [Footnote: The twenty-four are those enumerated in Isa. III, 18–24 q.v.] and then brought her to him! Thus it is written, *Thou wast in Eden the garden of God; every precious stone was thy covering, the carnelian, the topaz, and the emerald, the beryl, the onyx, and the jasper, the sapphire, the carbuncle, and the smaragd, and gold; the workmanship of thy settings and of thy sockets was in thee, in the day that thou wast created they were prepared* (Ezek. XXVIII, 13). The Rabbis and R[abbi] Simeon b. Lakish differ. The Rabbis say: There were ten canopies [Footnote: One of every precious stone enumerated in this verse.—Since God set up so many canopies, He must certainly have adorned her as a bride.]; R[abbi] Simeon b. Lakish maintained: There were eleven; R[abbi] Hama b. R[abbi] Hanina said: There were thirteen.[32]

To consider the similarities between the wedding in *Paradise Lost* and the wedding in the *Midrash Rabbah*, however, is not to present, or even to suggest, an argument about the sources or influences shaping *Paradise Lost*. It is, rather, to reveal similar emphasis on the literal meaning and the human story of Genesis ii, 22, as well as to note similar belief in the beautiful importance of love and marriage. So, just as Rabbi Hama, the son of Rabbi Hanina, announces rather forcefully that Eve was not an abandoned orphan God casually picked up for Adam "from under a carob tree or a sycamore tree," Milton carefully maintains her importance by detailing Eve's experience at the smooth lake where God comes to her, reasons with her, and finally persuades her to follow him to meet her future husband. The formally arranged wedding scene into which Eve is brought in both works also conveys the importance of the first bride and groom and the first marriage ceremony. The rabbis may argue a bit about the number of canopies God set up for the wedding in Eden, but their debate only impresses us with the beautiful, sacred dignity of the occasion. Milton mentions no canopies, of course, but he establishes the sense of the ceremonial by drawing more precise attention to Eve's actual entrance to the wedding. Conversing with Raphael, Adam fondly recalls the entrance of the bride and her Father, every measured step of their procession bringing a dream closer to reality and a bride closer to her waiting husband:

> When out of hope, behold her, not far off,
> Such as I saw her in my dream, adorn'd
> With what all Earth or Heaven could bestow
> To make her amiable: On she came,
> Led by her Heav'nly Maker, though unseen,
> And guided by his voice, nor uninform'd
> Of nuptial Sanctity and marriage Rites:
> Grace was in all her steps, Heav'n in her Eye,
> In every gesture dignity and love. (VIII, 481–89)

Adding to the lovely formality of the occasion are Milton's touches in evoking the air perfumed by "the fresh Gales and gentle Airs" and the "spicy Shrub" (VIII, 515, 517), the wedding song or "Hymenaean" sung by the "heavn'ly Choirs" (IV, 711), and the congratulations showered on the young couple by "the Earth," "each Hill," and all the other joyful wedding guests (IV, 513, 514).

Of central importance in both accounts, though, is the beauty of the bride God the Father brings to the wedding in Eden. Milton and the rabbis emphasize that Eve was especially groomed for the occasion of her marriage; the poem and the rabbinical commentary several times repeat the word "adorned." Just as the rabbis disagree about the number of canopies God erected for the wedding, they also fail to agree on precisely how God "decked . . . out" Eve. They establish beyond question, however, that she was "adorned" with her finery, whether with headbands, bracelets, scarves, festal robes, and other ornaments listed in Isaiah iii, 18, or with the topaz, jasper, sapphire, gold, and other precious gems listed in Ezekiel xxviii, 13. Avoiding such specific adornments, indeed even insisting that Eve comes to Adam "in naked beauty" (IV, 713), Milton nevertheless develops the same idea. Whatever may have been the gifts she received, Milton's Eve, like the rabbis' Eve, is adorned on her wedding day, "adorn'd / With what all Earth or Heaven could bestow" (VIII, 482–83).

For Jews and Christians alike, God established and sanctified marriage when he brought Eve to Adam. Because Milton chooses to disrupt the wedding procession in *Paradise Lost*, he cannot, as theologians and other poets can, easily and prominently affix the traditional divine-sanction interpretation to God's actual bringing of Eve. Following Eve's reminiscences in Book IV, however, the bard's hymn to "wedded Love" (IV, 750–70) presents one of the most well-known and admired elaborations of that divine-sanction view of marriage. Furthermore, by permitting Eve to flee from the wedding to which her Father leads her, and by then allowing Adam the opportunity to woo his future wife, Milton dramatically develops two unusually sensitive and important studies in the psychology of love. Milton's presentation of the garden wedding in the world's first spring therefore celebrates, with joy and dignity, both human love and divine love as they come together in the "mysterious Law" (IV, 750) of marriage.

University of New Mexico

NOTES

1. *Irenaeus Against Heresies*, trans. Alexander Roberts, in *The Ante-Nicene Fathers*, ed. Alexander Roberts and James Donaldson (Grand Rapids, Mich., 1956), I, p. 455. Augustine, *On Original Sin*, trans. Peter Holmes and Robert Ernest Wallis, rev. Benjamin B. Warfield, in *The Nicene and Post-Nicene Fathers*, ed. Philip Schaff (Grand Rapids, Mich., 1956), V, p. 251.

2. All references to *Paradise Lost* cite *John Milton: Complete Poems and Major Prose*, ed. Merritt Y. Hughes (New York, 1957).

3. Thomas Peyton, *The Glasse of Time* (London, 1620), sig. E3.

4. Clement of Alexandria, "On Marriage," *The Stromata or Miscellanies*, trans. William Wilson, in *The Ante-Nicene Fathers*, II, pp. 377–78. *Tertullian Against Marcion*, trans. Holmes, in *The Ante-Nicene Fathers*, III, p. 294. Chrysostom, "Homily IX," *Homilies on Second Corinthians*, the Oxford trans., rev. Talbot W. Chambers, in *The Nicene and Post-Nicene Fathers*, IX, pp. 323–24.

5. "Concerning the Pharisees and Scribes Tempting Him," *Commentary on Matthew*, trans. John Patrick, in *The Ante-Nicene Fathers*, X p. 506.

6. *Commentarii in Scripturam Sacram* (Paris, 1865), p. 80.

7. Sermon No. 17, in *The Sermons of John Donne*, ed. George R. Potter and Evelyn M. Simpson (Berkeley, 1955), II, pp. 335–36.

8. *A Preparative to Marriage* (London, 1591), p. 3.

9. *Lectures on Genesis, Chapters 1–5*, in *Luther's Works*, trans. Jaroslav Pelikan (St. Louis, 1958), I, p. 134.

10. *Commentaries on the First Book of Moses Called Genesis*, trans. John King (Edinburgh, 1847), I, p. 134.

11. *Patrologiae cursus completus*, ed. J. P. M. Migne (Paris, 1887), XXXIV, p. 196.

12. Ibid., p. 401.

13. *The Office and duetie of an husband*, trans. Thomas Paynell (London, 1553), sigs. C viii to C viii^v.

14. Ibid., sig. D iiii^v.

15. Trans. A. Marten (London, 1583), p. 431.

16. *The Works of the Right Reverend Father in God, Gervase Babington, Containing Comfortable Notes Upon the Five Books of Moses* (London, 1637), sig. C4^v.

17. *A Preparative to Marriage*, pp. 43–44.

18. *Commentaries*, p. 134.

19. *Lectures on Genesis*, I, p. 134.

20. Trans. Watson Kirkconnell, in *The Celestial Cycle* (New York, 1967), p. 232.

21. *Pious and Learned Annotations Upon the Holy Bible*, 2nd ed. (London, 1648), sig. B2.

22. "Milton and Cats," in *Essays in English Literature from the Renaissance to the Victorian Age: Presented to A. S. P. Woodhouse*, ed. Millar MacLure and F. W. Watt (Toronto, 1964), pp. 103–04.

23. *Commentarii*, p. 80.

24. *The Logical Epic: A Study of the Argument of "Paradise Lost"* (Cambridge, Mass., 1967), p. 85.

25. "Milton on Women—Yet Once More," in *Milton Studies*, VI, ed. James D. Simmonds (Pittsburgh, 1974), p. 5.

26. *Commentarii*, p. 80.

27. *Hexapla in Genesin* (London, 1608), p. 38.

28. Trans. Watson Kirkconnell, in *The Celestial Cycle*, pp. 434–47.

29. *The Life of Adam* (1659), trans. anon., ed. Roy C. Flannagan with John Arthos (facsimile rpt. Gainesville, Fla, 1967), pp. 17, 18, 22.

30. *DuBartas, His Divine Weekes and Works*, trans. Josuah Sylvester, in *The Complete Works of Josuah Sylvester*, ed. Alexander B. Grosart (1880; rpt. New York, 1967), I, p. 81.

31. *The Celestial Cycle*, p. 232.

32. *Midrash Rabbah*, trans. and ed. Rabbi Dr. H. Freedman and Maurice Simon (1939; compact ed. New York, 1977), I, p. 140–41.

ERUPTION AND CONTAINMENT:
THE SATANIC PREDICAMENT
IN *PARADISE LOST*

Jules David Law

WHEN MILTON's seraph Abdiel rises in Book V of *Paradise Lost* and advises Satan not to trouble himself any longer with the constraint of God's "yoke," the seraph assumes that a far harsher constraint is to follow: "That Golden Sceptre which thou didst reject," proclaims Abdiel, "Is now an Iron Rod to bruise and break / Thy disobedience" (V, 886–88).[1] However, no yoke ever replaces the one Satan disdains; Satan's fate—indeed, Satan's punishment—in *Paradise Lost* is a freedom far more radical than that which we consistently hear attributed to Adam and Eve throughout the poem. Just as Christ refuses to oppose Satan in *Paradise Regained,* so God removes all opposition and all constraint from Satan in *Paradise Lost.* Satan's predicament is defined not by any self-destructive eruption beyond the boundaries prescribed by God or Milton, or by any self-entangling attempt to argue away such boundaries, but rather by his very inability to fill up the enormous physical and rhetorical space given to him.

Ultimately, the degeneration or degradation of Satan, as perceived by Milton scholars, is a trick of perspective.[2] Satan's energies may dissipate, but they are never reduced or destroyed. The universe of *Paradise Lost*—like the universe of modern physics—is an expanding one, and Satan's energies are always compromised by extension rather than by limitation. Not only are we mistaken if we believe Satan to be limited, but there is a positive danger in such an assumption, a danger to which many of Milton's readers as well as his angels fall prey.[3] At any given moment, Satan can increase himself in stature. He can always be greater than he seems; he can simply never be great enough.

Although the angels in *Paradise Lost* seem to be ineffectual guardians of the earthly paradise, and hapless onlookers at larger cosmic events, their chief failure is far more subtle. Throughout the poem, they purvey a radical misconception of the nature of Satan's fall and punishment. The angels believe that the penalty for Satan's rebellion is to be

35

some form of containment, that he is to be bound or chained in eternal torment. "Who could have thought?" Gabriel laments after learning that Satan has "escap'd / The bars of Hell" (IV, 794–95). Gabriel demands of Satan, "Why hast thou . . . broke the bounds prescrib'd / To thy transgressions?" He later accuses Satan of trying to "scape his punishment" (IV, 878–79, 911). The seraph Abdiel warns Satan, "Yet Chains in Hell, not Realms expect" (VI, 186), and Raphael even admits to Adam that the angels had hoped, by ending the war in Heaven, to see "the Arch-foe subdu'd / Or Captive dragged in Chains" (VI, 259–60). Perhaps the most telling (and comical) instance of angelic ignorance concerning the nature of Satan's power occurs when Raphael tells Adam that a legion of angels had to be sent to guard the gates of Hell during the Creation, lest Satan escape. Raphael confides to Adam his fear that a Satanic eruption at the time might have caused God to mismanage the Creation:

> For I that Day was absent, as befell,
> Bound on a voyage uncouth and obscure,
> Far on excursion toward the Gates of Hell;
> Squar'd in full Legion (such command we had)
> To see that none thence issu'd forth a spy,
> Or enemy, while God was in his work,
> Lest hee *incenst at such eruption bold,*
> *Destruction with Creation might have mixt.*
>
> (VIII, 229–36; my emphasis)

Such a misconception of Satan's abilities has indirectly fueled almost two hundred years of Satanist criticism, ever since Blake decided that *Paradise Lost* was essentially a dialectic between Milton's Satanic (poetic) energies and his moralistic urge to restrain or confine them.[4] It is Blake who provides us with what E. M. W. Tillyard has called the "neatest statement" of what has come to be known as the Satanic school in Milton criticism.[5] In *The Marriage of Heaven and Hell*, Blake's Devil argues that energy (in this case "desire"), when restrained, "by degrees becomes passive, till it is only the shadow of desire," and adds that "The history of this is written in Paradise Lost."[6] The argument continues: "Note: The reason Milton wrote in fetters when he wrote of Angels & God, and at liberty when of Devils & Hell, is because he was a true Poet and of the Devil's party without knowing it." This much is familiar to students of *Paradise Lost*, but what is generally ignored is Blake's more subtle explanation of the relationship between energy and restraint, given further on in *The Marriage* and in a voice no longer attributed to the Devil:

Thus one portion of being is the Prolific, the other the Devouring: to the Devourer it seems as if the producer was in his chains; but it is not so, he only takes portions of existence and fancies that the whole.

But the Prolific would cease to be Prolific unless the Devourer, as a sea, received the excess of his delights.[7]

Blake might have added what his Devil has already demonstrated, that the Prolific is as much a misreader of his own situation as is the Devourer. While the Devourer mistakenly presumes to keep the Prolific "in his chains," the Prolific mistakenly feels that restraint must degenerate into passivity; in truth, Blake reveals, it is the very restraining pressure of the Devourer that defines and sustains the Prolific. Only when it is given an opportunity to struggle or break through containment can energy become *heroic* rather than merely dissipating into a "shadow of desire."

To the Romantic sensibility, epitomized here in Blake's early work, heroic energy resides in that liminal ecstasy which occurs in the eruption from bidden to forbidden territory. In "Ode on Melancholy," Keats describes the liminal moment of poisonous pleasure as the "burst" of "Joy's grape."[8] But no such Romantic eruption is allowed in *Paradise Lost*, simply because the boundaries of containment are forever receding before, below, and beyond Satan. Blake correctly recognized the relationship between energy and containment in *Paradise Lost*, but failed to see that neither Milton nor Milton's God ever attempts to restrain Satan. Subsequent criticism has accepted Blake's misconception of restraint, yet failed to understand how such restraint would, necessarily, have made Satan heroic. For the modern critic, containment is not involved in the definition of Satan's heroic energy; instead, it is Milton's attempt to control or delimit that energy. A. J. A. Waldock talks of Milton's continual efforts "to correct, to damp down and neutralize" Satan's speeches,[9] a view which implies a curious psychological chronology to Milton's construction of Satan: that Milton gave free rein to certain energies in order that Satan might be defined, and subsequently had to confine his creation. Naturally, then, C. S. Lewis takes great comfort in Milton's actually having conceived Satan's weaker speeches first; Lewis concludes that it was Satan's strengths—not his containment—that were retrospectively, and thus artificially, added: "Fortunately we happen to know that the terrible soliloquy in Book IV (32–113) was conceived and in part composed before the first two books. It was from this conception that Milton started."[10]

What both these critics assume—"Christian" and "Satanist" alike—is that Milton's poem depicts a Satan struggling against his containment.[11] The question then becomes whether it was Satanic energy or divine containment that was chronologically (and therefore thematically) precedent in Milton's mind. To either of these critics, the suggestion that Satan is never contained would imply that Satan in some way triumphs over both God and Milton. In fact, precisely the opposite is true. If we consider the original Romantic commentary on *Paradise Lost*, we can see how it follows from the complex relationship between energy and its suppression or containment—between the Prolific and the Devourer— that the removal of containment must bring the death, not the victory, of energy.

To posit a mutually dependent relationship between eruption and containment in Milton's poem is hardly to impose a Romantic aesthetic upon a seventeenth-century poem. Images of surfeit in Milton's Eden may serve as traditional Renaissance emblems of an overreaching pride, an ambition which must be cut down. But there is a curious twist: restraint seems to be imposed upon the botanical vitality of the garden precisely in order to stimulate growth rather than inhibit it. If Adam and Eve must "check" trees that have "reach'd too far," it is not to arrest fecundity but rather to prevent "fruitless imbraces":

> On to thir morning's rural work they haste
> Among sweet dews and flow'rs; where any row
> Of Fruit-trees overwoody reach'd too far
> Thir pamper'd boughs, and needed hands to check
> Fruitless imbraces.   (V, 211–15)

Here we can see that it is not containment, but the lack of it, which ultimately threatens Eden's botanical energy. Conversely, that energy is increased by restraint:

> Nature multiplies
> Her fertile growth, and by disburd'ning grows
> More fruitful, which instructs us not to spare.   (V, 318–20)

> the work under our labor grows,
> Luxurious by restraint.   (IX, 208–09)

By the time of the Fall, Adam and Eve are participating eagerly in this economy of transgression and restraint, and are encouraged (initially by Satan) to interpret God's interdiction as a kind of stimulus:

> [Eve:] but his [God's] forbidding
> Commends thee more.   (IX, 753–54)

[Adam:] if such pleasure be
In things to us forbidden, it might be wish'd,
For this one Tree had been forbidden ten.   (IX, 1024–26)

Adam, Eve, and the angels are not the only figures in the poem to think in terms of eruption and containment. Satan, Beëlzebub, and the other infernal spirits consistently assume that God has prescribed boundaries which must be overcome:

[Satan:] who overcomes
By force, hath overcome but half his foe.
Space may produce new Worlds;

. . . .

Thither, if but to pry, shall be perhaps
Our first eruption, thither or elsewhere:
For this Infernal Pit shall never hold
Celestial Spirits in Bondage.   (I, 648–58),

[Belial:] Or could we break our way
By force, and at our heels all Hell should rise
With blackest Insurrection.   (II, 134–36)

[Beëlzebub:] we dream
And know not that the King of Heav'n hath doom'd
This place our dungeon, not our safe retreat
Beyond his Potent arm, to live exempt
From Heav'n's high jurisdiction, in new League
Banded against his Throne, but to remain
In strictest bondage, though thus far remov'd,
Under th' inevitable curb, reserv'd
His captive multitude.   (II, 315–23)

[Satan:] let him surer bar
His Iron Gates, if he intends our stay
In that dark durance.   (IV, 897–99)

[Sin:] Hell could no longer hold us in her bounds.

. . . .

Thou hast achiev'd our liberty, confin'd
Within Hell Gates till now.   (X, 365–69)

Satan interprets even his voluntary metamorphoses in Paradise as a kind of perverse constraint imposed on him:

O foul descent! that I who erst contended
With Gods to sit the highest, am now constrain'd
Into a Beast.   (IX, 163–65)

A number of critics have agreed with Satan's assessment of this meta-morphosis and conclude that the animalism of Book IV is evidence of Satan's "decline."[12] However, changes of outward form which reflect inward spirit—though they may be convenient as moral signposts—are hardly "constraints" upon Satan, as tempting as it is to think so. Satan's energies and abilities, his choice of actions, and even the duration of his metamorphoses, are neither determined nor limited by the forms he chooses.[13]

Satan interprets not only his own situation but the entire created universe in terms of eruption and containment. Paradise was created, he speculates, to avoid overpopulation in Heaven and its attendant political consequences:

> a place foretold
> Should be, and, by concurring signs, ere now
> Created vast and round, a place of bliss
> In the Purlieus of Heav'n, and therein plac't
> A race of upstart Creatures, to supply
> Perhaps our vacant room, though more remov'd,
> *Lest Heav'n surcharg'd with potent multitude*
> Might hap to move new broils.   (II, 830–37; my emphasis)

Even when his tone becomes slightly ironic, Satan still betrays an obsession with enclosures and their violation. Of Adam and Eve, he says,

> Hell shall unfold,
> To entertain you two, her widest Gates,
> And send forth all her Kings; there will be room,
> Not like these narrow limits, to receive
> Your numerous offspring.   (IV, 381–85)

Yet Satan's notion of containment comes under suspicion as early as Book I, when we are forced to note that God has no intention of confining Satan to the burning lake, despite the "chains" (I, 48 and 210) which encourage us to imagine Satan bound:

> So stretcht out huge in length the Arch-fiend lay
> Chain'd on the burning Lake, nor ever thence
> Had ris'n or heav'd his head, but that the will
> And high permission of all-ruling Heaven
> Left him at large.
>
>   . . . .
>
> Forthwith upright he rears from off the Pool
> His mighty Stature.   (209–22)

In fact, we are consistently reminded that God has no intention of actively restraining Satan:

> Only begotten Son, seest thou what rage
> Transports our adversary, whom no bounds
> Prescrib'd, no bars of Hell, nor all the chains
> Heapt on him there, nor yet the main Abyss
> Wide interrupt can hold. (III, 80–84)

> So spake the false dissembler unperceiv'd;
> For neither Man nor Angel can discern
> Hypocrisy, the only evil that walks
> Invisible, except to God alone,
> *By his permissive will*, through Heav'n and Earth.
> (III, 681–85; my emphasis)

> for what can scape the Eye
> Of God All-seeing, or deceive his Heart
> Omniscient, who in all things wise and just,
> Hinder'd not *Satan* to attempt the mind
> Of Man. (X, 5–9)

Such statements come directly from God or Milton, but as we have seen, one of the most striking guarantees of Satanic freedom comes from the seraph Abdiel, who predicts Satan's true punishment when he tells the archfiend—just before the commencement of hostilities—"henceforth / No more be troubl'd how to quit the yoke / Of God's *Messiah*" (V, 881–83). Once we notice this peculiar and unexpected pronouncement, almost lost in the hubristic rhetoric which ends Book V, we may begin to discern curious double readings in similar pronouncements made by other figures. God tells the assembled angels in Book V that Satan will be "Cast out from God" and fall into a "place / Ordain'd without redemption, *without end*" (V, 613–15; my emphasis). Here, syntax makes endlessness seem almost as much a quality of space as of time. The result is that God seems a specific place (a not entirely accurate impression which we will examine later), whereas Satan's new "place" seems frighteningly unspecific and unbounded. A similar effect is achieved in Michael's proclamation to Satan, "Heav'n casts thee out / From all her Confines" (VI, 272–73), and in God's command to the Son, "drive them out / From all Heav'n's bounds into the utter Deep" (VI, 715–16), both of which place an uneasy emphasis on Satan's future lack of containment.[14]

This kind of verbal ambiguity provides an interesting retrospective

on earlier parts of the poem. Phrases like "profoundest Hell" (I, 251)
surely lend irony to the notion of containment,[15] as does the description
of Satan entering Eden. In the latter case, a passage resounding with
words and phrases such as "border" (IV, 131), "enclosure" (133), "access
deni'd" (137), "insuperable highth" (138), "verdurous wall" (143), and
"circling row" (146) comes to an ironic climax when Satan "At one slight
bound high over-leap'd all bound" (181), a line which employs the very
language of enclosure against itself. This is not the only instance of an
"eruption" which ends up stressing Satan's lack of containment. Sin
opens the doors of Hell to let Satan escape, but, prophetically for Satan
as well as for us, "to shut / Excell'd her power" (II, 883–84).

Perhaps nothing emphasizes Satan's freedom as significantly or as
ironically as his lines to Beëlzebub in Book I:

> To do aught good never will be our task,
> But ever to do ill our sole delight,
> As being the *contrary to his high will*
> *Whom we resist.*   (159–62; my emphasis)

It is important to remember that Satan does not fail to accomplish
anything he sets out to do: he escapes from Hell, traverses the abyss,
eludes the guardian angels, seduces Eve, and returns to Hell, having
established an intergalactic "Causey" (X, 415) between Hell and Earth.
He accomplishes all this, however, without ever acting "contrary to" or
"resisting" God's "high will." Even when confrontation with God's mar-
shals seems inevitable, Satan always manages to proceed without engag-
ing in the kind of "Duel" that we—like Adam in Book XII (386–87)[16]—
are so anxiously anticipating. Satan's boundaries continually recede beyond him, and it is only appropriate that his encounter with Gabriel in
Book IV, just like the meeting with Sin and Death in Book II, defuses
rather than erupts.

One of the results of this continual enlarging of Satan's physical and
dramatic space is to keep him ever "wandering." In Book I we are told
that one of the punishments of the fallen angels is to be sent "wand'ring
o'er the Earth" for God's "trial of Man" (I, 365–66). Satan's journey to
earth is described at several points as a "wandering" (II, 404, 830, 973;
III, 631), and Satan's paradoxical fate might well be summed up in his
own description of himself as "by constraint / Wand'ring" (II, 972–73). If
wandering is the state imposed upon the devils for their punishment,
then we may legitimately feel disturbed when it turns out to be a state
shared by other figures in the poem, most noticeably Adam, Eve, and
John Milton himself. At two crucial points in the poem, Milton de-

scribes his poetic endeavor as a potential wandering, at first pleasant, then more ominous:

> Yet not the more
> Cease I to wander where the Muses haunt
> Clear Spring, or shady Grove, or Sunny Hill,
> Smit with the love of sacred Song; but chief
> Thee *Sion* and the flow'ry Brooks beneath
> That wash thy hallow'd feet, and warbling flow,
> Nightly I visit.   (III, 26–32)

> Up led by thee
> Into the Heav'n of Heav'ns I have presum'd,
> An Earthly Guest, and drawn Empyreal Air,
> Thy temp'ring; with like safety guided down
> Return me to my Native Element:
> Lest from this flying Steed unrein'd, (as once
> *Bellerophon,* though from a lower Clime)
> Dismounted, on th' *Aleian* Field I fall
> Erroneous there to wander and forlorn.   (VII, 12–20)

Milton's admission—part vaunt, part fear—is important because it stresses the moral neutrality of wandering. Immediately after the invocation to Book VII ("Erroneous there to wander . . . "), the burden of "wandering" shifts from Milton to Adam and Eve:

> that sole command,
> So easily obey'd amid the choice
> Of all tastes else to please thir appetite,
> *Though wand'ring.*   (VII, 47–50; my emphasis)

It is no coincidence when, eleven lines later, we are reminded bluntly that Adam is "yet sinless" (VII, 61). Adam wanders before the Fall as well as after it (he and Eve ultimately leave Paradise "with wand'ring steps and slow, XII, 648), and the wandering thus carries with it no necessary moral disapprobation. Satan's "wand'ring" is another convenient but misleading moral signpost: his "constraint" to wander is his punishment, not his distinguishing moral condition. Significantly, before Adam and Eve even begin the wandering which is to be their punishment, the moral resonance of that action is countered by a proleptic reference to Christ's sojourn in the wilderness. This occurs when Michael leads Adam up a "Hill / Of Paradise" to survey the scene of Adam's and Eve's future exile:

> It was a Hill
> Of Paradise the highest, from whose top

> The Hemisphere of Earth in clearest Ken
> Stretcht out to the amplest reach of prospect lay.
> Not higher that Hill nor wider looking round,
> Whereon for different cause the Tempter set
> Our second *Adam* in the Wilderness,
> To show him all Earth's Kingdoms and thir Glory.   (XI, 377–84)

Before Adam's exile even begins, it is linked to the story of that other "wand'ring" undertaken for the redemption of mankind.[17] How the same condition can serve as a punishment to Satan but not to the regenerate (i.e., Milton), is a question to which we will return.

Satan's "wand'ring" in the first two Books is to a great extent enforced by the highly ambiguous nature of his surroundings. The description of Hell is full of indeterminacies which open wide geographic and semantic gaps.[18] Everything is paradoxically synesthetic, oxymoronic, and uncertain:

> Him the Almighty Power
> Hurl'd headlong flaming from th' Ethereal Sky
> With hideous ruin and combustion down
> To *bottomless* perdition, *there* to dwell.
>
> (I, 44–47; my emphasis)

> Nine times the Space that measures Day and Night
> . . . hee . . . / Lay vanquisht.   (I, 50–52)

> . . . darkness visible . . .   (I, 63)

> . . . boundless deep . . .   (I, 177)

> . . . till on dry Land / He lights, if it were Land.   (I, 227–28)

Indeterminacy recurs when Raphael describes Satan's fall to Adam in Book VI:

> a spacious Gap disclos'd
> Into the wasteful Deep; the monstrous sight
> Struck them with horror backward, but far worse
> Urged them behind; headlong themselves they threw
> Down from the verge of Heav'n, Eternal wrath
> Burn'd after them to the bottomless pit.
>   Hell heard th' unsufferable noise, Hell saw
> Heav'n ruining from Heav'n, and would have fled
> Affrighted; but strict Fate had cast too deep
> Her dark foundations, and too fast had bound.
> Nine days they fell;
>
>   .   .   .   .

> Hell at last
> Yawning receiv'd them whole, and on them clos'd.
>
> (VI, 861–75)

There is a constant interplay here between a sense of closure and a sense of infinite recess. Phrases such as "spacious Gap," "wasteful Deep," "bottomless pit," and "cast too deep" might suggest that Satan is ultimately exiled to Chaos rather than Hell,[19] but we are still left with a residue of disturbingly concrete images: the anthropomorphization of Hell, the "foundations" which are "bound" too "fast" to avoid receiving the fallen angels, and the "yawning" mouth which "on them clos'd."

This dual aspect of Hell's physicality is eventually imparted to the devils themselves. Michael Lieb argues persuasively that Satan's violations in *Paradise Lost* are a kind of "penetration," evidenced in the "sexual overtones" of Satan's vocabulary.[20] Nevertheless, in the same way that Hell is both an enclosure and an infinite recess, the rhetoric of Hell reveals simultaneously an impulse toward penetration and an anxiety about the absence of delineation or demarcation:

> [Beëlzebub:] who shall tempt with wand'ring feet
> The dark unbottom'd infinite Abyss
> And through the palpable obscure find out
> His uncouth way,
>
> . . . .
>
>   what strength, what art can then
> Suffice, or what evasion bear him safe
> Through the strict Sentries and Stations thick
> Of Angels watching round?   (II, 404–13)

Satanic wandering is not only a physical, but a rhetorical phenomenon. Harold Toliver observes: "Actually, all positions disintegrate under the relentless pressure of Hell's metaphysical bottomlessness. The speakers find each of their principles giving way beneath them."[21] The notion that the Satanic thought-process is ultimately defective is common to most twentieth-century criticism of the poem. C. S. Lewis in particular has argued so strongly for Satan's lack of intellectual rigor that even subsequent "Satanists" have admitted that Milton at least intended us to be unimpressed by Satan's rhetorical energies.[22] Nevertheless, it is crucial to realize that what strikes the reader of the poem is not so much Satan's illogicality as it is his inability to sustain the intensity of that illogicality. The resultant dissipation of his energy can be accounted for by the fact that Satan is given too much rhetorical space. In his most powerful speech in Book I, it is not the perverse irrationality of Satan's

"Hail horrors" which undercuts him, but his inability to keep his mental energies focused on the tremendous sense of immediacy, the sense of here-and-now he needs to fuel that irrationality:

> Is *this* the Region, *this* the Soil, the Clime,
> Said then the lost Arch-Angel, *this* the seat
> That we must change for Heav'n, *this* mournful gloom
> For that celestial light? Be it so.
>
> . . . .
>
> Farewell happy Fields
> Where Joy for ever dwells; *Hail* horrors, *hail*
> *Infernal world, and thou profoundest Hell*
> *Receive they new Possessor: One who brings*
> *A mind not to be chang' by Place or Time.*
>
> . . . .
>
> *Here* at least
> We shall be free; th' Almighty hath not built
> *Here* for his envy, will not drive us hence:
> *Here* we may reign secure, and in my choice
> To reign is worth ambition though in Hell:
> Better to reign in Hell, than serve in Heav'n.
> *But* wherefore let we then our faithful friends,
> Th' associates and copartners of our loss
> Lie thus astonisht on th' oblivious Pool,
> And call them not to share with us their part
> In this unhappy Mansion: *or* once more
> With rallied Arms to try what *may* be yet
> Regain'd in Heav'n, or what more lost in Hell?

> (I, 242–70; my emphasis)

The passage resounds with repetitions of "this," "Hail," and "here," but Satan partly compromises the rhetorical intensity that buttresses his infernal decision when he expands his focus to consider his companions ("But wherefore let we then our faithful friends . . . ");[23] he fully defeats it when he lets his thoughts drift once more up to the Heaven he has just just so forcefully shut out ("or once more / With rallied Arms to try what may be yet / Regain'd in Heav'n").

In other speeches, Satan's focus opens in a similar "wand'ring" manner. Intensity which relies upon the exclusion of other possibilities, questions, or consequences, becomes dissipated as Satan's scope of consideration expands. Willfully perverse conclusions abound, but it is the very space that opens up between their repetitions which makes Satan not absurd, not illogical, but perhaps a little tiresome.[24] At the beginning of Book IX, after lamenting his inability to enjoy Eden, Satan concludes with an illogical, but tremendously powerful assertion of will:

> Nor hope to be myself less miserable
> By what I seek, but others to make such
> As I, though thereby worse to me redound:
> For only in destroying I find ease
> To my relentless thoughts.　　　　　　　(IX, 126–30)

In Hell, the speech might have ended at this point or a little after, slightly diverted from its aim by Satan's necessary consideration of his audience, his turn away from an exclusive to an expanding context. Viewed simply in terms of length, the speech thus far falls perfectly within the range of speeches he has made in Hell.[25] But the solipsistic intensity of Satan's will, which was defused by the political context of Hell, is even further defused when that context is removed. Satan's audiences forced him away from himself, but they at least kept his discourses relatively brief and, therefore, relatively taut. Here in Book IX, Satan compromises the intensity of his conclusion by going on for another forty lines, only to arrive once more at the same conclusion: "Revenge, at first though sweet, / Bitter ere long back on itself recoils: / Let it" (IX, 171–73). We may admire willfulness when its intensity and concision seem to hold dynamic potential, but not when it simply repeats itself. Similarly, Satan's soliloquy at the beginning of Book IV reaches a crescendo after forty lines ("Which way I fly is Hell; myself am Hell"), but then digresses with two essentially redundant passages ("O then at last relent," 79; "But say I could repent," 93) before returning to the original conclusion: "all Good to me is lost; / Evil be thou my Good" (109–10).

It is perhaps in response to this distressing freedom, this "constrained wandering," that Satan and the devils seem continually to seek containment. The first project the devils undertake in Book I is to build an enclosure, and Satan later promises to "stand" as a "bulwark" for them against God (II, 28–29). The reference to Pandemonium as a "narrow room" (I, 779) is particularly ironic, because it is one of the first phrases used to describe Eden ("In narrow room Nature's whole wealth," IV, 207). In fact, the space created for Adam and Eve is continually referred to as the "room" that the devils have been expelled from:

> [Satan:] O Hell! What do mine eyes with grief behold,
> *Into our room* of bliss thus high advanc't
> Creatures of other mould.　　　　(IV, 358–60; my emphasis)

> to him [God]
> Glory and praise, whose wisdom had ordain'd
> Good out of evil to create, instead
> Of Spirits malign a better Race to bring
> *Into their vacant room.*   (VII, 186–90; my emphasis)

>   [Satan:]to spite us more,
> Determin'd to advance *into our room*
> A Creature form'd of Earth.   (IX, 147–49; my emphasis)

The devils in Hell, then, try to create the one aspect of Paradise that they most need: not "Nature's whole wealth," but the "narrow room" that encloses it.

In a sense, Satan's own survival as a political figure in Hell depends upon a very particular form of containment. After engineering his own nomination to undertake the mission to earth, Satan accepts and rises to forestall other choices:

>   Thus saying rose
> The Monarch, and prevented all reply,
> Prudent, lest from his resolution rais'd
> Others among the chief might offer now
> (Certain to be refus'd) what erst they fear'd;
> And so refus'd might in opinion stand
> His Rivals, winning cheap the high repute
> Which he through hazard huge must earn.   (II, 466–73)

Satan's political control over the fallen angels involves a containment or restriction of their choices which must be disguised. If it should become clear that they are being contained by him, their political energy would increase and his relative stature decrease. God alone can defuse the Prolific by refusing to be the Devourer; the same strategy is not available to Satan in his manipulation of the devils. Nevertheless, Satan manages an almost equally effective plan: he pretends not to be the Devourer. In either case, the relationship perceived by Blake is clearly at work.

If containment provides a desired end to "wand'ring," it also provides the antidote to a similar affliction, endless self-extension. Satan, who is described several times in the first two Books as a creature or vessel at sea, finds himself at the end of Book II "glad that now his Sea should find a shore" (1011). In this particular metaphor, Satan seems virtually to become the sea, and the shore seems not so much a symbol of relief from external chaos as an expression of the desire for self-containment; the anxiety at this point is not that consciousness and identity might be overwhelmed (like a vessel at sea), but rather that they might be extended infinitely (like shoreless sea) to the point of dissipation. Certainly, Satan suffers assaults in Chaos—"his ear . . . peal'd / With noises loud and ruinous" (II, 920–21–but assault does not present his greatest danger. In fact, he is rescued from Chaos only when he is "rebuff [ed]" by "some tumultuous cloud / Instinct with Fire and Nitre" (II, 936–37). It is not impingement, but the lack of it, which threatens Satan as he flutters vainly through the abyss: "and to this hour / Down had been falling" (II, 934–35). It is the threat of becoming a shoreless sea. Satan's predicament may be contrasted with the situation of God, who is temporally and spatially co-extensive with the universe. God proclaims in Book VII: "Boundless the Deep, because I am who fill / Infinitude, nor vacuous the space. / Though I uncircumscrib'd myself retire" (168–70). Satan is not unaware of this: "God in Heav'n / Is Centre, yet extends to all," he recalls in Book IX (107–08). God is neither bounded nor contained but because there is nothing beyond or outside him which is not him, his consciousness and identity lose nothing from extension. Satan, who brings Hell and is Hell whichever way he flies, faces the dilemma of either extending himself into a space he cannot fill or defining (and thus containing) himself against it. This dilemma, as we shall see, occupies the heart of the poem. Unlike God, who may "retire" without being "circumscrib'd," Satan must always be actively generating his identity (as Nancy Hoffman says, "his hell is process")[26] and at the same time looking for boundaries by which to define himself. Satan, like man, lives in "An Edifice too large for him to fill" (VIII, 104).

The problems of self-extension affect the rhetoric used to describe Satan as well as the rhetoric he uses himself. In both cases, Satan can no more fill up his rhetorical space than he can his physical space. Balachandra Rajan states that "Satan considered as a poetic force is different from Satan as a cosmic principle,"[27] but this is not so, and the epic similes, which Milton applies almost exclusively to Satan and the devils, are proof. Critical discussion of these similes has centered on the effects they produce as metaphors—the intellectual, imaginative, or even visual responses they provoke.[28] Nevertheless, the most immediate and striking effect of the extended similes does not depend so much on the status or relationship of the figures they present as upon the rhetorical and syntactic discontinuity they involve. The epic similes are rhetorical eruptions, proliferations of language, not unlike the lists, descriptive set-pieces, prayers, and invocations found throughout the poem. Syntactically, however, they share this unique and striking feature: though they are technically free to extend themselves indefinitely, their "as . . . so" construction creates a tremendous pressure for closure, a pressure which increases in direct proportion to length. Though most of the epic similes are static or slow-moving tableaux, in *formal* terms we experience them all in the way we experience the drama of this particular one:

> As when a spark
> Lights on a heap of nitrous Powder, laid
> Fit for the Tun some Magazin to store
> Against a rumor'd War, the Smutty grain
> With sudden blaze diffus'd, inflames the Air:
> So started up in his own shape the Fiend.   (IV, 814–19)

Milton does not have to tell us that the "sudden blaze" is only momentary; such is the very nature of an explosion. The spark touching the "heap of nitrous Powder" has all the force of the "As when" which begins the sentence: both betray an inevitable closure determined more by the inherent nature of the event than by any external pressure. In a sense, the explosion subsides before it has even occurred; the simile is syntactically complete the moment it gets under way. We wait for Satan's next move before he has even "started up in his own shape." The similes by which Satan is presented force us to jump ahead, to anticipate the inevitable end of their eruption, and thus to stand outside them.

Even if we consider the epic similes in terms of their secondary effects—the actual images they present—we witness Satan's consistent inability to fill his expanding physical environment. When applied to Satan, the epic similes generally portray him as a figure in a tableau or landscape. During the first four books, the shifting physical perspective of the similes moves us progressively further away from the objects of comparison, making those objects seem increasingly diminished in stature. The very first epic simile in Book I describes Satan as Leviathan, a creature so large and so physically proximate that the pilot in the tableau mistakes him for an island. Our physical perspective as readers/viewers allows us distance enough to see the real as well as the distorted image, but we are still fairly close to the scene, close enough to perceive with a chill the "fixed Anchor in his scaly rind." The next three times we see Satan at sea, he is a more distant, more imperiled figure:

> As when far off at Sea a Fleet descri'd
> Hangs in the Clouds.   (II, 636–37)

> harder beset
> And more endanger'd, than when *Argo* pass'd
> Through *Bosporus* betwixt the justling Rocks.   (II, 1016–17)

> And like a weather-beaten Vessel holds
> Gladly the Port, though Shrouds and Tackle torn. (II, 1043–44)

Yet, once again, Satan is not really limited. His reduction here, as always, is a trick of perspective or of rhetorical trope, as the self-conscious artistry of the simile makes clear. We encounter difficult problems if we allow ourselves to think that Satan is truly reduced. The point of the similes is not to show him contained by a landscape, but rather insufficient to fill it.

Because a sense of the "edifice" Satan cannot fill is crucial to our understanding of his ultimate eschatological dissolution, Milton constantly renews our awareness of distance, of the space in the poem's universe. He achieves this end in part with tremendous, sometimes abrupt, changes in the perspective created by his narrative telescope. The telescoping of perspectives begins even before the reference to Galileo's "Optic Glass" (I, 288). Almost immediately, the poem gives us evidence of Satan's prodigious, if somewhat awkward, telescopic powers:

> At once as far as Angels' ken he views
> The dismal Situation waste and wild,
> A Dungeon horrible, on all sides round
> As one great Furnace flam'd.
>
> . . . .
>
> There the companions of his fall, o'erwhelm'd
> With Floods and Whirlwinds of tempestuous fire,
> He soon discerns, and welt'ring by his side
> One next himself in power.   (I, 59–79)

Satan's rather cumbersome readjustment of focal length is our first clue that Hell is a place of optical illusions, a place where physical statures increase and diminish according to shifting perspectives. Satan's telescopic powers never diminish; they increase, rather, as his panoramic command of Eden later demonstrates (IV, 194–355). But, at the same time, Satan becomes more and more the object of a telescopic perspective, first as the point-of-view in the epic similes recedes and secondly as he comes under the increasing scrutiny of heavenly observers:

> Thus while he spake, each passion dimm'd his face,
> Thrice chang'd with pale, ire, envy and despair,
> Which marr'd his borrow'd visage, and betray'd
> Him counterfeit, if any eye beheld.
>
> . . . .
>
> Yet not anough had practis'd to deceive
> *Uriel* once warn'd; whose eye pursu'd him down
> The way he went, and on th' *Assyrian* mount

Saw him disfigur'd, more than could befall
Spirit of happy sort: his gestures fierce
He mark'd and mad demeanor, then alone,
As he suppos'd, all unobserv'd, unseen.   (IV, 114–30)

Uriel's observation of Satan is all the more striking because it has been
anticipated in the argument prefacing Book IV, where Satan is "discovered . . . by his furious gestures in the Mount." Thus when Uriel
sees Satan "disfigur'd," with "gestures fierce" and "mad demeanor," we
are not forced merely into a telescopic view of Satan, but into a recognition that what we should have been seeing all along was a telescopic
view. From the vantage point of the argument Milton tells us what
Satan looks like during his soliloquy; but when we descend into the
poem and down to earth, we forget this, and find no description of Satan
but that "his griev'd look he fixes sad" (IV, 28). The repetition of Uriel's
observation is not simply a double affirmation of Satan's "relative" stature. It reminds us of the tremendous amplitude of Milton's universe, a
universe which can be traversed only by narrative shifts in perspective,
and in which neither we nor Satan can be everywhere simultaneously,
for only God and Milton "fill the infinitude."

Significantly, no such aerial perspective is permitted in the Hell of
Books I and II. The epic similes provide some adjustment of focus, but
we are not allowed to fix the dimensions of Hell from a distance as we
might have, had the initial location of the poem been Heaven, or even
the cosmos. Milton explicitly keeps us out of Heaven in those first two
books in order that Hell's dimensions might seem more expansive. It is
a nice—and necessary—touch that Milton will only lament "O how unlike the place from whence they fell!" (I, 75), leaving the first actual
description of Heaven to Satan ("the happy Realms of Light" I, 85). This
is not to say that the telescopic perspectives developed later in the poem
make Satan's actual stature any more determinate or Hell's actual dimensions any more definite (Hell is still infinite for those who live in it).
However, the telescopic effect does reassure us of something we can
only suspect in the first two books: the imaginative and physical space of
Milton's universe—a space we are constantly being moved through—is
truly larger than Satan can possibly fill.

One of Satan's favorite occupations throughout *Paradise Lost* is pre-
dicting what life will be like after the Fall. Mostly, as we have seen, this
consists of promising more space for the various inhabitants of God's
creation. To the fallen angels, Satan promises "a spacious World, to our
native Heaven / Little inferior" (X, 467–68); for Sin and Death, he

guarantees a place "Created vast and round" where "ye shall be fed and fill'd / Immeasurably, all things shall be your prey" (II, 832, 843–44); with heavy irony, he prophesies for Adam and Eve "room, / Not like these narrow limits, to receive / Your numerous offspring" (IV, 383–85). Despite his capacious vision, however, Satan ultimately establishes a far more extensive domain than even he had anticipated, for the greatest "space" generated by the Fall is the space of history. As we find out in the final two books, Satan is to be cast out on the waters of history much as he was set adrift in the sea of Chaos in Book II (history, like Chaos, being a potentially open-ended "space," circumscribed only by God, and not circumscribed at all for the unregenerate). For Satan, history turns out to be an endless series of transformations. He makes his first historical appearance in the form of his son, Death, whose grisly aspect Adam first witnesses in Michael's presentation of the Cain and Abel story (XI, 429–47). Yet when Adam asks of Michael, "have I now seen Death?" the angel replies:

> Death thou hast seen
> *In his first shape* on man; *but many shapes*
> *Of Death*, and many are the ways that lead
> To his grim Cave.   (XI, 462, 466–69; my emphasis)

The protean nature of Satan's existence in history is emphasized to Adam once again in the familiar passage from Book XII, where Michael prophesies that Christ will redeem man, "Not by destroying *Satan*, but his works / In thee and in thy Seed" (XII, 394–95). Thus history provides an endless series of Satanic types (such as Nimrod, who "from Rebellion shall derive his name," XII, 36), and an endless succession of roles for Satan to play; but it offers him no definitive or sustaining role. Satan can never confront the limitations of action because he can never exhaust his role. We can see how this leads to what one critic has termed "Satan's impatience, in *Paradise Regained*, to have his story concluded."[29] Conclusion—or containment—is the single fate from which Satan is excluded, and this fact is enacted as inexorably in postlapsarian history as it is in prelapsarian space.

The assertion that Satan is never contained, and therefore never allowed the heroism of a true "eruption," finds further support in many commentators' view of the nature and construction of Milton's cosmos. The notions of form and formlessness are integral to Milton's cosmology, and the role of form in the Miltonic universe can be described briefly as follows: God is the one uncircumscribed being in the universe, and needs no boundaries or containment to define his identity (VII, 168–70); God circumscribes the beings of the universe, giving them individual form and identity (V, 823–25; VII, 225–27); outside containment (creation) there is only God and Chaos, the latter only a part of God which he himself has not put in order; to progress to a union with God is to willingly put off form and individuality, to become a spirit "of purest light" (VI, 660);[30] to try to circumvent one's own containment and yet retain one's own individuality, identity, and form, is impossible, and one eventually dissolves into Chaos.

The cosmological relationship of containment and dissolution is crucial to the main action of the poem. Adam and Eve fail to appreciate their containment, the security of their "Narrow room," and this is the flaw that Satan exploits. When Satan tempts Eve, he asks her to break containment by transgressing the one restriction set by God, but at the same time to assume another powerful, individual form: "by putting off / Human, to put on Gods" (IX, 713–14). This is precisely what is impossible, for God is the single entity in the universe whose identity is not defined by form; his uncircumscribed nature is, in fact, his very identity, as we have seen. Satan tells Eve that she may retain her individual identity and yet become God, but this is a contradiction in terms. Her containment has guaranteed her individuation and her safety. Stanley Fish writes that, "Apart from God there can be no stability and no true, that is internally consistent, self." He goes on to note that the "sameness of evil is the sameness of chaos, a stability of instability where the identity and form of any atom or cluster of atoms is a matter of chance unless an ordering power is imposed."[31] To break union with God, to break one's prescribed containment, is not merely to enter a state of moral chaos but of physical chaos as well. Abdiel tells Satan that God "made / Thee what thou art, and form'd the Pow'rs of Heav'n / Such as he pleas'd, and *circumscrib'd their being*" (V, 823–25; my emphasis). Thus when Abdiel proclaims "henceforth / No more be troubl'd how to quit the yoke / Of God's *Messiah*," he also warns him, "who can uncreate thee thou shalt know" (V, 881–83, 895). To have form and containment removed is either to become one with God's infinitude (to beome indistinguishable, to sing "with undiscording voice" in "endless morn of light"),[32] or to dissolve into Chaos.[33] The latter is exactly Satan's fate, as we shall see.

To have containment, to have limitation, is to have form, and thus to have meaning. Adam describes the forbidden tree as "The only sign of our obedience left" (IV, 428); it is the single check which keeps Adam and Eve from quitting the yoke of God's Messiah, from daring uncreation. It is a limitation which props them up. When Satan hears of the interdiction, he is overjoyed:

> all is not theirs it seems:
> One fatal Tree there stands of Knowledge call'd,
> Forbidden them to taste: Knowledge forbidd'n?
> Suspicious, reasonless. Why should thir Lord
> Envy them that? can it be sin to know,
> Can it be death? and do they only stand
> By Ignorance, is that thir happy state,
> The proof of thir obedience and thir faith? (IV, 513–20)

When Satan asks, "do they only stand / By Ignorance?" he emphasizes "Ignorance," but we must understand Milton's emphasis to be on "stand." The ultimate answer to Satan's question is *yes*. It would be a mistake to assent to Satan's censure of "Ignorance," but it would be an even greater mistake to think that ignorance is not the issue, that Satan is misrepresenting the choice. His characterization of the interdiction— "suspicious, reasonless"—is wrong, of course, but we must be careful not to reject the notion of forbidden knowledge just because we are uneasy with the word *ignorance*. Forbidden knowledge is not simply an arbitrary metaphor or an occasion for Adam and Eve to prove their obedience; the issue of limits and form and the issue of forbidden knowledge are one and the same.[34] Adam and Eve "stand" because they are contained—circumscribed by God; the outline of that containment is God's interdiction.

What provoked Blake's famous statement about Milton being one of the Devil's party is that spiritual energy—born of moral tension—is not easily distinguishable from that intellectual energy which is impulse without restraint. Both seem to merge into that precarious zone of mental activity so esteemed and so feared by the Romantics, what Coleridge calls "abstruser musings." The impulses behind Milton's invocation in Book III ("Yet not the more / Cease I to wander where the muses haunt . . . / Then feed on thoughts" III, 26–27, 37) and behind Belial's words in Hell ("for who would lose, / The full of pain, this intellectual being, / Those thoughts that wander through Eternity," II, 146–48) are disturbingly similar. We know they cannot be equivalent, but it is hard to say why they cannot. It is not sufficient to point out, as Lewis does, that the devils and Satan are really nonsensical; one can feel intellectual urgings and still make a poor logician (at least we as readers can feel Belial's mental urgings and still recognize his illogicality). We must do better than that to understand why Milton's "mind through all her powers" piercing into "things invisible to mortal sight" (III, 52, 55) does

not violate forbidden knowledge, and why it does not unconsciously
sanction Satan's and Belial's "thoughts that wander through Eternity."
We must go back to the distinction between the two things in Milton's
universe that lie outside containment: Chaos and God. Any desire to
pierce or see beyond one's own limitations must take one of two forms;
it must either merge into God's order, into the "endless morn of light,"
or become part of the Chaos, as void of meaning and knowledge as it is
of form. Belial's advice appears to oppose this latter choice:

> For who would lose,
> Though full of pain, this intellectual being,
> Those thoughts that wander through Eternity,
> To perish rather, swallow'd up and lost
> In the wide womb of uncreated night,
> Devoid of sense and motion?   (II, 146–51)

Belial wants nothing to do with Chaos, but of course it is too late. God
has already removed the "yoke" of containment, and for the devils, even
to pursue thought is to be "swallow'd up and lost." When they do try to
satisfy their intellectual yearnings, they find not that they are incapable
of reasoning, or that their judgment of fit subject is faulty, but simply
that they can come to no end:

> Others apart sat on a Hill retir'd,
> In thoughts more elevate, and reason'd high
> Of Providence, Foreknowledge, Will, and Fate,
> Fixt Fate, Free will, Foreknowledge absolute,
> And *found no end*, in wand'ring mazes lost.
>   (II, 557–61; my emphasis)

By contrast, Milton's own wandering is ultimately secure because it
assumes containment from which he has never broken. It is a wandering
analogous to the search for the "disserved pieces" of Truth which Milton
so poignantly describes in the *Areopagitica*, a wandering that is a pre-
liminary, rather than a permanent condition, because its resolution
awaits the Second Coming:

From that time ever since, the sad friends of Truth, such as durst appear,
imitating the carefull search that *Isis* made for the mangl'd body of *Osiris*, went
up and down gathering up limb by limb still as they could find them. We have
not yet found them all, Lords and Commons, nor ever shall doe, till her Masters
second comming; he shall bring together every joynt and member, and shall
mould them into an immortall feature of lovelines and perfection.[35]

Even Coleridge's "abstruser musings" had to come to some sort of
resolution. The Romantic hero and the Romantic lyric found their end

either in exhausted repose (Coleridge's "silent icicles / Quietly shining to the quiet Moon")[36] or in the self-destructive burst of "Joy's grape"— either in containment or in eruption. But for Milton's Satan, "in the lowest deep a lower deep / Still threat'ning to devour . . . opens wide" (IV, 76–77). There is neither containment nor eruption, and the banality of truly endless wandering and truly endless repetition becomes more acute as the poem progresses, manifesting itself in (though never being contained or defined by) nonsensicality, comicality, degradation, and bathos. Even in the end, we are mistaken if we think that Satan is to be contained in the eschatalogical future.[37] There are hints that this might be the case: God promises that he will "seal up" the "mouth of Hell / For ever" (X, 636–37), and Michael tells Adam that Christ will "surprise / The Serpent, Prince of air, and drag in Chains / Through all his Realm, and there confounded leave" (XII, 453–55). But the final word used in relation to Satan is telling: Christ will "dissolve / *Satan* with his perverted World" (XII, 546–47). In the end, the uncontained Satan is only to dissolve.

The Johns Hopkins University

NOTES

1. *John Milton: Complete Poems and Major Prose*, ed. Merritt Y. Hughes (Indianapolis, 1957). All quotations from Milton's poetry refer to this edition.

2. In *"Paradise Lost" and Its Critics* (Cambridge, 1947), A. J. A. Waldock writes that Satan "does not degenerate: *he is degraded*" (p. 83). Twentieth-century critics are divided on the question of Satan's diminishing stature; some see it as inherent in his moral nature (Waldock's "degeneration"), whereas others read it as an authorial imposition (Waldock's "degradation"). But all seem to agree that deflation occurs. In *The Fierce Equation: A Study of Milton's Decorum* (London, 1965), Thomas Kranidas claims that Satan "is shown in the process of de-energizing" (p. 126). Presenting "Further Thoughts on Satan's Journey Through Chaos," *Milton Quarterly*, XII, no. 4 (December 1978), Michael Lieb calls Satan's journey an "ironic debasement of the Arch-Deceiver in scatalogical terms" (p. 126). In "On Toads and the Justice of God," *Milton Quarterly*, XIII, no. 1 (March 1979), Dennis Danielson argues that Satan's metamorphosis signifies "decline" (p. 12).

3. Cf. Isabel Gamble MacCaffrey, in *"Paradise Lost" as "Myth"* (Cambridge, Mass., 1959), and Harold E. Toliver, "The Splinter Coalition," in *New Essays on "Paradise Lost,"* ed. Thomas Kranidas (Berkeley, 1969). MacCaffrey writes that Satan "shares the relevant human condition: he is sinful and *hedged about with limitations*" (p. 180; my emphasis). Toliver agrees that Satan "confronts his limits at every turn." He "receives all blows himself, passively unable to ward them off" (p. 56).

4. R. J. Zwi Werblowsky, *Lucifer and Prometheus: A Study of Milton's Satan* (London, 1952). Werblowsky writes that "until Blake's *Marriage of Heaven and Hell* (about

1790) nobody ever appears to have been seduced by Satan's Promethean charms" (p. 3). One might argue that Werblowsky overlooks Dryden. However, Dryden conceives of Satan as a hero only in formal terms; his admiration arises out of the technical sympathy that any creative artist must enter into with his villain. Blake, on the other hand, conceives of Satan as a hero in *moral* terms. See Jerome J. McGann, *Don Juan in Context* (London, 1976), for a similar distinction between Byronic Satanism and its eighteenth-century precursors (pp. 24–25).

    5. *Milton* (London, 1930), p. 276. Cf. Joseph A. Wittreich, Jr., "The 'Satanism' of Blake and Shelley Reconsidered," *SP*, LXV, no. 5 (October 1968), 816–33. Wittreich cautions both against the use of Blake as an emblem for Romantic criticism of Milton and against the notion of a consistently defined "Satanic School" (pp. 818, 832), and argues that, of the various definitions of Satanism, only the notion of Satan as an "admirable moral agent" seems "to provide reasonable grounds for labeling a critic a Satanist" (p. 818). Wittreich goes on to argue that only in *The Marriage of Heaven and Hell*, not in the later, more mature *Milton*, does Blake demonstrate any sympathy for Satan as a moral creature. Also see Edna Newmeyer, "Wordsworth on Milton and the Devil's Party," *Milton Studies*, XI, ed. Balachandra Rajan (Pittsburgh, 1978), pp. 83–98. Newmeyer argues that Wordsworth, even in his youth, never confuses Satan as an aesthetic conception with Satan as a moral conception, and that he was never of the Hazlitt-Byron-Shelley camp. For an analysis of Byron's and Shelley's views on Milton's Satan, see McGann, *Don Juan in Context*, pp. 23–31, and Stuart Curran, "The Siege of Hateful Contraries: Shelley, Mary Shelley, Byron, and *Paradise Lost*," in *Milton and the Line of Vision*, ed. Joseph A. Wittreich, Jr. (Madison, 1975), pp. 209–30. Romantic perspectives on Milton clearly cover a wide spectrum, as Wittreich implies. The present paper does not present Blake's views in *The Marriage of Heaven and Hell* as emblematic either of his final views or of the Romantics' views in general. Blake's work has been chosen because it exemplifies certain shared Romantic assumptions about the nature of energy and its relationship to containment, a set of assumptions which I believe to be manifest even in the poetry of the least Blakean of the Romantics, Keats.

    6. In *Complete Writings*, ed. Geoffrey Keynes (Oxford, 1966), p. 150.

    7. Ibid., pp. 150, 155.

    8. In *Poetical Works*, ed. H. W. Garrod (Oxford, 1970), p. 220.

    9. Waldock, *"Paradise Lost" and Its Critics*, p. 78.

    10. *A Preface to "Paradise Lost"* (Oxford, 1942), pp. 97–98. For Waldock, the evidence cited by Lewis indicates only that the "whole equilibrium" of Milton's work shifted when he abandoned tragedy for epic, and that the speeches imported into the epic from the tragedy do not indicate a priority of intent (*"Paradise Lost" and Its Critics*, pp. 84–85).

    11. I use Wittreich's terms as the most convenient distinction between two basic camps of twentieth-century Milton criticism ("The 'Satanism' of Blake and Shelley Reconsidered," p. 816).

    12. Irby B. Cauthen, Jr., "Satan 'Squat Like a Toad'," *Milton Quaterly*, VII, no. 4 (December 1973), 95–97; Ann Gossman, "Satan: From Toad to Atlas," *Milton Quarterly*, X, no. 1 (March 1976), 7–11; Danielson, "On Toads," pp. 12–14.

    13. Even the one form that we may consider to be externally imposed on Satan, the metamorphosis into a snake in Hell (Book X), is not of lasting consequence. See Cherrell Guilfoyle, "Adamantine and Serpentine: Milton's Use of Two Conventions of Satan in *Paradise Lost*," *Milton Quarterly*, XIII, no. 4 (December 1979), 133.

    14. Leonora Leet Brodwin, "The Dissolution of Satan in *Paradise Lost*: A Study of Milton's Heretical Eschatology," *Milton Studies*, VIII, ed. James D. Simmonds (Pitts-

burgh, 1975), pp. 165–207. Brodwin insists that a careful reading of God's commands (V, 612–15; VI, 52–55) reveals that Satan's fate is to be thrown not into Hell, but into Chaos (pp. 181–82).

15. Note a similar play on the double sense of "profound" to indicate psychological and physical depth in Marvell's "Mourning":

> How wide they dream! The *Indian* Slaves
> That sink for Pearl through Seas profound,
> Would find her Tears yet deeper Waves
> And not of one the bottom sound.

The Poems and Letters of Andrew Marvell, I, *Poems*, ed. H. M. Margoliouth (Oxford, 1927), p. 32.

16. Stanley Fish, *Surprised by Sin: The Reader in "Paradise Lost"* (New York, 1967), pp. 179–80.

17. *Paradise Regained*, I, 351–56; II, 245–46; IV, 596–600. See *Complete Poems*, pp. 470–530.

18. J. B. Broadbent, *Some Graver Subject: An Essay on "Paradise Lost"* (London, 1960), p. 71. Hell's indeterminacy does not depend on its literal infinity. As Walter Clyde Curry points out, in *Milton's Ontology, Cosmogony and Physics* (Lexington, 1957), Milton's universe is not "literally," but "hyperbolically" infinite, as infinite as the human mind can imagine, but nevertheless contained within the "Infinity of God" (p. 145).

19. Brodwin, "The Dissolution of Satan," p. 181.

20. *The Dialectics of Creation: Patterns of Birth and Regeneration in "Paradise Lost"* (Boston, 1970), pp. 116–17, 142–60.

21. "The Splinter Coalition," in *New Essays on "Paradise Lost,"* p. 49.

22. See Lewis, *Preface*, pp. 94–95, and Waldock, *"Paradise Lost" and Its Critics*, pp. 73–74.

23. Arnold Stein, *Answerable Style: Essays on "Paradise Lost"* (Minneapolis, 1953). Stein admits that although Satan's "stature" is greatest when he is "before his millions," it is at the cost of denying "his essential solitary self" (p. 5).

24. Lewis points out that the "Hell he carries with him is, in one sense, a Hell of infinite boredom" (*Preface*, p. 100).

25. The soliloquy begins at IX, 99, and reaches its first juncture at IX, 130. Satan's speeches to the fallen angels in Books I and II average approximately thirty-three lines; the longest is only forty-one lines. His seven speeches occur at I, 84–124, 157–91, 242–70, 315–30, 622–62, and II, 11–42, 430–66.

26. "The Hard-Hearted Hell of Self-Delusion," *Milton Quarterly*, VII, no. 1 (March 1973), 12.

27. *"Paradise Lost" and the Seventeenth Century Reader* (London, 1947), p. 94.

28. Three basic interpretations of the epic similes all rest on their subject matter rather than on their basic (and common) syntactic form. See James P. Holoka, " 'Thick as Autumnal Leaves': The Structure and Generic Potentials of an Epic Simile," *Milton Quarterly*, X, no. 4 (December 1976), 78–83; Kingsley Widmer, "The Iconography of Renunciation: The Miltonic Simile," *ELH*, XXV (1958), 297–308; Geoffrey Hartman "Milton's Counterplot," in *Milton: Modern Essays in Criticism*, ed. Arthur Barker (London, 1965), p. 389.

29. Patricia A. Parker, *Inescapable Romance: Studies in the Poetics of a Mode* (Princeton, 1979), p. 139. See Parker's similar point about Satan in *Paradise Lost* (p. 149).

30. Curry, *Milton's Onotology, Cosmogony and Physics*, pp. 36, 145, 162–63.

31. Fish, *Surprised by Sin*, pp. 337–38.

32. Milton, "At a Solemn Music," in *Complete Poems*, pp. 81–82.

33. Adam tells Eve, "I thought / I then was passing to my former state / Insensible, and forthwith to dissolve" (VIII, 289–91). Bodwin concurs: "Milton's materialism . . . causes his mortalist doctrine to be dissolutionist rather than annihilationist" ("The Dissolution of Satan," p. 173).

34. It is not the tree or the fruit that is forbidden, but knowledge itself. Milton's syntax is hardly arbitrary when he writes of the "tree / of interdicted Knowledge" (V, 51–52). In "A Better Teacher than Aquinas," *SP*, XIV (April 1917), Edwin Greenlaw claims that the Fall "immediately gains significance and interest if we recognize that the apple is but a symbol, and that Milton's real theme is to show how Adam fell because he did not stand the test of temperance" (p. 213). However, the apple does not represent temperance; in fact, it does not *represent* knowledge, but *is* knowledge itself. Accordingly, after the Fall, Adam admits that it was a mistake *to know more*, because "beyond is all abyss, / Eternity, whose end no eye can reach" (XII, 555–56). At a certain point, ignorance is containment, containment safety.

35. *Areopagitica*, in *The Prose of John Milton*, ed. J. Max Patrick (New York, 1968), p. 317.

36. "Frost at Midnight," in *Poetical Works*, ed. Ernest Hartley Coleridge (Oxford, 1969), pp. 240–42.

37. Brodwin, "The Dissolution of Satan," pp. 169–71. Brodwin argues that verbal ambiguity compromises even the certainty of God's final declaration that Hell will be shut forever (X, 636–37). Yet this is hardly a necessary argument, since Milton's last words on Satan (XII, 546–47) already support Brodwin's theory that Milton's doctrine was ultimately "dissolutionist."

TIME, FREEDOM, AND FOREKNOWLEDGE IN *PARADISE LOST*

R. D. Bedford

T HE READER of *Paradise Lost* who ventures into the mazes of determinism and free will can only do so with an awareness of the labyrinths of "providence, foreknowledge, will and fate, / Fixed fate, free will, foreknowledge absolute" (II, 599–60) and of Milton's reservation of such endless discussions to fallen angels.[1] Nevertheless, although *Paradise Lost* is a poem, not a dialogue on liberty and necessity, its author reveals both a subtle sense of the philosophical and logical problems involved (evidenced elsewhere by his strenuous concern with the issues in *Christian Doctrine*, and a commitment to what for him is an inviolable principle: without true freedom of the will, "liberty will be an empty word, and will have to be banished utterly not only from religion but also from morality" (*CD* I, iii).[2] It will be argued here that although Milton's casuistry may continue to generate speculation on the issue, his artistic and poetic solution to these problems depends largely on his resonantly ambiguous handling of the phenomenon of time in *Paradise Lost*.

It will be readily acknowledged that at the heart of the middle books of the poem lie questions of freedom, causality, determinism—and hence of responsibility—questions to which both Milton as poet and we as readers are forced to offer various shifts and stratagems. One of these characteristic questions is that if Adam's fall is in any sense caused (whether by external events or by his own actions is indifferent here) then it logically cannot be avoided; if something is caused, it cannot not happen. If we, or Milton, were to argue in response, recoiling from this idea of necessity, that Adam's choice is not caused, then the only alternative must be that it is an arbitrary event, an accident, for which no more responsibility can be adduced than for a necessitated act. Either way, we do not have what the poem seems to demand: a clear conception of free will acting with full responsibility and accountability.

It may be, of course, that we are looking for the wrong thing; a clear conception may not be possible. Adam's free will may be both an insurmountable logical problem and at the same time an article of

61

belief—which is after all a perfectly familiar theological position. When St. Augustine speaks of free will, the impression emerges that it is, in Adam's case, a kind of minimal theological requirement, a technicality sufficient to allow the apportioning of blame, but not to constitute the freedom to have chosen differently.[3] One mode of argument, like that of St. Augustine, would be to attribute to free will only the exercise of *rational* choice ("for reason is but choosing," as *Areopagitica* has it, and thus choosing is the act of reason); this argument would suggest that Adam is free only to act rationally or in proportion as he acts rationally. Adam's "half-abashed" response to Raphael's lecture on love, reason, and passion contains the defense that:

> I to thee disclose
> What inward thence I feel, not therefore foiled,
> Who meet with various objects, from the sense
> Variously representing; yet still free
> Approve the best, and follow what I approve.   (VIII, 607–11)

It is however a defense with ominous echoes, both of St. Paul and of Ovid's *Metamorphoses:* "I see the better, and I approve it too: / The worse I follow."[4] Raphael's farewell to Adam picks it up a little later: "take heed lest passion sway / Thy judgement to do aught, which else free will / Would not admit" (VIII, 635–36). The difficulty with the view that Adam is free only to act rationally (which is what Raphael appears to be saying here) is that it invites the problem that one cannot, in the same sense of the term *free will*, argue that it is by free choice also that he acts irrationally; otherwise one would be saying that Adam can freely will that which, should he ever will it, would not be freely willed.

Together with such logical conundrums regarding the moral position of free will lies the equally intransigent issue of causality. The moment one asks *why* Adam did this or that (whether it be a morning hymn to the Creator or the eating of the fruit), one seems to be talking about unavoidable acts in the sense that, if they have those causes, they must occur; there is only the possibility of other and different acts if there are other and different causes. Consequently, we have been encouraged to take up various positions toward Milton's narrative. The simplest is to acquiesce in the illogicality, admit the impossibility of the posited free will, and relish the comedy of the situation.[5] Another encourages us to shut our eyes to causes in the poem, or at least to recognize that Milton only offers "causes" as they come to hand, none of them sufficient or decisive. Milton, it is argued, is highly sensitive to the problems of causation, and hence of necessitated acts, and offers us free will *without* causation.[6] Yet others have persuaded us to recognize that Milton *stresses* the causes, plots the Fall from the beginning, offers us an unfallen Adam passionately fixated and an Eve petulantly contrary, but, at the same time, promotes the "official" view of a paradisal innocence with which these actions are subtly at variance. The object is to present moral freedom, which Adam forfeits, as provisional, relative, and contextual, depending on his acting within the scope of his true stature and not contrary to his higher knowledge and sense of moral obligation.[7] In the first strategy we are asked merely to see the joke; in the second we are asked to pretend not to have noticed and are (paradoxically) invited to be surprised by sin; in the third we are asked to untangle, or at least to endure, the riddles of Adam being in one sense free to sin or not to sin, but in another sense not free should he sin.

In the face of such difficulties, defenders of the doctrine of moral freedom from Plotinus and Boethius to Kant have characteristically acknowledged that true freedom cannot be conceived except outside of time. A dominant theological form of this acknowledgment stresses, as St. Augustine did, that freedom is proportional to our ability to escape from worldly and temporal processes and can be approached only through contemplation of the eternal and the immutable—that is, God.[8] Adam's excessive response to Eve and the critical confusion of loyalties of which Raphael sharply warns him make one significant strand in Milton's dramatization of events and may be numbered among the "causes." But another response to the possibility timelessness offers for escape from the riddles of freedom and causality is in a sense more searching and equally germane to Milton's treatment of the Fall.

One of the most poignant dimensions of the poem is its nostalgia for what might have been, for what is lost irrecoverably in time. It renders a particular time inaccessible and past in a peculiarly definitive way. It is, too, full of conditionals and second thoughts, which are, of course, the necessary conditions of acts of remorse and repentance. The sense of time is also the necessary condition for the exercise of free will and of choice itself: to choose involves deliberation; deliberation implies time as its condition. But is choice then an illusion? For time is also the necessary condition for causation; there can be no cause without sequence, and causation seems to contradict free choice. Where every action or event occurs in time, determined by the past and determining the future, freedom must seem a figment, for things can only be as they are or as they will be. Milton's approach to this dilemma involves two strategies: one is to assume a crucial difference between causal necessity and logical necessity, the other is to assume and demonstrate a God who is nontemporal and, despite his temporary descents to the grammar of the human mind, knows all actions and events without "before" and "after." The first strategy challenges us to distinguish between "this must happen" and "this will happen" and see where our distinctions may lead; the second enters into combat with yet another celebrated conundrum regarding Adam's freedom and responsibility (a conundrum to which the form of Milton's poem gives unavoidable exposure), the relation of man's will to God's foreknowledge. To both of these issues Milton's treatment of time is critical.

In *Surprised by Sin: The Reader in "Paradise Lost,"* Stanley Fish has persuasively conducted the reader of Milton's account of the Fall through the minefields of possible misunderstanding that Milton lays in his path. The ever-present tension between Adam's and Eve's innocence and our own foreknowledge is delicately invoked in Milton's instruction to the reader and in moments of poignant dramatic irony. While this effect unquestionably poses possibilities no imaginative writer could ignore, there may be a more rigorously philosophical questioning involved at the same time. When we have followed the course of Eve's and Adam's temptation and fall, have recognized that they, unlike us, cannot know the end of the story, and have recognized too that what we have thought "necessary" or "inevitable" has not been so to the protagonists at their moments of action (those actions have been more "free" than we may have supposed), there still remains a confusing nexus of riddles involving the multiple senses of the terms *necessary* and *impossible*. We may find ourselves wondering whether, if the Fall was not then "necessary" (in the sense that nothing may have "determined" it but our own foreknowledge), was it also therefore possible for Adam and Eve to have acted differently? We may have to conclude, accepting the argument from causation, that it was not for the overwhelmingly simple reason that the Fall occurred. So that although we may have avoided committing ourselves to the proleptical view that the Fall "must" occur, we have no answer to the assertions either that it will occur or that it has occurred, and, consequently, cannot have been otherwise. The upshot may seem to be that Adam and Eve had no other choice and therefore, no choice.

One of the assumptions involved here is that if it is logically necessary for the past to be what it has been and for the future to be what it is going to be (if it is logically impossible for the future not to be what it is going to be), then it follows that there is no point in doing anything about it or in speaking of free will. Whatever Adam has done must have happened anyway, and whatever Adam and Eve have not done could not have happened anyway, even if they had tried to make it happen. From this position, the possibility of a Miltonic freedom seems to vanish without trace, despite the poet's formal and repeated protestations of its reality.

And yet logical determinism, which asserts no more than that things are as they are and cannot be otherwise, need not involve us or Milton in causal necessity. The sense in which things "cannot possibly be otherwise" because they are what they are greatly differs from the sense in which things "cannot possibly be otherwise" because other things—Adam's uxoriousness, Eve's willfulness, Satan's "glozing lies," or even the absence of free will—cause or compel them to be what they are. To say that the future is logically determined is not to say that it is causally determined. Logical determinism is not fatalism; nor is logical necessity causal necessity. Milton presents a Fall in which a posited free will, though not compatible with fatalism, is perfectly compatible with a determinism which proposes that for everything that ever happens there are conditions, given which, nothing else could happen. I think that, despite the aggressively defensive stance and the desire to make sense of the issue in terms of God's "decrees," this awareness lies somewhere at the center of *Christian Doctrine*, where Milton discusses the paradox that "man fell, though not unwillingly, yet by necessity" (I, iv).

It may be true that all paradises are paradises lost, and the peculiar sense of loss in the poem depends in part for its effect on the possibility that although the future cannot be changed from what it is to be, it may be "altered" from what it might have been *if* our first parents had not taken the actions they did. The real moral issue here, of course, is not whether the future will (tautologically) be what it is to be, but whether *what* it is to be owes anything to our future or present efforts and activities. Fatalism asserts a present causally discontinuous with the future, in which all events occur by accident or by chance and in which free will is illusory.

This, at any rate, is Satan's view of the matter. Milton characteristically invites us to consider events in the poem as happening by chance, a word almost inevitable in introducing similes in which Satan participates: Leviathan is discovered "haply" (by chance) "slumbering on the Norway foam" (I, 203); the devils' new sense of purpose is like a "bark by chance" anchoring in a "craggy bay" (II, 288–89); the illuminated landscape of Book II occurs "if chance the radiant sun" (492); Satan approaches Eve by chance, both in the simile "if chance with nymph-like step fair virgin pass" (IX, 452) and in his mental picture of a universe in which events occur only by necessity or by chance—"He sought them both, but wished his hap might find / Eve separate, he wished, but not with hope / Of what so seldom chanced" (IX, 421–23). Milton even springs a little trap for the reader in his exclamation "hapless Eve," inviting us to think of her as a victim of bad luck caught in an accident (IX, 404). Milton's God, on the other hand, assigns chance only to Chaos, to which he chooses not to extend his form-giving goodness: "necessity and chance / Approach not me, and what I will is fate" (VII, 172). In Milton's usage "fate" means not fatalism, but "only what is *fatum*, spoken by some almighty power" (*CD* I, ii). Replying to Belial's optimistic yet deterministic hope of what "future days might bring, what chance, what change / Worth waiting," Mammon perceptively rebukes him: "him to unthrone we then / May hope when everlasting fate shall yield / To fickle chance, and Chaos judge the strife" (II, 231–33).

That is, if "everlasting fate" should ever yield to chance, the result would be chaotic, for "chance governs all" only in Chaos (II, 910). The alternative is an eternal providence which is logically determined, and logical determinism tells us no more than that the future will be what it is to be and cannot be otherwise. It tells us nothing, in other words, about free will's relation to the apparent alternatives of chance and causal necessity; it can be invoked without implying either of them.

As we read Milton's account of the Fall, both our own fore-knowledge of events and our difficulties in distinguishing logical determinism from causal necessity and from fatalism may interfere with our understanding of his assertions of man's freedom. Much more intractable an issue, however, is raised by the presence in the action of the poem of a God who knows all events, a God who has to be presented as in a sense "neutral" (noninterfering, not-determining) with regard to man's actions and yet whose defined attributes of omnipotence and omniscience seem to render such neutrality logically impossible. And it is clear from Milton's wrestling with free will and divine foreknowledge in *Christian Doctrine* that he was sharply aware of all the devious and complex implications of these problems.

Paradise Lost embodies the end-in-the-beginning of an accomplished theological as well as poetic structure. That the Alpha and Omega who knows all truths from the beginning of time presides over its action gives a powerful imaginative appeal to the suggestion of a determinism militating against free will's operation in time. One response to the paradox is to pretend that it isn't there and to fall into the trap of incoherence about the concept of "the future": "The relation between cosmic time and human time depended upon Adam's action and God's response to it; now the outcome of the Fall has altered the future of all human history"; "this is the final purport of all Michael's teaching."[9] This view appears to suggest either that God has a number of possible futures up his sleeve and selects the right one for the circumstances, or that he just got it wrong.

Let us look a little more closely at the nature of this problem. At noon on the thirty-second day of the action of *Paradise Lost*, Eve reached for the forbidden fruit, "she plucked, she ate" (IX, 781). Prior to noon on the thirty-second day, God knew that Eve would eat the fruit at that precise moment. It would therefore seem, from our general theological and logical assumptions about the nature of God—his eternity, omnipotence, omniscience, and infallibility—that at the time of the action Eve was not able, it was not within Eve's power, to refrain from eating the fruit. Eve's eating of the fruit cannot be accounted a voluntary action since, it seems safe to assume, no action is voluntary if it is not, at the time, within the power of the agent to refrain from its performance. From this blunt statement of affairs, which Milton must handle in his account of the Fall, it is perhaps necessary to get the details of the issue as clear as possible. Among the assumptions central to the nature of God are first, the claim that God is infallible and second, the claim that God knows the outcome of human actions in advance of their performance. Related to these claims is the assumption of God's omniscience, that God knows all facts, and that it is conceptually impossible for an individual who is God to hold a false belief or to be mistaken; also crucial is the assumption of God's eternity, that God has always existed and will always exist, and that he extends indefinitely both forward and backward in time. To suppose, therefore, that Eve could act in such a way as to render false a belief previously held by God or an item of knowledge previously known by God would be to suppose that at the time of the action Eve was capable of something having a conceptually incoherent description, namely, something that would render false an item of knowledge held by God, who is infallible. Of course, the same argument holds had Eve *not* eaten the fruit.

What then is Milton to make of this situation? Of the claim that God knows in advance the outcome of human actions, Milton writes; "God has complete foreknowledge, so he knows what men . . . will think and do, even before they are born and even though these thoughts and deeds will not take place until many centuries are passed" (*CD* I, ii). But into the hiatus I have excavated here Milton drops the words—in this context, I think, inconsistent words—"who are free in their actions." He also takes up the issue of infallibility. Concerning God's decrees, he argues that they may be merely contingent: "God makes no absolute decrees about anything which he left in the power of man, for men have freedom of action" (CD I, iii). Hieronymous Zanchius provides a classic text revealing the interior of the problem Milton is probing: "Now if God foreknew this, He must have predetermined it, because His own will is the foundation of his decrees, and His decrees are the foundation of His Prescience; He therefore foreknowing futurities, because by His predestination He hath rendered their futurition certain and inevitable."[10] Briefly acknowledging the host of adherents on each side of this issue, Milton appeals to human common sense ("if it is allowable to apply the standards of mortal reason to divine decrees") and tilts at the paradox, about which the Reformed theologians themselves appear to have been sensitive, of absolute predestination, which seemed to conclude that what was necessary for eternal life was not any human will or exertion, "but only some sort of fatal decree" (CD I, iv). God made his decrees conditional, Milton argues, "for the purpose of allowing free causes to put into effect that freedom which he himself gave them"; freedom is destroyed, "or at least obscured," "if we admit any such sophisticated concept of necessity as that which, we are asked to believe, results not from compulsion but from immutability or infallibility. This concept has misled and continues to mislead a lot of people" (CD I, iii). He then offers as plain a statement of affairs as possible: "The divine plan depends only on God's own wisdom. By this wisdom he had perfect knowledge of all things in his own mind and knew what they would be like and what their consequences would be when they occurred" (CD I, iii). But then comes the question, "how can these consequences which, on account of man's free will, are uncertain, be reconciled with God's absolutely firm decree?"[11] Milton says simply that God does not always absolutely decree; he points out that the decree in Genesis ii, 17–"do not eat of this, for on the day you eat it you will die"—"itself was conditional before the Fall" (CD I, iv). He draws a distinction between things happening of necessity and God foreknowing that they will happen, and he argues that Adam's fall was certain but not necessary (CD I, iii).[12]

It is of course evident that *Christian Doctrine* keeps to the context of Arminian-Calvinist oppositions over the doctrine of free will. Milton conducts his argument entirely in terms of that debate. He frequently refers, at times in a rather weary way, to the nature of the language being used in this sort of discourse about God, who is, in one of Milton's listed attributes, incomprehensible (cf. *PL* III, 705–07; VII, 112–14); he warns, for example, that "when we talk about God, it must be understood in terms of man's limited powers of comprehension," and he shows exasperation with such debate: "but really, if we must discuss God in terms of our own habits and understandings." In this treatise his defense of man's free will and God's noninterference rests upon two basic arguments, contingency and human analogy, both of which remain within the terms of formulations about God's foreknowledge.

The argument from contingency, as offered by Milton in *Christian Doctrine* and, in another form, by Leibniz in *Theodicee*,[13] contrasts "necessary" to "conditional" or "contingent" and also opposes "necessary" to "voluntary." To say that Eve's eating of the fruit is true or certain (because it is foreknown by God), but not *necessarily* true or certain, does not salvage the issue of free will. St. Augustine, as the Reformers well knew, says that if God foreknows actions, then they *are* necessary in the sense that they are not voluntary. The conditional or contingent response does not solve the problem that, if Eve's action were only contingently necessary, and if Eve were able, contingently, to refrain from eating the fruit, then either she was able, contingently, to act in a way which would have falsified an item of God's knowledge or she was able, contingently, to act so that God held not that item of knowledge, but some other. Neither of these possibilities is acceptable; each fails to touch the issue in hand.[14] The argument from human analogy, also espoused by St. Augustine as an approach to this question, suggests that since our own human prescience of another's actions does not involve compulsion, then neither does God's.[15] God knows in advance, it is argued, that a given person is going to choose to perform a certain action at some specific time in the future. And yet this argument, too, is not without its problems, since God is required to know both that Eve will eat the fruit at noon on the thirty-second day (an item of knowledge which cannot be other and is therefore necessary, not free) and also that she acted freely. God is thus discovered holding a false belief. In other words, the human analogy is not a parallel to God's foreknowledge in relation to determinism, for the crucial difference is that human foreknowledge, unlike that of a being who is God, is not infallible. St. Augustine therefore proceeds to attack the notion of infallibility, while on another front, both he and, later, Boethius attack that other assumption involved in the complex, the notion of God's knowing in advance.[16]

In Part 5, section iii, of *The Consolation of Philosophy*, Boethius said, like St. Augustine, that if God is infallible and knows the outcome of all human actions in advance of their performance, then no human action is voluntary.[17] At the same time, Boethius held that some human actions are voluntary. He was therefore obliged to deny either that God is infallible, or that he knows beforehand how human beings will act. Boethius chose to deny the second. He denied that God can have temporal extension. A timeless being cannot know the outcome of human actions in advance of their performance, since the cognition of such a being is not located in time relative to the action in question. In Section vi of the fifth book he offers the view that it is not possible to speak of a timeless being knowing prior to, at the time, or after. God's knowledge is present tense only and cannot involve time-qualified predicates. This attack on assumptions about the nature of God's duration would seem to reach the heart of the issue, for, without locating God's cognition in the past relative to the actions it knows, there appears to be no way of formulating the problem of divine foreknowledge.

We should now return to *Christian Doctrine*. At one or two moments, Milton seems about to break out of the charmed circle of predestinarian debate. At one point early in the discussion, he observes that "It is absurd . . . to separate God's decrees or intention from his eternal resolution or foreknowledge and give the former chronological priority. For God's foreknowledge is simply his wisdom under another name, or that idea of all things which, to speak in human terms, he had in mind before he decreed anything."[18] His hint here that the very notion of foreknowledge is merely a human mental fabrication and has nothing to do with God's perception (for with God there is no latter or former, no "chronological priority") and that foreknowledge for a being who is God is simply knowledge is, surprisingly, not developed or incorporated into the discussion. Following St. Augustine's concept of eternity, where "nothing is flitting, but all is at once present,"[19] Boethius' celebrated formulation of God's "interminabilis vitae tota simul et perfecta possessio" ("simultaneous and complete possession of infinite life"),[20] and Aquinas' "nunc stans," other commentators saw the crucial issue readily enough, though they may have made very different things of it. For Luther, "there is no Dinumeration of tyme with God," for whom "all thynges are lapped up as it were in one bundle."[21] Even for Calvin, God "holds and sees" all things at once "as if actually placed before him."[22] For Sir Thomas Browne, there is in eternity "no distinction of Tenses"; with God there is "no prescious determination of our Estates to come," for "what to us is to come, to His eternity is present, His whole duration being but one permanent point, without Succession, Parts, Flux or Division."[23] Why then does Milton give no prominence to such views in *Christian Doctrine*, and why does he appear to ignore the Augustinian and Boethian solutions to the problems of determinism?

It has been noted that Milton was "one of the few great writers of the Renaissance to depart from the traditional view of time."[24] Where for St. Augustine time did not exist before the Creation ("the world was made with time, and not in time"),[25] Milton counters that "there is certainly no reason why we should conform to the popular belief that motion and time, which is the measure of motion, could not, according to our concepts of 'before' and 'after,' have existed before this world was made" (*CD* I, vii). In *Paradise Lost*, Raphael makes it clear to Adam that time reaches behind the Creation and that there is time in Heaven, though it differs from human time:

> As yet this world was not, and Chaos wild
> Reigned where these heavens now roll, where earth now rests
> Upon her centre poised, when on a day
> (For time, though in eternity, applied
> To motion, measures all things durable
> By present, past, and future) on such a day
> As heaven's great year brings forth.   (V, 577–83)

A possible explanation for Milton's lapse from orthodoxy (or his original adaptation of it) may be that in *Paradise Lost* a timeless stasis before the Creation would make action utterly intractable, eliminating or rendering inconceivable of execution any dramatic or narrative possibilities depending upon suspense, movement, and sequence. Milton may have other issues on his mind in *Christian Doctrine*, where his antitrinitarianism, the subordinate position of the Son and the Holy Spirit and the Son's generation *in time*, requires not timelessness, but duration in eternity.

While there may be special reasons for Milton's tactics in *Christian Doctrine*, it may be acknowledged that *Paradise Lost* is not a poem which gives great prominence to antitrinitarian views (though they may be there) or to any other theological novelties. Milton's reasons for insisting upon time before the Creation and in Heaven (until, for Milton as for St. Augustine, time will cease and, after the Last Judgment, "stand fixed")[26] may have something to do with theology, but a good deal also to do with artistic and poetic judgment. For one thing, time renders extraterrestrial action narratively possible, and for another, it allows, in its "mythic" use of times within times, vertically rather than sequentially (hence, causally) organized perspectives upon which many of the poem's most moving and dramatic moments turn. Such perspectives present the Fall and Satan's decline so that they seem to occur almost continuously, from the time when seamen moor alongside Leviathan in the opening epic simile to the time of Adam's capitulation to "what seemed remediless." It is a unique poem, not least for its energetic confrontation with the problem of time posed by Milton's "grand design." Milton expects his readers to be alert and adaptable, to be aware of simultaneous and layered times.

While he pays detailed attention to the measurement of time, to precise chronology, to significant sunrises, noons, and sunsets, Milton also gives attention to dimensions where "time and place are lost" and to an empyrean where God sits in an eternal present indicative (III, 77–78). Milton invites us to explore the ironic paradoxes of introducing poetic material for simile and comparison derived from a world surviving the event in hand; he invites us to recognize through classical, biblical, and seventeenth-century analogues the simultaneity of an action in which sequential ordering is merely a deceptive narrative convenience. He insists on the paradox of the present in the past, where "before," and "now," and "after" may be conflated in one continuum. Uriel, for instance, glides down a sunbeam to the newly created earth and is transformed into a shooting star observed by both an Homeric and a seventeenth-century mariner (IV, 555–60). The sun, as significant symbol, measures time as it passes and signals crisis and judgment, yet remains a static archetype, emblematic, out of time. Events constantly repeat themselves. We begin and end the poem with a picture of the sea swallowing Pharoah/Satan "with all his host," God crazing "their chariot wheels," and the "sojourners" surviving to "gain their shore" (I, 304–11; XII, 190–215). As we read, we grapple with the stratified accumulations of a sequence of events complicated by flashbacks but unfolding in time, with the relation of these to historical time and to a vividly present, seventeenth-century time (what is Galileo doing itemizing Satan's armor?), and with the relation of all these to the time of the reading experience itself. All of this is further complicated by another, cosmic time that exists in Heaven, surmounted by a God who views all times simultaneously from a point altogether outside time. In other words, in *Paradise Lost* if not in *Christian Doctrine*, Milton asserts the Boethian view and all its implications.

We therefore have in this extraordinary poem a density of texture which offers logically incompatible but poetically energetic perspectives. As Milton scholars often note, Milton's God articulates the essentials of the foreknowledge-and-necessity issue like an inspired summary of *Christian Doctrine*.[27] Such discussions are not limited to a single section of Book III.[28] Both the speaking God of *Paradise Lost* and the customary theological language—whether of "foreknowledge," "prevenient grace," or "the promised seed"—that embodies such time-qualified perspectives exist in the poem simultaneously with a timeless Boethian God and a poetically realized disintegration of temporality.

In his discourse on predestination in Book III, Milton's God propounds a liberal anti-Calvinistic view which, like that expressed in *Christian Doctrine*, is so defined as to hope to exclude "necessity" or "determinism." Whatever the problems and limitations of that particular nexus of arguments, Milton also indicates the timeless being who is dramatically rendering such a discourse. He does this in part by assigning to God a totally random use of tenses which allows the Fall to be at some points future ("till they enthrall themselves," 125), at others present ("They trespass, authors to themselves in all / Both what they judge and what they choose," 122–23), and at others past ("they themselves decreed / Their own revolt," 116–17). When the Son responds to offer "life for life," Milton again presents a supratemporal view, a timeless present sub specie aeternitatis, without precise chronological sequence (256–65). Similarly, God's later words deny time's limitations:

> So heavenly love shall outdo hellish hate
> Giving to death, and dying to redeem,
> So dearly to redeem what hellish hate
> So easily destroyed, and still destroys.   (298–301)

God involves us in tenses which could imply that the Fall has already occurred and is occurring; his words sustain the impression created earlier in Book III—"that he may know how frail / His fallen condition is" (180–81)—the impression of timeless meditation by a being whose knowledge comprehends many different temporal perspectives and who is not himself "in" any of them.

Through Satan's misconceptions and confusions, Milton ironically affirms aspects of God's nature, most notably, of course, the omnipotence (which Satan regards as mere potency) and the creativity (which Satan thinks contingent on his own initiatives). In other ways, Satan is equally mistaken: he garbles the Neoplatonic notion of God as an infinite sphere whose center is everywhere and whose circumference nowhere (IX, 107–09), and he scoffs at an omnipotent God who requires *time* to create "and who knows how long / Before had been contriving" (IX, 138–40). We are intended to note these Satanic aberrations and to translate them into alternative propositions.

Milton locates God in his empyrean, but time itself, although it approaches very close to God, is *contained* within a cave "fast by his throne," "where light and darkness in perpetual round / Lodge and dislodge by turns" (VI, 6–7). Although there is time in eternity (there is in Milton's imaginative view, which contradicts both Plato and St. Augustine, motion in eternity), it is conceived not as a passage or a process but as a form of relation between events. In Heaven that relation is "grateful vicissitude." In Satan's mind time conceived as a process provokes the bad theology of a God capable of "second thoughts" (IX, 101); but more urgently, time is the relation between "the bitter memory / Of what he was, what is, and what must be / Worse" (IV, 24–25). In Adam, after the indulgence of despair at a falsely deterministic response to his own foreknowledge of future history (XI, 763), time registers as a form of relation between disobedience and repentance. The moral "actions" of the poem are narrated in time, or times: the harangues, rebellions, falls, the discharging of debts, the repentances. The moral "postures" of the poem—love and hate, obedience and disdain—are expressed as conditions, not as events; they are not time-related. Conditions or aptitudes realized in action constitute the poem's narrative process, but at the same time deny process. In other words, *Paradise Lost* is a myth, and like all myth, it requires a temporal dimension in which to unfold, yet uses time only to obliterate it.

Milton thus presents events—angelic and human falls—which take place both within times and outside time. For the human understanding and the grammar of the human mind, they are in time; for God, they are outside time. From one point of view there is causality, suspense, sequence; there is remembrance, knowledge, and foreknowledge. From another, there is, in a phrase with which Jackson Cope has described *Paradise Regained*, "only the exfoliation of the eternally given into time." It is part of Milton's genius to make demands on his readers' ability to comprehend the length of the narrative with all its recurrent themes, back-references, and parallels, to grasp correctly the whole range of the story as it is unfolded. But Milton also reminds them that the story unfolding in their time ultimately works to deny the reality of time. One of the poem's most ambiguous words is "now." In such a mythic utterance (and despite Milton's failure to resist the temptation of a literary tour de force which temporarily traps his articulate God in the toils of human grammar), the presiding Boethian God lies outside time, causality, sequence, or proleptical decrees. In the poetic universe of *Paradise Lost*, the fact that Satan's or Adam's, Mulciber's or Abraham's, Charles I's or Galileo's "future" actions exist in the space-time manifolds observed by God does not mean that they come to each action independently of what they have done in the meantime, or that they come fated despite their wills. In such a mythic utterance, God's angelic and human creations go about their business of falling and of standing again, "known" of God, but not "foreknown."

University of Exeter

NOTES

1. All quotations from *Paradise Lost* are cited from *The Poems of John Milton*, ed. John Carey and Alastair Fowler (London, 1968).
2. Trans. John Carey, in *The Complete Prose Works* (New Haven, 1973), VI. All quotations cite book and chapter of this edition of the *Christian Doctrine (CD)*.
3. See *De Gratia et libero arbitrio*, XV, 31, in *The Fathers of the Church*, LIX (Washington, 1968), p. 285.
4. Trans. George Sandys (Oxford, 1632), VII, 20–21.
5. See, for example, William Empson, *Milton's God* (London, 1961) and K. W. Gransden, "Milton, Dryden and the Comedy of the Fall," *Essays in Criticism*, XXVI (1976), 116–33.
6. See, for example, Stanley Fish, *Surprised by Sin: The Reader in "Paradise Lost"* (London, 1969).
7. See, for example, J. B. Savage's penetrating and stimulating "Freedom and Necessity in *Paradise Lost*," *ELH*, XLIV (1977), 286–311.
8. See *De musica*, VI, 11, 29, in *The Fathers of the Church*, II (New York, 1947), p. 355.
9. Laurence Stapleton, "Perspectives of Time in *Paradise Lost*," *PQ*, XLV (1966), 734–48.
10. *The Doctrine of Absolute Predestination*, trans. A. M. Toplady (London, 1930), p. 91.
11. Cf. Turretinus, *Institutio theologiae elenticae*, IV, iii, 3–4, cited in *Reformed Dogmatics*, 3rd ed., ed. and trans. John W. Beardslee (Grand Rapids, Mich., 1977).
12. Cf. *Paradise Lost*, III, 111–23, and Milton's *The Art of Logic* (1672), I, v, in *The Works of John Milton*, ed. Frank Allen Patterson et al. (New York, 1931–38), vol. XI.
13. *Theodicee*, trans. E. M. Huggard (New Haven, 1952), part I, sec. xxxvii.
14. Cf. Thomas Hobbes's comment: "for whatsoever God hath *purposed* to bring to pass by *man*, as an instrument, or foreseeth shall come to pass; a man, if he hath liberty, such as his Lordship affirmeth, from *necessitation*, might frustrate, and make not to come to pass, and God should either not *foreknow* it, and not *decree* it, or he should *foreknow* such things shall be, as shall never be, and decree that which shall never *come to pass*." *To the Lord Marquis of Newcastle: Of Liberty and Necessity*, in *English Works*, IV, ed. Sir W. Molesworth (London, 1840), p. 278.
15. *De libero arbitrio*, III, 3, sec. vi, in *Augustine's Earlier Writings*, trans. J. H. S. Burleigh (Philadelphia, 1955).
16. St. Augustine's and Boethius' arguments on this question receive lucid discussion in a study to which I am indebted here; see Nelson Pike, *God and Timelessness* (London, 1970), chap. 4.

17. *The Consolation of Philosophy*, V, Prose vi, trans. W. V. Cooper (London, 1902).

18. *CD* I, iii, and Milton's definition of God's eternity, I, ii. Cf. the rather different view set forth in his *The Art of Logic:* "Here [among the adjuncts of circumstance] is put *time*, to wit, the duration of things past, present and future. Thus also God is named, who is, who was, and who is to be. (*Apocalypse*, 1, 4, and 4, 8.) But to God everlastingness or eternity, not time, is generally attributed, but what properly is everlastingness except eternal duration . . . ?" (I, xi).

19. *Confessions*, XI, 11, trans. William Watts (1631), ed. W. H. D. Rouse (London, 1912), 2 vols.

20. *The Consolation of Philosophy*, V, Prose vi.

21. *A Commentarie . . . uppon the twoo Epistles Generall of . . . Peter, and Jude*, trans. Thomas Newton (London, 1581), fol. 158.

22. *Institutes of the Christian Religion*, III, 21, trans. John Allen (Philadelphia, 1813), II, 145.

23. *Religio Medici* (1642), I, xi, in *Sir Thomas Browne: The Major Works*, ed. C. A. Patrides (Harmondsworth, 1977), pp. 72–73.

24. C. A. Patrides, "The Renaissance View of Time: A Bibliographical Note," *N&Q*, CCVII (1963), 408–10.

25. *De civitate Dei*, XI, 6, trans. John Healey (1610), revised R. V. G. Tasker (London, 1942), 2 vols.

26. *Paradise Lost*, XII, 555; cf. *Ad Patrem*, i, 131, and *On Time*, in *The Poems of John Milton*, pp. 148–55, 165–66.

27. See, for example, Maurice Kelley, *This Great Argument* (Princeton, 1962).

28. Also see *Paradise Lost*, V, 535–38 and 66–67; VI, 911–12.

"PARDON ME, MIGHTY POET": VERSIONS OF THE BARD IN MARVELL'S "ON MR. MILTON'S *PARADISE LOST*"

Kenneth Gross

If one wants to have a friend one must also want to wage war
for him: and to wage war, one must be *capable* of being an enemy.
In a friend one should still honor the enemy. Can you go
close to your friend without going over to him?
In a friend one should have one's best enemy. You should be
closest to him with your heart when you resist him.

—Nietzsche

In the prison of his days
Teach the free man how to praise.

—Auden

ANDREW MARVELL's dedicatory verses to the second edition of *Paradise Lost* (1675) stage an encounter between two poets and two friends: the one a Puritan revolutionary, author of iconoclastic, Ciceronian prose tracts, two biblical epics, and a hybrid tragedy; the other a canny liberal member of Parliament, a defender of religious toleration, a brilliant satirist, a strange and serious lyrist.[1] Responding to the "evil days" and "evil tongues" of the Restoration, the poem's first aim is public: it defends the career of a man condemned for his politics and religion, accused of sacrilege in his writings, and even mocked for his blindness, which his enemies insisted was a punishment from God for his service to the regicides. As a study in the rhetoric of reputation, the verses speak very much to their historical moment and complement Marvell's quite different vindication of Milton in the second part of *The Rehearsal Transpros'd* (1673). But for all the richness of their topical allusions, Marvell's lines map out a truly inward critique of the epic and may introduce the reader of *Paradise Lost* to a subtler knowledge of its complexities than is evident on a first reading. For in questioning, praising, and defending his author, Marvell continually adapts dramatic stances, metaphors, key words (not to mention the larger systems of

77

value which these imply), many of which derive from that author's major poetry. One might say that Marvell examines and cross-examines Milton by speaking to him in his own voice, paints him in his own colors, disguises and reveals him with his own masks. This he does with great sympathy and respect; yet at the same time he is always striving to put his subject in perspective and to maintain the integrity of his own poetic mode, if only because it is his individual liberty of vision, rather than his skill at imitation, that is the truest measure of his admiration. The poem may in fact be read as a quiet agon between Marvell's desire to offer knowing praise to the poet who awes him, and his equal desire for freedom, self-definition, and self-esteem. To commend and echo Milton as he does, and yet keep imaginative space open for himself, is a task which requires all of Marvell's resources of humor and faith.

Marvell unfolds his initial thoughts on *Paradise Lost* in the dramatic and visionary scene of reading which occupies the first two verse paragraphs. Quite simply, he fears the poet and his poem. And although he utters his fears in a tentative, hypothetical manner, he undoubtedly means us to recall many of the particular criticisms leveled at Milton by contemporaries like Richard Leigh, who attacked Milton's obscurity of diction and his willful distortions of religious truth, or Samuel Parker, who in *A Reproof to "The Rehearsal Transpros'd"* revived the old claims about Milton's blindness. These and other slurs have been discussed in an important article on Marvell's poem by Joseph Anthony Wittreich, Jr.; but while they provide us with a useful historical analogue, the fact is that none of the writers Wittreich cites ever reimagines his own anxieties in so broad, balanced, and shrewdly dialectical a fashion as Marvell.[2] Nor do they show anything like his insight into the moral and imaginative challenge which the epic thrusts upon its readers. I therefore want to risk abstracting the argument of the first sixteen lines of the verses, as much as possible in their own terms, after which I can comment in more detail on the matter of Marvell's debt to the poetics of Milton:

> When I beheld the Poet blind, yet bold,
> In slender Book, his vast Design unfold,
> *Messiah* Crown'd, *Gods* Reconcil'd Decree,
> Rebelling *Angels*, the Forbidden Tree,
> Heav'n, Hell, Earth, Chaos, All; the Argument　　　　5
> Held me a while, misdoubting his Intent,
> That he would ruine (for I saw him strong)
> The sacred Truths to Fable and old Song,
> (So *Sampson* groap'd the Temples Posts in spight)
> The World o'rewhelming to revenge his Sight.　　　　10

Yet as I read, soon growing less severe,
I lik'd his Project, the success did fear;
Through that wide Field how he his way should find
O're which lame Faith leads Understanding blind;
Lest he perplext the things he would explain,   15
And what was easie he should render vain.³

Here Marvell tries to distinguish two "technical" problems facing the author of a biblical epic, and thus two ways of violating the sacred materials adapted in such a poem. First, although Milton is able to encompass with such grand eloquence and epic style all that the Bible presents in a difficult array of books, parables, histories, and prophecies—sometimes lucid, sometimes gnomic—is it not possible that such literary enrichment, such poetic rather than religious power, might trivialize or gloss over the austere text of Scripture, so much more sublime than any romance? By the sheer mastery of its fiction, might not Milton's poem suggest that the Bible's literal history is merely moral fable, or even worse, matter only for secular "old Song"? Milton's epic architecture, his competitive strength of poetic design, might then "ruine" rather than "justify" the revelation which ought to sustain it (as if his were a prophetic voice which, in the words of Jeremiah i, 10, could only "pluck up and break down" and not "build and plant" as well).

A second, contrasting difficulty is set forth in the next verse paragraph. If *Paradise Lost* avoids reducing Scripture either to entertainment or allegory, it might go to the other extreme by superadding complications to those truths which Scripture presents with great simplicity. As a result, Milton might not only confuse the understanding of his readers, but block the message of those "simple" dicta, proverbs, and eloquent structures of parable which allow shaky human faith to survive. By moving so easily through the field of Scripture, by so effortlessly compassing its theological complexities, Milton might overawe the already uneasy mutuality of "lame Faith" and "understanding blind" by which man seeks a path to his God. Marvell apparently fears that Milton's ponderous learning and strong imagination might enchain even a faithful reader's liberty to confront Scripture in its own terms, to believe according to the dictates of his own conscience—a freedom for which both men had long fought.

Marvell's defense *of* Milton begins, then, as a defense *against* Milton. The poet of *Paradise Lost* is ultimately absolved of both crimes suggested above. But the opening lines remind us that in that time of tense religious controversy, when even prophecy was seen as predominantly a matter of inspired interpretation (not God's voice, but its written echo), the crucial test of such a work was not simply the integrity of the poet's imaginative myth, but its relation to the authority and influence of the revealed Word.[4] Marvell's *The Rehearsal Transpros'd* (Part 1, 1671; Part 2, 1673) employs exactly the criteria of reverence and violation that are implicit in the first verse paragraph to prove the writings of Archdeacon Parker as vile as those of Milton are praiseworthy:

> I thought his profanation of the Scripture intolerable; For though he alledges that 'tis only in order to shew how it was misapplyed by the Fanaticks, he might have done that too, and yet preserved the Dignity and Reverence of those Sacred Writings, which he hath not done; but on the contrary, he hath in what is properly his own, taken the most of all his Ornaments, and Imbellishments thence in a scurrilous and sacrilegious stile. . . . Methought I never saw a more bold and wicked attempt than that of reducing *Grace*, and making it meer *Fable*, of which he gives us *the Moral*.[5]

Milton, by contrast, treats of divine things "in such state / as them preserves, and Thee, inviolate." In fact, the poet's chaste treatment of Scripture eventually raises in Marvell a further concern about the reverence which others, Marvell included, must rightfully accord to *Paradise Lost*.[6] Marvell's uncertainty regarding the fitness of his own evaluation and praise is again paralleled by comments at the very end of *The Rehearsal Transpros'd*, Part 1: "And now I have done," he says, feeling a need for some sort of self-absolution, "And shall think myself largely recompensed for this trouble, if any one that hath been formerly of another mind, shall learn by this Example, that it is not impossible to be merry and angry as long time as I have been writing, without profaning and violating those things which are and ought to be most sacred."[7]

In his concern over the possible violation of both his own and others' virtue and integrity, Marvell recalls certain figures from his lyric poetry—the retiring, tree-loving speaker of "The Garden," the inward-turning, fragile, yet religious soul in "On a Drop of Dew," and perhaps even the erotically wounded "Nymph Complaining," who mourns for and yet transfigures her slain faun.[8] The opening of the poem on *Paradise Lost* curiously mirrors the first stanza of "Upon Appleton House," with its picture of the devastating work of the "Forrain Architect," "Who of his great Design in pain / Did for a Model vault his Brain"; its depiction of Milton also recalls the antipastoral violence of Cromwell in "An Horatian Ode."[9]

Without tracing any of these likenesses in detail, one can still see a quite characteristic Marvellian drama being set up in the opening of the poem on *Paradise Lost*. But one of the devices which gives Marvell's

anxieties such a surprising and powerful shape is the Miltonic ventrilo-
quism that emerges here and works more or less throughout the piece.
Most of the poem's critics have noted something of this; Rosalie Colie,
for instance, observes that in the first ten lines "Marvell pays Milton the
tribute of approximating his 'Number, Weight and Measure,' and in the
poem as a whole the greater compliment of not daring to dispense with
his own support, the rhymes."[10] She is referring primarily to Marvell's
rather fine use of long, enjambed sentences and a periodic, Virgilian
syntax, but the influence of *Paradise Lost* goes far beyond matters of
style. In fact, despite their tone of reticence and respect, the verses
become a testing ground for some of the most radical metaphors and
religious claims of Milton's poetry.

For example, the very drama of amazement in the opening lines
seems to reflect Milton's interest in the dilemmas of the witness, in the
moral imperative of beholding all phases of spiritual good and evil.
Compare to Marvell's "When I beheld . . ." the following passage from
the close of Book I of *Paradise Lost:*

> Behold a wonder! they but now who seemd
> In bigness to surpass Earths Giant-Sons
> Now less than smallest Dwarfs, in narrow room
> Throng numberless, like that Pigmean Race
> Beyond the *Indian* Mount; or Faerie Elves,
> Whose midnight Revels, by a Forrest side
> Or Fountain, some belated Peasant sees,
> Or dreams he sees, while over head to the Moon
> Sits Arbitress, and nearer to the Earth
> Wheels her pale course: they on thir mirth and dance
> Intent, with jocond Music charm his ear;
> At once with joy and fear his heart rebounds.   (777–88)[11]

Marvell, another belated watcher, likewise witnesses a vision of tremendous spiritual and phenomenological ambiguity, a vision which tests his
powers of recognition, resistance, and choice, suspending him in doubt
about both his object and himself.[12] In the lines from *Paradise Lost*, the
Virgilian *mirabile dictu,* with its self-reflexive indication of the poet's
own rhetorical difficulties, gives way to the more urgent optative of
"Behold a wonder!" Milton actually posits two witnesses, an earthly and
a celestial one, and juxtaposes the ambiguous motions of the devils in
Pandemonium with those of more benign, Shakespearean daimons. For
both the reader and the peasant there is no single, fully adequate perspective for judgment; the impression shifts, quite as it does in Marvell's
poem, among surprise, fear, sedate wonder, and even a sense of the

ridiculous. Marvell's attention to the contrast between the "slender book" and its "vast Design" does recall the paradoxes of scale so lovingly described in lyrics like "A Drop of Dew" and "Upon Appleton House." But in the poem on *Paradise Lost*, as in the lines quoted above from Book I, references to such curious perspectives and ambiguities of dimension convey a more pressing sense of imaginative danger, the moral threat of chaos and enchantment.

The religious burden placed on such a witness is difficult to define. It entails a self-consciousness rather different from that involved in the schematic, highly visual, and often dramatic strategies of formal meditation which, as Louis Martz has shown, so appealed to the metaphysical poets.[13] For Marvell is not struggling to recall or visualize a critical scriptural topos (indeed, his eye can hardly fix itself within the flux of "places") and so question, cure, or humble his conscience. On the other hand, there is something more than a feeling of sheer, untrammeled awe. The stance of the witness is more likely derived from prophetic and apocalyptic literature, where the alienated reader and speaker are set to watch the conflict between the false visions of history and the true, providential design of God.[14] Book I of *Paradise Lost* again provides an example, a severe one, in the lines which foretell the earthly career of the demon Thammuz as the god of a mystery cult that will seduce the "daughters of *Sion*,"

> Whose wanton passions in the sacred Porch
> *Ezekiel* saw, when by the Vision led
> His eye survayd the dark Idolatries
> Of alienated *Judah*.   (454–57)

Marvell, too, stations himself at the threshold of what should be a sacred house, not knowing whether he beholds true religion or abomination. He lacks the inspired certainty of truth and falsehood which he later seems to gain, and for the moment we remain unsure as to who is idolater and who is prophet. In the text to which Milton alludes (Ezekiel viii, 3–15), the prophet stands at a gate of the Temple "where was the seat of the image of jealousy," a pagan idol whose name yet ironically points to the jealousy of the One God and of the seer who defends him. It is a feeling which Marvell will show only in the third verse paragraph, when he grows jealous of those who would violate a poem which he begins to recognize as sacred.

There is no question that Marvell might have adapted the prophetic or apocalyptic stances which I have noted from sources other than Milton, that is, from the Bible and contemporary religious writing. Yet such stances have little place in Marvell's other poetic work and on the whole seem rather alien to his own more introverted, hermetic mode. This circumstance, as well as the poem's very curious way of setting the prophetic elements in perspective, suggests that, whatever their ultimate source, Marvell's use of them in the poem was formally and thematically controlled by this particular encounter with Milton's work.

As I have suggested, the important point is that Marvell first sees the blind poet and his work through one of that poet's own dramatic models of ambivalent or alienated vision. Though primarily a figure for the relation of the reader Marvell to the writer Milton, the fact that Marvell himself is writing about another poet's reading of the Bible puts all easy distinctions between writing and reading into question. The very opening line of the poem, in fact, suggests a visionary symbiosis between Marvell and Milton by means of the alliteration which links Marvell's "I beheld" to the adjectives "blind" and "bold," which describe the object of the beholding. Still, we must see that Marvell does not allow his perspectivizing imitation of his subject to collapse into blind identification; nor does he turn into an unwitting idolater under the mask of a critic. Marvell is not simply aping a Miltonic form of encounter; rather, he shrewdly reshapes the details of that poem whose unfolding he witnesses. His list of the epic's main topics, for instance—"*Messiah* Crown'd, *Gods* Reconcil'd Decree, / Rebelling *Angels*, the Forbidden Tree, / Heav'n, Hell, Earth, Chaos, All; the Argument"—pointedly alters their real sequence, both as they are summarized in the invocation to Book I, which runs from "Man's first disobedience" to the recovery of "one Greater Man," the Messiah, and as they occur in the epic as a whole, which opens with the fallen legions of Satan. Marvell's lines tend to suppress the connections between the various events, realms, and persons of the poem. He traces a descending path from the Messiah to the forbidden tree (leaving out all mention of "Man," which holds together Milton's opening lines), moves from Heaven to Hell, back to earth, then to Chaos, as if undoing the entire sequence of creation. "Chaos," the penultimate item in the list, seems a not unironic glance backward over the whole work just surveyed. And it is difficult to determine whether Marvell's "All" refers to the actual universe or to the book which aspires to contain it.

"All" is one of Milton's favorite words, as William Empson pointed out some time ago, and Marvell manages to give it much of the resonance it possesses in *Paradise Lost*. As Empson tells us, the word "seems to be suited to the all-or-none man. All else is unimportant beside one thing, he is continually deciding. . . . The generosity of the proud man also requires the word; when he gives, he gives all. It is as suited to absolute love and self-sacrifice as to insane self-assertion. The self-centered man, in his turn, is not much interested in the variety of the world, and readily lumps it all together as 'all.' "[15] Milton is blind, yet boldly claims to see all the truth there is to see. The problem is that in Marvell any discrete design or argument dissolves into the equally confusing alternatives of "All" or "Chaos." The hurried survey of the epic suggests not plenitude or generosity, but a world in ruins; Milton's poem becomes a false apocalypse, not a revelation of a new world, but simply the overwhelming of the old by the poet's own catastrophic phantasmagoria.

The undoing of creation is a design of Satan's, yet rather than explicitly compare the poet's work to that of his archvillain, Marvell choses another, equally problematic destroyer:

> That he would ruine (for I saw him strong)
> The sacred Truths to Fable and old Song,
> (So *Sampson* groap'd the Temples Posts in spight)
> The World o'rewhelming to revenge his Sight.

Samson Agonistes had appeared five years before these lines, and the analogy which Marvell suggests here may not have been terribly surprising. What is astonishing is the picture of Samson's act as willfully destructive, rather than redemptive. The scandal or stumbling-block for most readers of the dedicatory poem is that while Milton's tragedy suggests that the hero's pulling down of the Philistine temple represents "a good purgation of hatred" and "a regained public consciousness of covenantal power and destiny," Marvell attaches to the act a purely selfish motive.[16] In the article already mentioned, Wittreich even goes so far as to suggest that the Samson/Milton analogy must be read as a palpably ironic relation and that the lines point to a strong contrast between the self-slain Samson and the providentially preserved poet.[17] Wittreich quite justly takes to task those critics who have willfully misconstrued the plain meaning of "spight" in order to give the text a gentler, more orthodox sense. Yet it seems to me no less plain that Marvell is asserting a real likeness between the two men of power. The syntax of the couplet actually helps to confuse the two, for while Marvell's reference to Samson is, strictly speaking, confined to a one-line parenthesis, the clause which describes him seems continuous with the line following (as might be expected in the case of a couplet), so that the possessive pronoun in the phrase "his Sight" may refer to Samson or to Milton.

I had at one point thought that this ambiguous allusion might begin to make poetic sense if we were to assume that Marvell is speaking through a persona. His error, if it is that, would then be quite consistent with the poet's intention to represent his experience of *Paradise Lost* in its earliest, most uncertain stages. Such a misprision of Samson's motivations—not unlike that of Manoa or the chorus in the play itself—would show that Marvell's speaker has his own blindness to overcome. He is tested by the very Miltonic masks which he is himself testing. While he sees an authentic analogy between Milton and Samson, he has not yet comprehended the full dialectic by which self-destruction can become, if not creation, then heroic and divine self-fulfillment.

Such an interpretation may still prove serviceable, but it requires at least two qualifications. First, as I shall argue below, even in the later portions of the poem Marvell evades any confrontation with the difficult moral and redemptive ironies of the tragedy. He wants somehow to supersede the prior images of ruin, rather than directly to reject or reinstate them; the chaotic opening vision is never truly opposed or displaced (though it is an open question whether Marvell deceives himself that it has been). Second, it is important to see that in misrepresenting Milton's play, Marvell has at the same time more accurately represented the starker picture of Samson in Milton's biblical source: "And Samson called unto the Lord, and said, O Lord God, remember me, I pray thee, and strengthen me . . . that I may be at once avenged of the Philistines for my two eyes" (Judges xvi, 28). It is not simply a question of Marvell's exposing Milton's misappropriation of this text, for Marvell's reductive return to such fundamental violence also serves as the basis for his own surprising extension of the original narrative. In the context of a poem defending the integrity of sacred Scripture, Marvell's reference to "the Temple" suggests that Samson tore down a Hebrew, rather than a Philistine, place of worship, just as the following line suggests that this act of violence encompasses not one enemy race, but the entire world.

In lines 11–16, Marvell's fear of a chaos wrought by a sacrilegious poetic strength yields to the contrasting suspicion that the theologian in Milton is erecting a labyrinth, a temple that is overbuilt and overcomplicated. Instead of trivializing Scripture, the blind poet may overwhelm his readers' "Understanding blind" (Marvell's repetition of "blind" here forcing us to wonder whether the literally sightless Milton shares the metaphorical affliction as well and, in general, to consider how the tropes of seeing relate to sight's realities). The problems created by Milton's intellectual obscurity are real, but as if to demonstrate the poetic uses of learning, Marvell goes on to attempt a very Miltonic sort of Latinate punning. Line 15, "Lest he perplext the things he would explain," which states the speaker's fear most succinctly, deploys the opposed words "perplext" and "explain" so that their etymological meanings ("tangle together" and "smooth out") reinforce the figurative representation of thought and faith in terms of travel and topography, as in Milton's "on th'*Aleian* Field I fall, / *Erroneous* there to wander and forlorne" (*Paradise Lost*, VII, 19–20; emphasis mine).

Lines 17–22 shift from anxious hypothesis to prophetic satire

> Or, if a Work so infinite he spann'd
> Jealous I was that some less skilful hand
> (Such as disquiet always what is well,
> And by ill imitating would excell)   20
> Might hence presume the whole Creations day
> To change in Scenes, and show it in a Play.

Such a decreation of the Creation would at least be certain of obeying the unity of time. Marvell is presumably mocking John Dryden's project for making a rhymed "opera" of *Paradise Lost*, although the lines may also allude to Davenant's praise of epic drama in the "Preface to *Gondibert*."[18] Of more immediate interest, however, is that Marvell's attack on what seems to him literary parasitism continues to employ terms of evaluation uncannily like those in Milton. Taken in isolation, the lines about writers "Such as disquiet always what is well, / and by ill imitating would excell," refer as aptly to the political program of Satan, his aim being "out of good still to find means of evil" (I, 165). No form of the verb "to imitate" occurs anywhere else in Marvell's poetry, and although it may recall classical notions of literary mimesis or *imitatio*, equally important is the fact that Milton always applies the word to forms of demonic mimicry. There are a number of examples of this in *Paradise Lost* (II, 270, 511; V, 111), but Marvell's phrasing recalls more precisely Christ's rebuke to Satan in *Paradise Regained:*

> Our Hebrew Songs and Harps in *Babylon,*
> That pleas'd so well our Victors ear, declare
> That rather *Greece* from us these Arts deriv'd;
> *Ill imitated,* while they loudest sing
> The vices of thir Deities, and thir own
> In Fable, Hymn, or Song, so personating
> Thir Gods ridiculous, and themselves past shame.
>   (IV, 336–42; emphasis mine)

By an allusive stroke worthy of William Blake, Marvell aligns Dryden's presumptuous, neoclassical dramaturgy with the temptations of a debased Hellenism which Satan offers the Son. Without anticipating too much, it would also be useful to compare Marvell's later scorn of false and alluring rhyme (lines 45–50) to the verses in *Paradise Regained* which immediately follow those quoted above:

> Remove thir swelling Epithetes thick laid
> As varnish on a Harlots cheek, the rest,
> Thin sown with aught of profit or delight,
> Will farr be found unworthy to compare
> With *Sions* songs, to all true tasts excelling,
> Where God is prais'd aright, and Godlike men,
> The Holiest of Holies, and his Saints.   (343–49)

Marvell's poem, though it imitates Milton, also seeks to praise aright that God-like man. Still, he does not directly address the epic poet until the beginning of the fourth verse paragraph, just about the midpoint of the poem: "Pardon me, *mighty Poet*, nor despise / My causeless, yet not impious, surmise." This sudden recognition of the poet as a presence of authority and regard is the major turn of the poem. It is also the moment when Marvell remembers and comments upon his own words, for he specifically asks the poet to pardon his "surmise," that is, the satirical prediction of his previous verse paragraph. The force of the turn is that Marvell has suddenly been enabled to set aside the religious anxieties which had so distanced him from Milton in the earlier verses, and can speak to him with such confidence. Marvell later returns to the question of Milton's reverence for Scripture and vindicates the poet of sacrilege. But his conviction is not won through any reasoned demonstration within the poem itself; in fact, his later words of praise tend to beg the questions he had before so urgently posed to himself and Milton. Marvell's vindication of Milton seems to depend on a more hidden moment of recognition, one in which he realizes the power of his own "surmise."[19] For his apology to Milton makes it suddenly clear both to reader and speaker that in the act of imagining other writers' "ill imitating," the earlier anxieties about Milton's relation to Scripture have been turned around and directed toward Milton's text itself. That is to say, the poem has begun to regard *Paradise Lost* as a scriptural or sacred work in its own right—at least insofar as such a work can be defined by the claims it makes on its readers and interpreters. Milton's poem turns out to be equally susceptible to violation by sacrilegious writers, so much so that even the author who defends it must guard against seeming "impious."

The poet's crucial coincidence with his subject on the question of a surmise may owe something to a similar turn in Milton's *Lycidas*. There too, the speaker emerges from the uncertainties of grief at the point where he begins to think about both the consolations and the limitations of his fictions about another poet: "For so to interpose a little ease, / Let our frail thoughts dally with false surmise." Even Marvell's way of entering into his causeless, satirical, if not completely false surmise shows something of Miltonic character. The third verse paragraph ("Or if a Work so infinite he spann'd . . . ") opens with that very subtle "or" which, as Leslie Brisman has argued in detail, so characterizes Milton's poetry.[20] Rather than merely contrast two different terms, this conjunction sets up an urgent moment of choice between certain real or fictive alternatives, the matter of selection and rejection becoming a continual part of the process of self-denial, self-revision, and self-election by which the poet orients himself toward a higher vision. Likewise, Marvell's sudden access to a stance of unqualified regard emerges from the negative act of rejecting his surmise, rather than from any more rational process of argument. The turn is quite literally a conversion, a leap out of the flux of literary and religious opinion into the certainty of faith.

To map such discontinuities in the progress or argument of a poem is difficult without recourse to some falsifying, genetic logic. What can be said, however, is that the second half of the poem must be judged for its renewed rhetorical assurance, rather than as a direct, reasonable answer to the questions raised in the first half. The paradox of this section is that while Milton's poetry has now begun to be accepted at its authentic value, the presence and pressure of the Miltonic *voice* are considerably lessened. One is more conscious of Marvellian urbanity keeping oratory in control. The anxious, unstable stances of the opening, the images of disorder, perplexity, and discontinuity—all of these disappear, and while Milton's poetry is still figured through images of power and sublimity, these are generally subdued, even domesticated. Lines 25–30, for instance, praise Milton's vast design for its exacting fitness and plenitude, rather than as a chaotic flood of vision:

> But now I am convinc'd, and none will dare
> Within thy Labours to pretend a Share.
> Thou hast not miss'd one thought that could be fit,
> And all that was improper dost omit:
> So that no room is here for Writers left,
> But to detect their Ignorance or Theft. 30

Lines 29 and 30 are in some ways the most astonishing of the poem. They can be read as an uncanny prediction of the anxiety felt by many eighteenth- and nineteenth-century poets that any attempt at writing a sublime poem after Milton could find a place within the imaginative space he had usurped only if it could violate, in retrospect, or willfully forget the greater poet's priority. The historical fulfillment of this prophecy (studied in different ways by Walter Jackson Bate and Harold Bloom) is not within the scope of this essay. But Marvell's own relation to his pronouncement is, and what militates against any simplistic acceptance of his hyperboles is that Marvell himself has all along pretended a share in the labors of his poet. This local irony points to a broader problem in the poem. One might justify Marvell's half-truth by saying that his bold theft of some of *Paradise Lost*'s ample store of tropes aims only at achieving a subtler critical perspective. Yet no such chrestomathy of echoes and imitations as this poem can really escape some subversion of its source, and it only enlarges the dialectical ironies of the poem to say that Marvell also subverts his own idealizings of that source.

Our awareness of this carefully balanced undermining of the praiser and the praised must qualify, although it does not in any way disqualify, the further hyperboles of the next four lines. These, in their subtly opposed images of sacred and secular power, claim for Milton both the integrity and the inviolability which had previously seemed so uncertain:

> That Majesty which through thy Work doth Reign
> Draws the Devout, deterring the Profane;
> And things divine thou treatst of in such state
> As them preserves, and Thee, inviolate.

Marvell's use of "Majesty" may seem a rather good joke, Christopher Hill remarks, coming as it does in verses dedicated to a former servant of the regicides.[21] But Marvell is not only joking here. His deeper point is that, even with the Restoration, true kingship could not be realized as a political fact, but only as an internalized poetic preeminence, as if majesty survived the Puritan revolution only within the realm of trope. As Hill himself goes on to say, such majesty ensures rather than challenges the inviolability of "things divine," since it represents the majesty of God, to whom the poet dedicates his career. The poet, too, remains inviolate, set apart from danger like those Marvellian figures mentioned above, although the lines from the commendatory verses do not fully convey Milton's acute awareness of both prophetic election and Orphic vulnerability.

Lines 35 and 36 continue to revise the speaker's initial impressions of Milton, substituting for his violent shifts between fascination and fear the assertion that "At once delight and horrour on us seize, / Thou singst with so much gravity and ease" (although this still recalls the ambivalences of the belated watcher in Book I: "At once with joy and fear his heart rebounds"). The chiastic arrangement of the four nouns in this couplet has the surprising effect of letting delight parallel gravity, horror ease. Painful and gentle feelings thus not only relieve but transform each other, so that the idea of poetic "ease" no longer resembles the innocent "easie" of line 16 or that playful, meditative easiness one finds in "Upon Appleton House." Instead, Marvell evokes something closer to the intense, visionary condition which Milton describes when he calls on his "Celestial Patroness,"

> who deignes
> Her nightly visitation unimplor'd
> And dictates to me slumbring, or inspires
> *Easie*, my unpremeditated Verse.
>
> (*PL*, IX, 21–24; emphasis mine)

The next couplet echoes two other invocations from *Paradise Lost*, those in Books I and VII, particularly the images of the poet pursuing "things unattempted yet in Prose or Rhyme" (I, 16) and soaring "Above the flight of *Pegasean* wing" (VII, 4) to describe the great war in Heaven. Marvell's lines, however, match their initial suggestion of transcendence with a controlled decrescendo, a leveling out of such flight: "And above humane flight dost soar aloft / With Plume so strong, so equal, and so soft." Miltonic sublimity is identified with a force more genial, sweet, and controlled than either sheer rising or destructiveness; the epithet "strong," which earlier described the temple-breaking Samson, here refers to a strength of continuity and elevation. Lines 39 and 40 take this process of subduing the Miltonic sublime even further. They compare the poet's flight not to the presumptuous ascent of Pegasus, but to that of the ever-flying but more terrestrial bird of paradise, bound to the atmosphere if not to the surface of the world. Yet lest he be accused of distortion, Marvell slyly places on Milton himself the responsibility for this not terribly sublime simile, referring to the bird as one "named from the Paradise *you* sing."

This vision of a mild, almost Spenserian Milton, a poet of earthly continuities rather than prophetic discontinuities, is not in itself entirely false, as critics like Geoffrey Hartman have taught us.[22] But the next verse paragraph, a scant four lines, makes a sudden leap toward a more obviously sublime conception, both more severe and less catastrophic than Marvell's opening vision. In lines 41 and 42, Marvell reassesses the confusing array of spatial tropes by which he had earlier characterized

Milton's poem—worlds, skies, plains, chaos—and localizes its power within a wholly inward space: "Where couldst thou Words of such a compass find? / Whence furnish such a vast expense of Mind?" It is words which inhabit and measure the poet's world. Taking advantage of the ambiguities of seventeenth-century orthography, Marvell makes of the poet's mind both the source of that heroic outpouring, that *expense*, of intelligence and the near infinite *expanse* which that intelligence fills. This remarkable couplet may remind us that Marvell was a contemporary of Descartes. Yet, lest this suggestion of imaginative autonomy collapse into the Satanic claim that "the mind is its own place," Marvell suddenly displaces the power he describes to somewhat remoter origins and answers what might have seemed purely rhetorical questions with a sudden assertion of Milton's prophetic calling.

The comparison of Milton to the Greek seer Tiresias is worth looking at carefully, not only because it again possesses Milton's authority (see *PL*, III, 36), but because it explicitly parallels the earlier comparison of the poet to Samson. The greater assurance of the later simile marks the distance the speaker has traveled from his fearful, ambivalent representations to glorification of Milton's mythic and poetic identity:

> (So *Sampson* groap'd the Temples Posts in spight)
> The World o'rewhelming to revenge his Sight.

> Just Heav'n thee, like *Tiresias*, to requite,
> Rewards with *Prophesie* thy loss of sight.

Milton's power is justified as God's reward, rather than as a man's revenge, the energy of his spiteful selfhood. The design of *Paradise Lost* thus coincides with the design of the revealed Word because they are equally productions of prophetic speech. To suggest, as I think Wittreich does, that Marvell is betraying the truly revolutionary nature of Milton's poetic enterprise and reconciling him with orthodox theology is not quite fair.[23] This powerful act of evasion and elevation sets aside the specific question of doctrinal reverence. The prophetic voice granted to Milton obviates any lesser questions of his fidelity to textual authority. Marvell may be qualifying his extreme claim by comparing Milton to a classical rather than an Hebraic prophet, but he means quite precisely what he says: here is a man of divine vision. Thus Marvell's own stance has altered; he is no longer only a defender or a giver of praise. To announce another's divine powers is to become, like John the Baptist, oneself a prophet.

In the coda of this poem, secure for the moment in his sense of Milton's worth, Marvell returns with new enthusiasm to more strictly literary matters, particularly to the question of rhyme. He takes Milton's part in scorning those who, lacking any purer and more severe inspiration, take refuge in the seductive, fashionable music of tagged lines. Milton's poetic *virtù* is measured in the end by the stand he takes against rhyme, and the poem quickly drops its harsh, satirical voice for what seems to be praise even higher than that already offered:

> I, too, transported by the *Mode* offend,
> And while I meant to *Praise* thee, must Commend.
> Thy verse created like thy *Theme* sublime,
> In Number, Weight, and Measure, needs not *Rhime*.

The final verse echoes Wisdom xi, 21, "Thou hast ordered all things in measure, number and weight," but Marvell's slight reshuffling of this passage subtly signals his reappropriation of the scriptural text for his peculiar poetic needs. The allusion raises Milton's achievement above prophecy by intimating that he possesses a creative power like that of the deity. This ideal is admittedly something of a commonplace for artists in the Renaissance, but the distinctive wit of Marvell's lines lies in their discovery of a divine creativity embedded in the most immediate, technical facts of prosody. Number, measure, and weight refer literally to a poem's meter as well as figuratively to its mythopoesis or power of world making (an implicit warning to any critics or theologians who, on the authority of the verses from Wisdom, would foist elaborate numerological allegories on sacred texts, rather than follow the Protestant rule that one must read them with strict attention to an integrated, literal sense).[24] Such curious word play, at once arch and profound, is more Marvellian than Miltonic; yet these lines still point forward to the great moral and symbolic significance with which Milton will invest his choice of meter in his note on "The Verse," which directly follows Marvell's poem in the edition of 1674. Marvell's coda in fact warns the reader that Milton's stern talk about "ancient liberty" and "the troublesome and modern bondage of Riming" is of an order of seriousness far beyond the witty, paradoxical criticism of rhyme's "fetters" and "false weight" in a poem like Ben Jonson's "A Fit of Rime against Rime."

Yet Marvell cannot help but write as an ally of the unhappy party—whether God's or the Devil's—of rhyme, and he knows it well. Still drawing on key words and ironies derived from Milton's poems, his apology for his own tagged lines continues to show an archness which calls the easy self-deprecation into question. The hyperbolic "transported" in line 51 recalls God's mocking use of the word in Book III of *Paradise Lost*, at line 81, to describe the angry but impotent Satan's excursion through Chaos—as if Marvell the rhymer would now take on himself the demonic guise he cast before on Milton and Dryden. But the irony in the poet's account of himself may not be so simple; Adam too uses the word, and with a triumphant wonder, to describe his newly discovered capacity for sexual delight: "transported I behold / Transported touch" (VII, 529–30).[25] Marvell even implies that the bondage for which he mocks himself, the need to find a rhyme for "offend," is the real reason that he can redeem his offense by rising from mere praise to the increased confidence and responsibility entailed in the act of commendation.[26]

The final charm and marvel of the poem is, in fact, that while it allows Milton the highest possible justification for his choice of blank verse, the poet refuses to concede his own God-given right to rhyme. As tags and jingling bells, as "bushy-points" on the modish coats of poetasters, rhymes may be absurd. But they are crucial instruments for this most pointed of versifiers. The last words of the poem simultaneously declare Milton's liberty—he "needs not" match line ends—and show the necessity which holds Marvell—he "must" match "offend" to "Commend," "sublime" to "Rhime." The last rhyme, however, is neither a simple admission of fatality nor a subtle mockery of Miltonic sublimity— the poetry of rhymelessness being chained to its enemy by an unbreakable likeness of sound. The effect is rather more like a smiling, noble, liberating bow to subjectivity. Without directly challenging his ideas, Marvell implies that Milton's vatic castigation of rhyme is more private than public. The prophetic poet has set forth an antithetical law which makes imaginative sense and possesses imaginative authority within one particular poem, *Paradise Lost,* a world for which his verse was "created," as earth for man or Hell for the fallen angels. Marvell's distinction at once helps to invest Milton's choice of blank verse with greater tropological force and places the literal circumstances and conventions of Restoration rhyming effectively beyond the reach of his prosodic strictures. One might easily bring out the defensiveness which glimmers through this half-humorous gesture of self-limitation. Even if it could be said that Marvell wholeheartedly embraces his own position as a minor author facing the major Milton, the gesture still depends on Marvell's contrasting himself with a slightly distorted version of the latter, a version on the whole less effective than the darker, almost parodic vision of the poet offered in Marvell's opening lines. The main burden of the ending, however, is to allow rhyme and the sublime to stand independent of one another, each with its own proper work. This much at least the poet achieves. In the closing couplet, Marvell's elusive and allusive wit fixes a boundary to his own imaginative endeavors, but it is a boundary which allows him freedom, admiration, and something very like truth.

Yale University

NOTES

1. A detailed, if slightly biased, discussion of the friendship and political relations between the two poets can be found in Christopher Hill's essay, "Milton and Marvell," in *Approaches to Marvell: The York Tercentenary Lectures*, ed. C. A. Patrides (London, 1978), pp. 1–30.

I would like to thank Professors George deF. Lord and John Guillory of the Yale University Department of English, as well as Wendy Wipprecht of the *Yale Review*, for reading earlier versions of this essay.

2. "Perplexing the Explanation: Marvell's 'On Mr. Milton's *Paradise Lost*,'" in *Approaches*, pp. 280–305. The comments of Richard Leigh, from his *The Transproser Rehears'd: or the Fifth Act of Mr. Baye's Play* (1673), and those of Samuel Parker are reprinted in William R. Parker's *Milton's Contemporary Reputation* (Columbus, Ohio, 1940), pp. 113–17; for earlier slurs on Milton's blindness, see pp. 77, 83, 87, 99–103, and 107 (also cited by Wittreich, "Perplexing the Explanation," p. 302).

3. All citations are from *Andrew Marvell: Complete Poetry*, ed. George deF. Lord (New York, 1968).

4. For a discussion of prophetic literature's relation to the exegetical tradition, and its place in Protestant theology, see William Kerrigan, *The Prophetic Milton* (Charlottesville, Va., 1974), pp. 17–124.

5. *"The Rehearsal Transpros'd" and "The Rehearsal Transpros'd," Part the Second*, ed. D. I. B. Smith (Oxford, 1971), p. 143.

6. For an excellent discussion of Marvell's complex attitude toward praise, satiric criticism, and violation, especially as reflected in his political poetry's manipulation of the topoi of epideictic oratory, see Annabel Patterson, *Marvell and the Civic Crown* (Princeton, 1978), pp. 50–110. Patterson's findings are directly applicable to the verses on *Paradise Lost*, although there the problem is complicated by the fact that the source for images of both praise and blame is often Milton himself.

7. P. 145. It is worth noting here that much of Marvell's eloquent defense of Milton in Part II of this tract is devoted to denying Parker's charges that Milton helped Marvell put together Part I. Like the poem discussed in this essay, his defense serves the additional purpose of vindicating Marvell's literary independence.

8. Among the many studies of Marvell's introverted, overdetermined, or redundant metaphors of the self, I would cite Christopher Ricks's " 'It's own resemblance'," and John Carey's "Reversals Transposed: An Aspect of Marvell's Imagination," in *Approaches*, pp. 108–35 and pp. 136–54, respectively.

9. One might even say that the Cromwell of the Horatian ode is identical with the Milton of the prefatory verses. What distinguishes the latter work is that the violence Marvell fears is tropological, rather than literal, so that the poem is more capable of subduing that violence on its own terms.

10. *"My Ecchoing Song"*: *Andrew Marvell's Poetry of Criticism* (Princeton, 1970), p. 5.

11. All quotations of Milton's poetry are taken from *The Poetical Works of John Milton*, ed. Helen Darbishire (London, 1958).

12. On the place of *choice* as a central imaginative act in Milton, see Leslie Brisman, *Milton's Poetry of Choice and Its Romantic Heirs* (Ithaca, 1973), pp. 9–54.

13. *The Poetry of Meditation* (New Haven, 1954), pp. 1–24.

14. My own notion of "witnessing" relates only marginally to the scriptural concept of the "witness," a legal metaphor used to refer to any figure whose words, actions, or death have testified to the saving presence of God in history. (The English word "martyr" comes from the Greek word for "witness.") More relevant is the drama of perspectives which Kerrigan sees as central to prophetic writings, where the anxious visionary becomes simultaneously spectator and actor in a cosmic masque staged by God. See *The Prophetic Milton*, pp. 112–18 and 195–99.

15. *The Structure of Complex Words* (Ann Arbor, 1967), p. 101.

16. Kerrigan, *The Prophetic Milton*, p. 218, and Sanford Budick, *The Poetry of Civilization: Mythopoeic Displacement in Milton, Dryden, Pope and Johnson* (New Haven, 1974), p. 45.

17. "Perplexing the Explanation," pp. 294–95. In his notes, and in the essay " 'A Poet Amongst Poets': Milton and the Tradition of Prophecy," in *Milton and the Line of Vision*, ed. Wittreich (Madison, 1975), pp. 97–142, Wittreich appeals to contemporary Protestant commentaries that viewed Samson as a ruinous villain, and offers an interpretation of *Samson Agonistes* which makes Samson's suicide into a demonic parody of Christ's triumph over Satan and Self in *Paradise Regain'd*. This dark reading of the play reminds us forcibly of the real difficulty in accommodating the catastrophic ending to the traditional dialectics of Christian salvation. Despite his citation of contemporary commentaries, the general argument, tone, and language of Wittreich's discussion here suggest that he has invented a strongly Blakean reading of the drama, opposing Samson as fiery, self-entrapping Orc to Milton as creative Los. I honor the power of Wittreich's stance, but I am still uneasy about his stripping Samson of any shred of redemptive heroism. At the end of the tragedy, Samson is truly a hero, though a very different kind of hero from Christ Tempted, who is himself a hero of a different sort than Christ Crucified. At the risk of being outlandish, I would say that Milton's Old Testament giant resembles most the ironic hero of faith, Abraham, as described in Kierkegaard's *Fear and Trembling*.

18. Dryden's *The State of Innocence and the Fall of Man*, a dramatic version of *Paradise Lost* in rhymed couplets, was not completed until 1674, and remained unpublished until 1677, but it is possible that Marvell got wind of the project before he wrote his poem. Wittreich rightly questions the traditional assumption that Marvell's mockery of rhyme in lines 45–50 is aimed at Dryden, and that it recalls the playwright's famous request that Milton give him leave to "tag" his lines ("Perplexing the Explanation," pp. 288–89). Certainly it is odd that, if Marvell intended an allusion to Dryden's project, he kept his references to a dramatic version of the epic and to the fashion of rhyming quite separate.

19. In *Wordsworth's Poetry: 1787–1814* (New Haven, 1964) pp. 8–9, Geoffrey Hartman notes the expanded importance of the "surmise" in Milton and later in the Romantic poets. What was originally a simple figure of classical rhetoric becomes a major trope for drawing presence out of absence, for giving visionary authority to what is otherwise merely a hypothetical construct or compensatory fiction.

20. *Milton's Poetry of Choice*, pp. 12–24.

21. "Milton and Marvell," p. 24.

22. See, for instance, "Milton's Counterplot" and "Adam on the Grass with Balsa-mum," in *Beyond Formalism: Literary Essays 1958–1970* (New Haven, 1970), pp. 113–23 and pp. 124–50, respectively.

23. "Perplexing the Explanation," p. 300.

24. Maren-Sofie Røstvig, in "Structure as Prophecy: The Influence of Biblical Exege-sis Upon Theories of Literary Structure," in *Silent Poetry: Essays in Numerological Analy-sis*, ed. Alistair Fowler (London, 1970), pp. 32–72, cites Marvell's line as testimony that Milton's contemporaries were prepared to see numerological patterns in his poetry. My analysis should make it clear that the line actually subverts any such suggestions or at least gives them no real support.

25. The reader need not accept either of the passages I have cited from *Paradise Lost* as necessary subtexts for Marvell's use of the word "transported." But since the first citation is probably better known, I thought it wise to mention the latter as well, and so free Marvell's text from the infection of a single, isolated echo.

26. The *OED* provides no absolute evidence for deciding on the relative strength of "praise" and "commend." In "Perplexing the Explanation," Wittreich summarizes various opinions on the matter, then argues convincingly that "commend" is stronger because it "involves an expression of faith and confidence on the part of the bestower who ascribes glory but, more importantly, places the person commended under his own protection" (p. 287).

PATIENCE AND THE HUMBLY EXALTED HEROISM OF MILTON'S MESSIAH: TYPOLOGICAL AND ICONOGRAPHIC BACKGROUND

Gerald J. Schiffhorst

T HE CHRISTOCENTRIC theme of *Paradise Lost*, emphasized during Raphael's account of the war in Heaven (VI, 710–893), takes on special significance if we see the Son's triumph over the rebel angels as part of the patience tradition.[1] Without speculating on additional sources for Milton's scene, I wish to suggest that some typological background and iconographic analogues, especially to Christ the Suffering Servant and Supreme Judge, may reinforce our understanding of the scene and its significance. Because the Messiah is both *Christus victor* and *Christus patiens*, his heavenly triumph expresses his divine exaltation and concomitantly suggests his humiliation on the cross. Milton's vision of the patient heroism of the Son triumphant over sin is in part made possible by the use of biblical typology both to prefigure the Redemption and to remind us of the inseparability of the exaltation and humiliation. From the perspective of patience, which has redemptive as well as apocalyptic implications, we are led to see in the Son's defeat of Satan's forces the meaning of Christ's Passion and hence of his other victories over evil.

Focusing on Satan as the demonic counterpart of *Christus patiens* in the epic, Albert Labriola has observed that Milton, in conceiving the Son's exaltation and humiliation, has in mind the Redeemer's heroic manifestation of patience.[2] Developing this idea from different perspectives, I suggest that the poet has subtly enriched our picture of the Son's victory over his foes by imaging the victory of Calvary. In a traditional yet uniquely Miltonic conflation of the Messiah as judge and savior, Milton reveals how the triumph over disobedient evil, positioned at the exact center of the epic,[3] begins the fulfillment of the Son's exaltation (III, 276–343) as the obedient Messiah and prepares for the explicit definition of patience as it applies to Adam near the end of the poem: "Suffering for truth's sake / Is fortitude to highest victory" (XII, 569–70).

Patience, I think, is central to Milton's idea of Christian heroism, just as the triumph of the patient Son is central to the poem's structure. The Messiah, as the exemplar of a major virtue for Milton and his age, is dramatically active at the center of *Paradise Lost* in a way that prepares us for the education in patience which the final books of the poem entail.

Like the studies of most other critics, Stella Revard's important discussion of the Son in Book VI as the supreme spiritual warrior does not relate the Messiah or Milton's concept of Christian heroism to the tradition of patience, perhaps in part because this virtue is more obvious and explicit in *Paradise Regained* and *Samson Agonistes*.[4] Revard, John Steadman,[5] and others have shown how Milton's notion of glory and heroism is to be understood, yet the centrality of patience as a virtue encompassing the active and the passive, the present and the future, the divine and the human, the humble and the exalted, is also worth discussing. To do so is to appreciate fully how the Son of Book VI, prefiguring Christ the Suffering Servant, completes the promise of Book III and leads us poetically to what Adam will learn: that man must patiently await and freely serve God (XII, 557–73).

The Renaissance treated patience, variously and extensively, as a virtue essential to Christian salvation.[6] Due in part to the Neostoicism of Justus Lipsius and others, it received new emphasis as the highest kind of spiritual fortitude, as a virtue expressing, paradoxically, both calm submission and quiet passivity, on the one hand, and active, positive heroism on the other. Because of its supernatural meaning as redemptive suffering and its relation to hope, calm expectation, temperance, and constancy, patience was seen as the ideally balanced emotional and spiritual strength of those who can profit from afflictions and be affirmatively reconciled to the values of perseverance. The many homiletic and doctrinal renderings of the virtue produced, for example, in Milton's England stressed patience as a key part of the *imitatio Christi*, for it is the Christian's response to adversity.

When Milton speaks of "patience as the truest fortitude" (*SA*, 654), he is relying on many centuries of biblical, patristic, and late medieval commentaries on a virtue which, by the Renaissance, had become so widespread a homiletic theme and iconographic attribute as to be commonplace. Along with its closely related virtues of hope and perseverance, patience meant something much more than the passive endurance of Stoic fortitude; it meant active virtue, a positive response to God's will in the face of suffering. Often interchangeable with fortitude, patience as a Christian virtue was called God-like because it follows the example of Christ. Patience signifies the spiritual strength of the Christian armed with grace who accepts adversity while awaiting with readiness what Providence reveals. Patience, writes Nicholas Breton in "The Praise of Patience" (1605), expresses the qualities of the Christian soldier and servant. In contrast to the Stoics' unemotional Apathy, the Christian virtue stresses charity, forgiveness, and humility. With its root meaning of suffering, patience invariably leads to Christ, whose example makes affliction the remedy for evil and whose triumph over death makes him the unique hope of mankind. Referring to Christ on the cross, Lipsius says, "That is patience."[7]

In Milton's *Christian Doctrine*, the "better fortitude" of patience, especially as it is associated with the Mediator's functions as prophet, priest, and king, necessarily includes obedience, suffering, humility, and waiting. It means enduring present afflictions in the hope of future fulfillment. Milton defines the related virtue of hope as "a most assured expectation through faith of those future things which are already ours in Christ."[8] And fortitude, Milton says, is "exercised in the resistance to, or the endurance of evil" (CM, XVII, pp. 246–47). The proof texts for the interrelated virtues cited in *Christian Doctrine* reveal that patience and spiritual fortitude are inseparable and are keys to all other virtues needed by man because of the pattern of Christ. His humiliation and exaltation as Redeemer make him the archetype of patient heroism. The essential link between Christ's humiliation, his role as Suffering Servant, and his divine role as Supreme Judge is made clear in *Christian Doctrine* (CM, XV, p. 311), where Milton tells us what the exaltation means: "having triumphed over death and laid aside the form of a servant, he was exalted by God the Father" to immortality and glory for the benefit of mankind. That human regeneration is made possible by the Redemption (CM, XV, pp. 367–77) and that the imitation of Christ involves man's willingness to undergo suffering after the manner of Christ (1 Peter ii, 19), is basic to Scripture, *Christian Doctrine*, and Milton's other work. Moreover, as Labriola reminds us, humility is the essence of the *imitatio Christi*, since it is the remedy for the pride which caused the sin of man and the fall of Lucifer.[9] A full discussion of Milton's treatment of patience and its many associations and manifestations in the epic would require a separate study. It suffices to say here that this virtue is central to his theology of Redemption and that his explicit definition of patience in *Christian Doctrine* (CM, XVII, pp. 67, 69) in terms of obedience, reliance on God's power and goodness, and endurance of suffering, is just what we see the Father asking of and receiving from the Son in *Paradise Lost*. The poem reveals a pattern of heroism developed in terms of an ethos heavily indebted to Christian patience.

Especially apposite to the emergence of the Son in Book VI as one who obediently waits for the fulfillment of the divine will before he acts in his own right are several sections in *Christian Doctrine* in which Milton discusses patience. First, he stresses the "patient waiting for Christ," citing 2 Thessalonians iii, 5, Hebrews x, 36, and James v, 7 (CM, XVII, p. 67); he implies the readiness of the Christian armed with patience who awaits what providence will unfold. In the same section, he links patience with obedience. Second, discussing the "good temptation" as one in which God tries the righteous "for the purpose of magnifying their faith or patience" (CM, XV, p. 87), Milton's comments apply not only to Christians but also to the Son in *Paradise Lost*.[10] The Messiah's patient heroism, that is, includes the maturity of readiness which comes to those who not only suffer but also obediently wait. To be humbled in order to be proved by patience means that "one may become wiser by experience, and others may profit by their example" (CM, XV, p. 89). Milton cites Psalm xxvi, 2 ("examine me, O Jehovah, and prove me") along with James i, 2–3 ("the trying of your faith worketh patience"). As Robert Wickenheiser has shown, submissive Son develops into active Messiah in the epic, although all he represents as Son of God is constant and intensified; finally, he emerges as the Judge, Mediator, and Redeemer, thus expressing God's plan for man.[11] Just as the Son obediently undertakes the Redemption and stands ready to enact the Father's will, so man's role in providence is to wait patiently and serve freely. Patience is thus basic to the Son's humiliation; as a result, he becomes in Book XI (22–44) what the angels proclaimed in Book III (410–14) because of his deeds in Book VI, where his heretofore passive patience becomes for the first time heroically active. Steadman has shown that, in further contrast to worldly heroes who seek glory, regal dignity, and divine titles, the Messiah submits voluntarily to divine justice by taking on the "form of servant" (X, 214), foreshadowing his role as Suffering Servant. Just as this humiliation provides the pattern of Christian heroism in the epic, the exaltation is the reward for the humiliation, as the Father makes clear (III, 305–17). In both *Paradise Lost* and *Paradise Regained*, Steadman says, "the supremely heroic enterprise is Messiah's ministry of Redemption, and in the twofold aspects of his ministry—Messiah's humiliation and exaltation—lies the perfect exemplar of Christian heroism and its rewards."[12]

Patience is widely depicted as an iconographic attribute, as in Peter Brueghel the Elder's rendering of the virtue that separates the seven deadly sins from the seven virtues. She is treated (in the tradition of female, warring vices and virtues stemming from Prudentius' *Psychomachia*) by dozens of emblematists and other artists, though never as richly—or as appropriately for the present study—as in the eight allegorical engravings of Maarten van Heemskerck, *Patientiae triumphus* (c. 1555), in which Patience leads a triumphant procession of the virtue's other personifications.[13] Two of these, "The Triumph of David" and "The Triumph of Christ," are especially revealing for the background they provide for our picture of the victorious Son in terms that suggest the patience tradition. My point, of course, is not that Milton relied on these specific works, but that they conveniently summarize many of the symbolic motifs associated with patience and suggest many of the scriptural sources known to the poet.

In the fourth engraving of this series, David, riding a lion, wears elaborate armor and a crownlike helmet.[14] He carries a cross-topped staff and banner—symbolic of the resurrected Christ's victory—which include the emblematic bridle of temperance. His victory over Goliath, pictured in the background, is in keeping with the medieval tradition whereby David's slaying of Goliath is linked with Christ's triumph over Satan. In the *Biblia pauperum* and the *Laudes Sanctae Crucis* (c. 1180),[15] among other medieval sources, David's fight with Goliath parallels Christ's battle with Satan. A related motif is the parallel between David driving the evil spirit out of Saul by playing the harp and Christ's driving out of evil spirits, as seen, for example, in the fourteenth-century *Concordantia veteris et novi testamenti*. David played his harp before the ark of the Old Convenant (2 Kings xiv, 22), and he often appears in representations of the Crucifixion, in which the cross is identified with the ark of the New Covenant.[16] The influence of *Speculum humanae salvationis* on David-Christ typology (as, for example, in David's appearing with the *arma Christi* on the facade of the north side of Chartres) is especially significant in the evolution of David as a figure symbolic of Christ as priest, prophet, and king. The "Mirror of Human Salvation" links David's conquest of the lion and bear (1 Samuel xvii, 34–36) with the temptation of Christ, Shimei's cursing of David (2 Samuel xvi, 5) with the crown of thorns.[17] More apposite to Milton's picture of the victorious Son are two attributes in Heemskerck's allegory which make David a patience figure (see fig. 1): his harp, suggesting his Orphic power to calm beasts (hence his virtue as a patient ruler, as a type of Christ the king and peacemaker); and his armor, suggesting the Christian soldier defined by St. Paul (Ephesians vi, 13, 17) and in Erasmus' *Enchiridion militis Christiani* (1503).[18] The armor of salvation is often emblematic of patience-related virtues which enable one to with-stand oppression, as St. Ignatius of Antioch reveals in his letter to Poly-carp: "Your baptism shall be your shield, faith your helmet, your love a lance, and patience your armor." In the influential *Hypnerotomachia Poliphili*, helmeted patience is accompanied by the inscription: "Patien-tia est ornamentum, custodia at protectio vitae" ("Patience is the orna-ment, the safeguard, and the protection of life").[19] Clothed in virtuous armor, then, David emerges in Heemskerck's engraving as an allegory of the Christ-like knight or regal warrior. It is not by accident that Milton's Son is armed with "mildness" as he prepares to overcome Satan in Book VI.

Examining the scene in Book VI, we see that Milton uses images of victorious kingship, including allusions to David, to suggest that the patient heroism of the Redeemer is being applied to the Son.[20] In con-trast to the explicit references to David in Book XII, where Christ is foretold as the descendant of David's "Royal Stock" (325), or to the dozen messianic references to the throne of David in *Paradise Regained*, the presence of the Old Testament king is only indirectly suggested here, in echoes of Psalm cxxxix (VI, 734) and 2 Samuel xxii, 11 (VI, 771). In Book VI, David becomes most apparent as a source of allusion when the Son, having put on the Father's "mildness" (735) and "arm'd" him-self with the divine might, looks forward to a victory in which he will sing "Unfeigned *Halleluiahs*" (744). This recalls the exaltation (V, 600–41), with its heavenly harmonies, and is echoed when, after the Son roots the rebel angels out of Heaven, the saints sing "Triumph" to the "Victorious King" (VI, 886).[21] So too the "radiant *Urim*" of the Son's "breastplate of judgment" reminds us that David is a major type of Christ become perfect warrior-hero. Riding "on the wings of Cherub" (VI, 771), as Merritt Hughes notes, the Son recalls the cry of David (2 Samuel xxii, 11); he, along with Moses and Noah, may be considered one of the poem's "Shadowy Types" of Christ as Redeemer, just as the prophets (Isaiah xi, 1) saw the Messianic King as David *redivivus*. In short, we see that the Son, wearing the armor of divinity and eager to sing "Hymns of high praise" (VI, 745), resembles David, who similarly disarmed his enemies; we are thereby reminded of the incarnate Mes-siah's human patience and divine kingship. Thus the analogy with David, both as the type of the king, victor, and peacemaker and as the unarmed slayer of Goliath, helps to illuminate the Son's heroism in his two further victories over Satan.

Equally important to this scene in Book VI are overtones of the Son's exalted, yet humble status as the heroically patient victor. First,

Figure 1. "The Triumph of David," no. 4 in the series *Patientiae Triumphus* by Maarten van Heemskerck. Duke University Art Museum.

the blazing "Sign" of the Messiah (776), from Matthew xxiv, 30, reminds us of another manifestation of Christian patience—that of the Son of man at the end of time; it also signifies the cross, specifically, as Gertrud Schiller observes, as the symbol of the victory that legitimizes the crucified Christ as judge and foreshadows the Resurrection.[22] Second, the Son's climactic speech before leaving the "right hand of Glory" (747) and ascending the "Chariot of Paternal Deity" (750) begins with references to his exaltation and obedient submission; as Hughes notes, these lines recall Christ's prayer before the Crucifixion: "Father, the hour is come; glorify Thy Son that Thy Son also may glorify Thee" (John xvii, 1). This speech also reminds us of the Father's earlier prophecy of the Son's Incarnation, Redemption, and enthronement as the "Anointed universal King" (III, 317). In *Christian Doctrine* (CM, XV, p. 297), Milton discusses Christ's kingship as simultaneously entailing his humiliation by using a revealing typological text, Ezekiel xxxvii, 25: "my servant David shall be their prince forever."

If "The Triumph of David" sheds some light on Milton's picture of the Son's heroism, the final and climactic engraving of *Patientiae Triumphus*, "The Triumph of Christ," sheds even more (see fig. 2). First, Christ is depicted in the pose of *Majestas Domini* (or, more precisely, the supreme Judge), the elevated and triumphant Christ of the Second Coming, described, for example, in Hebrews xii, 2: "let us keep our eyes fixed on Jesus, the author and finisher of the faith, who, having set joy before him, endured the cross, despising the same, and now sits on the right hand of the throne of God." This passage, like Heemskerck's engraving, reminds us that patience is eschatologically conceived as the virtue of those who fervently await the Last Judgment. In the New Testament, patience nearly always implies the Second Coming (Revelation i, 9; ii, 3, 19; iii, 10). Patience not only leads to fulfillment in Christ (1 Thessalonians i, 3), but is the lively, energetic power of faith (Revelation xii, 11) perfected in Christ; it merges with hope and faith in the Son of God at the end of time. Especially significant for this notion of patience is the Epsitle of James: "Be patient therefore, brethren, unto the coming of the Lord" (v, 7–11). Patience involves a sense of time which transcends present afflictions in the hope of future fulfillment.

In keeping with the tradition for representing the Supreme Judge, Heemskerck's Christ is seated, like Milton's Messiah, on a terrestrial globe and rainbow in a chariot decorated with three of the animals described in Ezekiel (i, 5–13) and in the Apocalypse (iv, 6–7).[23] His iconographic glorification, summarizing the various themes and motifs of the other engravings, is indebted to the tradition of *Majestas Domini*,

Vnica Cunctipotens hominum Spes, veraq; vita
CHRISTVS, morigerus fuit æternovq; Parenti
Ad mortem, mortemq; crucis scelerolam.

æthera celsa super iam cernimus, omneq; nomē
Euectū, atq; triumphantē, post Tartara Mundii,
Dæmona, Peccatum, trucidentos depopulata.

Figure 2. "The Triumph of Christ," no. 8 in the series *Patientiae Triumphus* by Maarten van Heemskerck. Duke University Art Museum.

Christ the Ruler enthroned, gesturing in blessing.[24] As Maren-Sofie Røstvig has shown, Milton found in Ezekiel's vision of the chariot "his chief image of perfection" because the four-wheeled chariot with a man in the center (Ezekiel i, 10) is usually interpreted as Christ imposing harmony (or unity) through the four corners of the universe. Christ's middle position in the chariot, which is in keeping with centuries of biblical belief in *Christus medium tenet*, signifies *aequalitas*, "the most glorious of all structural images of perfection."[25]

Representations of Christ enthroned on the rainbow, symbolic of the ark of the covenant promised to Noah, often appear after the ninth century as frontispieces in Gospel books, indicating the harmony of the four Evangelists and their mystical unity in Christ. The victorious banner which Christ carries in Heemskerck's engraving bears the *arma Christi*, as in various representations of the Last Judgment, including Michelangelo's frescoes in the Sistine Chapel. These weapons of course signify the Passion and symbolize both the Redeemer's patient endurance and his dual triumph over evil, for the *arma Christi* are conventionally associated with the weapons Christ uses against Satan. Since to imitate Christ is to endure suffering, the *arma Christi*, like patience itself, can also be called part of the *imitatio Christi*. As the heraldic device of Christ as savior and judge, the *arma Christi*, Tate says, fuse "the imagery of the armored virtue with that of the patient ruler who endures. . . . They are transformed into weapons with which evil can be vanquished. With regard to the virtue patience, the *arma Christi* can be seen as symbolizing the two-fold essence of her character, that she obediently endures and through her suffering ultimately triumphs."[26] The conception of Christian patience as both triumphantly active and obediently passive is basic to Milton's use of the virtue in *Paradise Lost*, as we see in his view of the Messiah as its principal archetype.

The iconography of the rainbow throne in *Paradise Lost* (VI, 758–72) as part of the symbolism connecting the Son to the Supreme Judge at the end of time is briefly sketched by Roland Frye, who leaves no doubt that the poet's overall indebtedness to the visual arts is nearly as extensive as his reliance on biblical, patristic, and other written sources.[27] Not mentioned in Frye's treatment of the Son's triumphant throne is the "Eagle-wing'd Victory" (762–63) at his right hand. This detail connects the chariot-throne not so much with Greek war chariots but with the resurrected Christ in terms of a symbolic tradition with more ancient roots (cf. Hughes's note on VI, 762). J. H. Adamson has shown how Ezekiel's chariot of the Logos, which became a sacred part of the Jewish mystical tradition, symbolized the harmony of all being with the divine will. Milton's chariot of the Logos, metaphorically combined with Ezekiel's vision of a chariot of light, appears at the critical moment of the war in Heaven, suggesting the Son's triumph and, by extension, man's redemption. "As there is a triumphant Logos, so there is an indwelling Logos in the mind of man which, aided by prevenient grace, can also triumph."[28] The metaphorical triumph of the virtues in the *Patientiae Triumphus* is a convenient way of seeing how Milton's poetic syncretism works: the Son's victory over Satan and the rebel cohorts implies his irenic victory on the cross and thus his relation to human salvation, the core of the poem. St. Ambrose recounts how, at the Ascension, Christ climbed into a chariot like a triumphant conqueror;[29] yet Revard wisely remarks that Milton's idea of heroism and glory is much more than kingly triumph: the Son's glory is in his return to the Father.[30]

Enriching the chariot is the eagle, whose role as the king of birds may be seen, according to one source, to signify the majesty of emperorship, as in the heraldic spread eagle of the Holy Roman Empire.[31] More important is the bird's Christian association with the Ascension in medieval typology, which may have been inspired by Deuteronomy xxxii, 11 and by the eagle as symbolizing the heaven-bound soul on classical sarcophagi.[32] Because the eagle flies to the sun to renew its youth, it takes on phoenixlike associations and so is emblematic of the Resurrection.[33] That the spread wings may also signify the cross is suggested in the twelfth-century commentary of Honorius of Autun: "the eagle flies higher than any other bird, and it is the only bird which can look directly into the fiery light of the sun. It lovingly cares for its young and teaches them to do likewise. So also is Christ in heaven, who sits on the right hand of God the Father, raised endlessly above all the elect. He has spread the wings of his cross above all of us."[34] Stephen Batman's *A christall glasse of christian reformation* (1569) defines victory as the reward of constant faith in Christ;[35] compare Milton's own words about suffering as "fortitude to highest victory" as well as the conventional victory of the resurrected Christ. Since Milton's patience-related personification is also defined as "Eagle-wing'd," and since the eagle in his source (Ezekiel i, 10), as in the Revelation of St. John, carries associations with the striving of the crucified Christ's spirit for the grace of God,[36] I suggest that the image implies the redemptive nature of the Christian virtue tradition, expressed by patience. Although it is impossible to know the exact extent of the poet's typological assimilation, it is safe to say that the Son's "Eagle-wing'd Victory" is more than a classical allusion; it contains as well some of the eagle's associations with the Son

of man victorious over death. Clearly, the image of the eagle reinforces
Milton's predominantly majestic conception of the Supreme Judge as he
undertakes his triumph over evil.

That patience is crucial to the redemptive implications of the Son's
victory can be seen, finally, if we focus briefly on the Transfiguration
tradition as a means of interpreting Christ as Judge, Suffering Servant,
and Man of Sorrows. The Transfiguration was the only time on earth
that Christ allowed his divine glory to shine through his humanity.
Since the synoptic Evangelists connect Christ's sufferings with his
glorification, we are well advised to follow Labriola's suggestion that
the Transfiguration or glorification of Christ is an appropriate scriptural
and iconographic key to the exaltation. I would add that it also reveals
how patience, because it looks to future glory in the present, links the
humiliation with the exaltation.[37] St. Paul says that Jesus was obedient
unto death, and for this reason God exalted him (Philippians ii, 5–11).
Moreover, that the same three disciples were present both at the
glorification, as recounted by Matthew (xvii, 1–9), Mark (ix, 2–9), and
Luke (ix, 28–36), and in Gethsemane provides an additional link between the Passion and the Transfiguration.[38] The Fathers of the church
also construe the Transfiguration as prefiguring Christ's return to earth
as Judge (*parousia*), an interpretation which adds further background
to an established tradition enabling Milton to connect the Messiah as
Judge with Christ as Suffering Servant–and to expect us to make such
a connection. Discussing the relation between the Suffering Servant
and the Man of Sorrows, Schiller shows how artists of the late Middle
Ages transferred the liturgical King of Glory or Judge of the World to
the tradition of the Man of Sorrows, as part of the *imitatio Christi*.[39]
According to this tradition, the Redeemer is present in his eternal
suffering, as one who is both dead and alive; he is the Judge because
in the Passion and in death, he has obediently endured. Patience,
then, is again a key to an iconographic-theological tradition which sums
up the essential nature of the Redemption within and beyond time.
The Man of Sorrows is a figure of mercy and judgment; so, too, Milton's Messiah is both *Christus victor* and *Christus patiens*.[40] Because
the messianic prophecy of Zachariah xii, 10, taken up in Revelation i,
7, links the crucified Christ with the Christ of the Second Coming,
Milton's conflation of the Son as Supreme Judge with the crucified
Savior is traditionally sound.[41] The wounds evident in Heemskerck's
Christ capture this tradition.

How have the various patience-related traditions sketched here—
the biblical Suffering Servant, the iconographic Man of Sorrows, and the

typological victorious king with their many overtones and associations—helped us to understand the meaning of the picture at the center of Milton's epic? First, we see how *Christus victor* as implying *Christus patiens* points to the exaltation and humiliation as concomitant parts of Milton's idea of heroism, a concept that includes obedience, humility, and the active readiness of patience. Book VI thus poetically completes the theological pronouncements of Book III by portraying the Son as the Messiah, the King of Glory, in a triumphant scene that prepares us for Michael's prophecy in Book XII. It also adds to the Son's development, begun in Book III, as he takes on his "Filial Godhead" and becomes an increasingly active exemplar of heroism. Books VI and III thus jointly express the "joy of obedience fulfilled."[42]

Second, coming as he does on the third day of the heavenly battle, the Son is not only majestic Judge but also also victorious Savior, whose Resurrection on the third day signified his triumph over sin and death. We see his coming in thunder and chariot as it affects the rebel angels who, "astonisht all resistance lost, / All courage; down their idle weapons dropped" (VI, 838–39). From this perspective, we realize that the effect of the Son's powerful, climactic victory contravenes the false heroism of Satan and his followers, who, with "a pleasing sorcery," earlier thought that they could arm themselves "With stubborn patience" (II, 569) and be victorious against the throne of God. But, when we recall that Book VI is also the climax of Raphael's education of Adam, we realize that the scene has broader implications for Milton's readers: it images the patient triumph of the Messiah in his other victories on the cross and at the end of the world. From the perspective of man, the scene emphasizes Milton's Christocentric theme by placing the Son's victories in and beyond human history at the core of the poem.

The Messiah of Book VI, then, is the timeless, majestic soldier and the triumphant, future Judge of Revelation as well as the glorious, redemptive victor whose past humiliation and exaltation make him the perfect, eternally present pattern of heroic Christian patience. His heavenly triumph, in short, becomes correlative with his Redemption, a victory subtly but traditionally introduced to Adam and the reader at a climactic moment in the poem. Unlike the more typically subdued, passive pose of the "patient Son of God" sitting "unappall'd" amid the storm in *Paradise Regained* (IV, 420), the Redeemer's position as archetypal hero of *Paradise Lost* is presented in the context of a tradition which defines his patience as dramatically active. In a picture rich in symbolic scriptural and typological details, the Son rides forth majestically as a hero to vanquish the "cursed crew" in a triumph that looks forward to his two other triumphs over evil. Milton makes vividly concrete what the Father has proclaimed (III, 276–343); the Son's exaltation as ruler and judge will entail his willingness to undergo the humiliation on the cross. By visualizing this doctrine in terms of patience, a virtue signifying active as well as passive fortitude, present endurance as well as future expectation, the poet places the paradox of the Incarnation's fulfillment at the center of his epic and so emphasizes the paradox of patience by which the Messiah is the suffering victor, obedient king, and humbly triumphant exemplar of Christian heroism.

University of Central Florida

NOTES

1. All references to Milton's poetry follow *John Milton: Complete Poems and Major Prose*, ed. Merritt Y. Huges (New York, 1957).

2. "The Medieval View of Christian History in *Paradise Lost*," in *Milton and the Middle Ages*, ed. John Mulryan (Lewisburg, Pa., 1982). I am most grateful to Professor Labriola for allowing me to consult this essay prior to publication. His essays, "The Aesthetics of Self-Diminution: Christian Iconography and *Paradise Lost*," in *Milton Studies*, VII, ed. Albert C. Labriola and Michael Lieb (Pittsburgh, 1975), pp. 267–311, and " 'Thy Humiliation Shall Exalt': The Christology of *Paradise Lost*," in *Milton Studies*, XV, ed. James D. Simmonds (Pittsburgh, 1981), pp. 29–42, have also been of value in this study. For background on the theology of exaltation, see W. B. Hunter, "The War in Heaven: The Exaltation of the Son," in *Bright Essence*, ed. W. B. Hunter et al. (Salt Lake City, 1971), pp. 115–30.

3. Gunnar Qvarnström, *The Enchanted Palace: Some Structual Aspects of "Paradise Lost"* (Stockholm, 1967), p. 64.

4. *The War in Heaven: "Paradise Lost" and the Tradition of Satan's Rebellion* (Ithaca, N.Y., 1980).

5. *Milton and the Renaissance Hero* (New York, 1967), and *Milton's Epic Characters: Image and Idol* (Chapel Hill, 1968), esp. pp. 23–101.

6. Gerald J. Schiffhorst, ed., *The Triumph of Patience: Medieval and Renaissance Studies* (Gainesville, Fla., 1978), pp. 1–64.

7. Justus Lipsius, *Monita et exempla politica* (Antwerp, 1625), p. 208. Many centuries earlier, Gregory the Great referred to Christ "armed with unshakable patience" on the cross. See Gertrud Schiller, *Iconography of Christian Art*, trans. Janet Seligman (Greenwich, Conn., 1971), II, p. 2.

8. *Christian Doctrine*, I, xx, in *Works of John Milton*, ed. Frank Allen Patterson et al. (New York, 1931–38), XV, p. 407, hereafter cited in the text as CM. Note the many references to Philippians ii, 5–9 (the Suffering Servant) in Chapter xv, "Of the Ministry of Redemption." On patience, see CM, XVII, pp.67, 69, where Milton cites Job i, 22, Matthew xvi, 24, Luke xxi, 19, Romans viii, 25, 2 Thessalonians iii, 5, and 1 Peter ii, 19, as perhaps the most important proof texts associating patient waiting with suffering for both Christ and man. See also constancy (CM, XVII, p. 47) and temperance (XVII, pp. 213–23).

9. "The Aesthetics of Self-Diminution," p. 280.

10. Steadman discusses the good temptation in relation to Samson (*Milton's Epic Characters*, pp. 54–57).

11. "Milton's 'Pattern of a Christian Hero': the Son in *Paradise Lost*," *Milton Quarterly*, XII (1978), 3.

12 *Milton's Epic Characters*, p. 59. Steadman cites Milton's comments on humiliation and exaltation as the normative pattern for all believers and notes relevant theological comments by Polanus and Wollebius (p. 61).

13. I am greatly indebted to Priscilla L. Tate for sharing many insights from her study of the *Patientiae triumphus*. This is the subject of her 1974 master's thesis, "The Triumph of Patience," at Duke University, where we studied the original engravings under the expert tutelage of W. S. Heckscher, to whom I am also indebted. A redaction of her thesis appears in Schiffhorst, *The Triumph of Patience*, pp. 107–37.

14. The lion is one of many revealing details connecting David with Christ, who is sometimes seen riding a lion, as in Nicholas Reusner's *Emblemata* (Frankfurt, 1581), no. 40. The source of the lion and the tribe of Judah, the origin of David's and Christ's common lineage, is Genesis xlix, 9–10; the source of David's triumph over the lion and bear is 1 Kings xvii, 34–36, an account sometimes seen to prefigure Christ as the Good Shepherd. For the legendary temperance and regal fortitude of the lion, see Hrabanus Maurus and Isidore of Seville, in *Patrologiae cursus compeltus: Series Latina*, ed. J. P. Migne, CXI, col. 217; LXXXII, col. 434.

15. *Codex Latinus Monacensis* (National Library, Munich), XIV, p. 159.

16. Gustav Heider, "Beiträge zur Christlichen Typologie," *Jahrbuch der Kaiserlichen-Königlichen ZentralKommission*, V (1861), 116.

17. Thorns become a common attribute of emblematic Patience, as in Cesare Ripa's influential *Iconologia* (Rome, 1603), p. 381.

18. See also "The Christian Knight" engraving in Joesph Fletcher, *The History of the Perfect-Cursed-Blessed Man* (London, 1628), reproduced in S. C. Chew, *The Pilgrimage of Life* (New Haven, 1962), fig. 73.

19. Francesco Colonna, *Hypnerotomachia Poliphili* (Venice, 1499), facsimile ed. J. W. Appel (London, 1899), fig. 14. Dorothea Forstner, *Die Welt der Symbole*, 2nd ed. (Innsbruck, 1967) cites the passage from St. Ignatius (p. 480).

20. On David as a type of Christ in *Christian Doctrine*, see CM, XIV, p. 201, where Milton cites Jeremiah xxx, 9. For the priesthood of Christ as king, "whence the name of Christ is derived," Milton cites Psalm ii, 6–7, John i, 49–50, and Luke i, 32. In *The Prophet-King: Moses Traditions and the Johannine Christology* (Leiden, 1967), Wayne A. Meeks notes that the Messiah as eschatological king was conventionally seen as the descendant of David, just as Christ as prophet is a distinct eschatological figure related to the Mosaic tradition (p. 20). For some interpretations of David's many roles in literature, see *The David Myth in Western Literature*, ed. Raymond-Jean Frontain and Jan Wojcik (West Lafayette, Ind., 1980). Note that for many Renaissance artists, David symbolized the ideal of man confronting the adversities of the world, a secular extension of the traditionally patient waiting for delivery into the next world. That he was also viewed as a religious hero is apparent in the many brief epics composed between 1550 and 1650, especially in Michael Drayton's *David and Goliath* (1630) and Abraham Cowley's *Davideis* (1656), which can been seen as preparing for Milton's notion of a heroism based not on martial deeds but on Christ-like mercy.

21. John G. Demaray, "The Thrones of Satan and God: Backgrounds to Divine Opposition in *Paradise Lost*," *Huntington Library Quarterly*, XXXI (1967), 21–33, shows how

the enthroned Father (III, 58) is surrounded by harmonious sound, as in a court masque. See also his *Milton's Theatrical Epic* (Cambridge, Mass., 1980).

22. *Iconography of Christian Art*, II, p. 186.

23. The source of the "Majesty of the Lord" signifying the fulfillment of the covenant is the same that Milton draws on for the scene in Book VI, Ezekiel xliii, 4–5. See also Meeks, *The Prophet-King*, p. 305. Meeks notes that the refusal to accept Christ as the Messiah (in the scene before Pilate) exposes the world as condemned in God's judgment; thus the "trial" before the Passion becomes Christ's enthronement as king and judge and, simultaneously, the judgment of the world.

24. Briefly discussed by Roland M. Frye, *Milton's Imagery and the Visual Arts* (Princeton, 1978), p. 158.

25. "Images of Perfection," in *Seventeenth-Century Imagery*, ed. Earl Miner (Berkeley, 1971), pp. 11, 21. Note Miner's frontispiece: a 1617 title page showing Christ in a chariot of the world very similar to Milton's rendering in VI. Røstvig also shows how the chariot was a type of obedience in the work of John Diodati, Gasparius Sanctius, and Antonius Fernandius (p. 21).

26. "The Triumph of Patience," p. 130

27. *Milton's Imagery*, p. 158. See also Schiller, *Iconography of Christian Art*, II, p. 186, for the *etimasia* (throne prepared for the Judge of the World) as a sign of the Son of Man.

28. "The War in Heaven: *The Merkabah*," in *Bright Essence*, p. 114.

29. Schiller, *Iconography of Christian Art*, II, p. 2.

30. *The War in Heaven*, p. 262. In her revealing discussion of the chariot, Revard reminds us that the coming of the Son in the chariot, suggesting the Resurrection and Second Coming, was a popular image in seventeenth-century sermons (pp. 123–26, 256–60). She argues that the chariot be seen not as a battle chariot (as Hughes's note on line 762 suggests), but as a symbol of divinity, a vision of the Son of God when he is to come in the last days (p. 257). The vision of the chariot, she says, symbolized the key to Christ's divinity for the seventeenth-century reader (p. 259). Note also her citations from Peter Sterry, William Greenhill, and other Protestant contemporaries of Milton. That the chariot anticipates the Last Judgement has also been observed by Joesph Summers, *The Muse's Method* (Cambridge, Mass., 1962), p. 135; John Knott, *Milton's Pastoral Vision* (Chicago, 1971), pp. 71–74; and William Madsen, *From Shadowy Types of Truth* (New Haven, 1968), p. 111.

31. Carel van Mander, *Het Schilderboek* (Haarlem, 1604), 130v–131r.

32. Suggested by W. S. Heckscher, "Petites Perceptions," *Journal of Medieval and Renaissance Studies*, IV (1974), fig. 9.

33. See Psalm ciii, 5: "Thy youth shall be renewed like the eagle's."

34. I follow Tate's translation of the text, found in J. M. M. Timmers, *Symboliek en Iconographie der Christelijke Kunst* (Roermond-Maaseik, 1947), par. 1790. For the *Opera omnia* of Honorius, see *Patrologiae Latina*, CLXXII, cols. 39–102.

35. Summarized by Chew, *The Pilgrimage of Life*, p. 92.

36. Forstner, *Die Welt der Symbole*, cites this interpretation by Irenaeus (p. 340).

37. Labriola presents these ideas in "The Transfiguration and *Paradise Lost:* Medieval Commentaries and the Iconographic Tradition," an unpublished paper in which he notes that triptychs of the Tranfiguration in the *Biblia pauperum* portray Christ in the triumphant, apocalyptic pose as judge seated on the rainbow throne.

38. Schiller, *Iconography of Christian Art*, I, pp. 145–62.

39. *Iconography of Christian Art*, II, p. 198. Schiller cites Roberto Oderisis' fourteenth-century painting *Christ as the Man of Sorrows*, which includes the *arma Christi*.

40. Ibid., II, figs. 713, 714. Here the Man of Sorrows appears as judge, signifying the Son of Man to come at the end of time. He is also the obedient, sacrificial victim who, as priest, intercedes with the Father (pp. 197–229).

41. Ibid., II. Schiller cites numerous iconographic analogues to Milton's picture: fig. 646, the Judge of the World enthroned on a rainbow; figs. 647, 648, 651, and 652; fig. 537, Cranach's *Christ Slays Death and the Devil*, (1547). Compare I, fig. 427, *Christ in Triumph*.

42. Revard, *The War in Heaven*, p. 253.

SION'S BACCHANALIA:
AN INQUIRY INTO MILTON'S LATIN
IN THE *EPITAPHIUM DAMONIS*

John K. Hale

W HAT INTEREST does Milton's Latin poetry possess for us now? Of course, anything which extends our knowledge of a great writer's mind has some interest, yet Milton's Latin verse might after all rank with Bishop Berkeley's encomia upon tar-water. Again, though his Latin poems tend to be more autobiographical than his English verse of the same period and tell us important things about his emotional development and his plans for writing, translations suffice most readers for most purposes. Indeed, even if *poems* in Latin are a special case because poetry is precisely that quality of words which defies translation, they might still be dismissed as too derivative of the Roman poets, as eccentric where they depart from Roman practice, or (somewhat unreasonably) as both, or they might simply stand condemned to obscurity by the poet's choice of a learned and now dead language. My purpose in this essay is to explore Milton's most ambitious Latin poem, the *Epitaphium Damonis*, with three ends in view. I examine selected features of his diction and prosody to see what these aspects of his Latin accomplish. Then I examine the Latin form in which he has conceived the pastoral of the *Epitaphium*, which naturally invites comparison with his earlier pastoral in English, *Lycidas*. Finally, on these foundations, I argue that Latin is the living flesh of the poem, indispensable equally to its beauty and to its conviction.[1]

We should be clear at the outset that to Milton himself only Latin could have seemed the appropriate medium for this particular poem. The *Epitaphium* is written in Latin because it is written to Charles Diodati. The two friends had exchanged Latin verses since their schooldays together at St. Paul's: Latin verse was their usual and tradition-sanctioned means of personal communication. Accordingly, since the *Epitaphium* honoring Diodati's death is the last of these communications, it is entirely fitting that it should be in Latin, just as it is fitting that this should be Milton's most ambitious and his last major Latin

115

poem. Indeed, this sense of fitness extends to his discussing our own underlying question, the respective claims on the poet of Latin and English (168–78).[2] In various ways, then, the poem is an occasional poem, and to that purpose the use of Latin is integral.

Our question, however, is not whether Latin was appropriate for Milton in 1639 or 1640, but whether it is expressive for readers of any time, and in particular whether the diction and prosody pull their weight. To show, first, that the diction is adequate to the design, I consider two instances where objections have been made to it.

At line 60, the shepherd Thyrsis, whose lament for the dead Damon represents Milton's for Diodati, declares of his solitary grieving that "Hic serum expecto, supra caput imber et Eurus / Triste sonant, fractaeque agitata crepuscula silvae" ("Here I await the evening, while above my head the east wind and its rain make a dismal noise, and the twilight of the shattered wood, lashed to and fro by the wind, echoes that noise"). E. M. W. Tillyard commented that "the last four words may not be good Latin, but they are certainly good poetry."[3] I am tempted to say that if they are good poetry they *are* good Latin, but I forbear to say it. Why does he smell false Latin? Perhaps it is the fusion of a concrete with an abstract, the conception of a twilight being tossed about or making a noise; or should we speak of a transference to the twilight of the wood's agitation? Perhaps the Latin phrase betrays an English sensibility beneath it, but the reader of Milton will more likely admire the elaborate fusion of sense impressions and respond to the mood which these impressions project. Twilight, which we see, is linked with sound—"sonant . . . crepuscula"—and takes on motion, "agitata," so that it becomes an easy further step to impute a metaphorical turbulence to the agitated poet-shepherd. Moreover, the phrase is an aural masterpiece. Its sibilants hint at the wind's whistling in the treetops. It imitates the sound-filled darkness in the u-sounds of "crepuscula" and the rapid movements of shadow in the rhythm of "agitata," while the consonants suggest a sharp cracking of branches in "fractaeque . . . crepuscula." Placed at the climax of the verse paragraph, the phrase activates several of our senses at once, to corroborate the thought of loneliness ("At iam solus agros," 58) by giving us its tactile counterpart, a shiver caused by the sound and the movement of the words.

In the present instance, then, I find Milton's diction neither imitative nor obscure, but individual and creative: he is extending what Latin can express, just as he does elsewhere for English. Yet a problem results from this very lack of a strict precedent in his Latin masters. Since such bold phrases do not occur all the time, may not the reader who is more conversant than I am with the Roman poets find in Milton an uneasy mixture of the usually derivative with the intermittently, and jarringly, idiosyncratic? There may well be a point at which familiarity with the models rather works against than enhances enjoyment of Milton, or at which the Miltonist must always find more of interest than the true classicist can.

A different example will clarify what I mean and will bring me to my provisional conclusions about diction. At line 53, as a detail of a picture of high summer contentment which nonetheless reminds Thyrsis of his loss of Damon we read: "Pastoresque latent, stertit sub sepe colonus" ("The shepherds hide from the heat, and the farmworker snores under the hedge"). The inhabitants of classical pastoral have more dignity and cultivation than to behave like this. But the visual half-humorous detail would not be out of place in Breughel, and readers who feel no discrepancy here between Milton and his models probably welcome within the bland pastoral fiction a humanizing touch of realism. I myself find the detail in keeping with Milton's feeling for variety within the pastoral mode, a zest for its possible particulars, like the distinction in sound between the hissing of roast pears on the fire and the crackling of roasting nuts ("sibilat . . . strepitat," 47–48). But there may indeed be a parting of ways here, between the enjoyment of both new and old details of pastoral for those who know Milton better than his models, and the unease he creates in those who come to him from the models. Or are Milton's zest for variousness and concomitant willingness to stretch decorum part of a larger phenomenon, that slow dismantling of the classical strictness of decorum which Erich Auerbach ascribes, ultimately, to Judeo-Christian tradition?[4] At all events, Milton's diction combines absorption of his Latin exemplars with independent use of them. It shows not imitativeness but true imitatio, what Ascham called "similis materiei dissimilis tractatio" and "dissimilis materiei similis tractatio" ("the dissimilar treatment of similar material" and "the similar treatment of dissimilar material").[5]

Milton's hexameter prosody shows a similar combining of fidelity to exemplars, especially Virgil, with ease and independence. I illustrate the point from his opening paragraph, discussing first its effect as a whole and then some individual effects:

Himerides nymphae (nam vos et Daphnin et Hylan,
Et plorata diu meministis fata Bionis)
Dicite Sicelicum Thamesina per oppida carmen:
Quas miser effudit voces, quae murmura Thyrsis,
Et quibus assiduis exercuit antra querelis,

Fluminaque, fontesque vagos, nemorumque recessus,
Dum sibi praereptum queritur Damona, neque altam
Luctibus exemit noctem loca sola pererrans.
Et jam bis viridi surgebat culmus arista,
Et totidem flavas numerabant horrea messes,
Ex quo summa dies tulerat Damona sub umbras,
Nec dum aderat Thyrsis, pastorem scilicet illum
Dulcis amor Musae Thusca retinebat in urbe.
Ast ubi mens expleta domum, pecorisque relicti
Cura vocat, simul assueta seditque sub ulmo,
Tum vero amissum tum denique sentit amicum,
Coepit et immensum sic exonerare dolorem.

[O you nymphs of Himera—for you remember Daphnis and Hylas, and Bion's long-lamented fate—sing your Sicilian song through the towns beside the Thames. Sing about the cries and laments poured out by Thyrsis in his misery, and the ceaseless lamentations with which he disturbed the caves and rivers, the rambling rivulets and hidden groves while he lamented for Damon, snatched from him prematurely. Thyrsis filled even deep night with his grief, wandering about in places all else had deserted. Already the grain-stalk had twice arisen with its green beard, and the granaries had counted in two golden harvests, since the day of Damon's death had borne him down to the world of shadows; and still Thyrsis the shepherd was absent, detained by sweet love of the Muse in a Tuscan city. But when he had filled his mind there and was called home by concern for the flock he had left behind, and was sitting beneath his usual elm tree—then, then indeed he felt how his friend was lost to him; and began in these words to unload his immeasurable burden of grief.]

Like the Roman poets, Milton achieves variety within his verse paragraph by using only sparingly the maximum number of dactylic feet which the Latin hexameter admitted (cf. 3). Like Virgil in particular, he begins a line with a dactyl more often than not, so as to suggest the underlying dactylic pulse at the outset yet without laboring the point: the poem's proportion of first-foot dactyls, about 65 percent, is close to Virgil's norm. Again, like all the major Roman poets, Milton seeks variety in the interplay of spondees and dactyls in the first four feet: in the first ten lines, only lines 1 and 4 and lines 7 and 10 have matching rhythm in this respect. Similarly, Milton keeps to Roman practice in the fifth foot, which is almost always dactylic so as to reassert the basic pulse as each line is concluding and, more important, to assure that at this point of the line accent and ictus—the rhythms of the spoken words and the metrical scheme, respectively—must fully coincide ("Dáphnĭn ĕt Hýlān," "fātă Bĭónīs," and so on). More like Virgil in particular is Milton's treatment of the relation between accent and ictus in the fourth

foot. As Jackson Knight demonstrated, Virgil prefers a clashing or con-
flicting of these two in the fourth foot, a practice in marked contrast to
his predecessors';[6] Milton, whose pastoral lament follows Virgil in many
other respects, follows him in this more hidden way too, to such an
extent that the conflict of accent and ictus in 62 percent of the poem's
lines corresponds closely with the figures for the whole of Virgil's
Eclogues.

Naturally, however, we ask whether such a recondite consideration
as the coincidence or conflict of ictus with accent in the fourth foot of the
hexameter can affect our imaginative participation as we read the poem.
It does indeed. The coinciding of ictus with accent in the fourth of the
six feet must align the two kinds of rhythm at a point in the line earlier
than if they conflicted in the fourth foot; as a result, their counterpoint-
ing must be more abbreviated and less rich. It follows that by making
conflict in the fourth foot the norm both poets gain special force when
they depart from their norm to a coinciding, and even more so to a run
of coincidences or to a pattern of conflicts and coincidences. But rather
than summarize Jackson Knight, I shall consider two excellent examples
Milton provides. Lines 9 and 10 both contain fourth-foot coincidence of
a sort which achieves at least three small but useful aural effects. The
coincidences ('sūrgébāt," "nŭmĕrábānt") come after three successive instances of conflict and so give variety. They also give contrast, supporting the syntactic and semantic move (9) to a new aspect of Thyrsis' grief.
Moreover, the lines' parallel coincidences support their parallelism in
other formal respects. Again, in lines 14 to 17, the conclusion of the
paragraph takes on added weight and finality with the patterning of
conflicts and coincidences. Lines 14 and 15 have conflict ("dómūm,"
"āssuétā"), but the last two lines have coincidence ("dénĭquĕ,"
"ĕxŏnĕrárĕ"). Not only does the balancing of pairs of lines assert symmetry at the close of the passage after considerable variety earlier, but the
emergence from conflict into coincidence is itself coinciding with the
movement in syntax from paired subordinate clauses ("ubi . . . -que")
into paired main clauses, the latter in fact initiating the lament proper,
the words of Thyrsis/Milton. Thus Milton, like Virgil, is attentive to
both small and large units of structure. In following his procedure in the
fourth foot we see how, as in other ways, he supports the large units by
what he does with the small ones.

Prosody can alert us not only to large effects and the hidden, small
ones which assist them, but to striking and self-sufficient local effects in
which Milton exhibits a word-music and a power of mimesis that recall
Virgil, yet remain distinct and personal. For economy, I consider the

same two examples from the opening, though such later instances as line 61 and the whole ending are more striking. In lines 9 and 10, which share many stylistic features, including several metrical ones, the poet gives himself the option of a heightened effect in whatever does differ. Our attention may be drawn to such shifts as that from "viridi" to "flavas," from ˇˇˇ to ˉˉ and from one strong, euphonious color word to another; or to that from "surgebat" to "numerabant," from ˉˉˉ to ˇˇˇˇ, from the stalk of the grain rising to its garnering. That is, the two lines only appear to say the same thing; on closer inspection, to which small metrical variations amid much metrical and other repetition encourage us, the lines testify not to the sameness of seasons or years but to the inexorable passing of seasons and years and friendships (cf. 94–111). A more prominent prosodic effect comes at the climax of the paragraph, at "exonerare" in line 17. In noting the fourth-foot coincidence which this word yields and the fourth-foot patterning to which its line contributes, we have not explained all that it does and expresses. For a number of further reasons it positively arrests attention. Since it is the first word of five syllables in the poem and contains almost two whole dactyls (ˇˇˇˇ), it contributes an especially strong fourth-foot coincidence (ˊˇˇˊˇ). All these aural considerations emphasize the word's meaning, the beginning of Thyrsis' effort to "unburden" himself of his grief; but by placing *this* word at *this* point of *this* line in the paragraph, Milton yokes diction and prosody to imitate the very movement of the mourner's mind, the strenuous, almost levering effort of giving tongue to loss and maybe of easing grief by speaking it. Perhaps too much may seem by this interpretation to hinge on a single word. Yet my point is that the word chosen has exactly the aural qualities and metrical placing to make a good hinge; for in this word—and in the opening, only here—is insinuated the prospect that Thyrsis may not merely ease but dispel his grief, may finally rid himself altogether of the "burden."

I am certain, therefore, that Milton's diction and prosody are the obedient servants of his thought in the *Epitaphium*, and that he makes them assist each other to that end. They enliven and energize yet also objectify the very personal statement which the poem is making.

Milton's use of pastoral in this poem and its relationship to *Lycidas* are less easy to assess with equity. Responses to Milton's pastoral tend to polarize into dismissiveness and defensiveness. Thus, many readers echo Samuel Johnson: "where there is leisure for fiction there is little grief" (yet one might say the same, with as little truth, of the urge to make a *poem* from suffering). Others readers, more appreciative of the genre, but perhaps led on by the humility of pastoral's ready concession that it is a small, vulnerable, unreal or lost place, lapse into unnecessary deprecation. Comparing it to *Lycidas*, which is rightly admired, one can fault the slightly later *Epitaphium* both for resembling it and for not resembling it. I nonetheless pursue both questions together for the interest of seeing what Milton found pastoral to be capable of: to him, at any rate, there must have been great scope in the genre since he used it twice, in this case to lament the loss of his dearest and oldest friend.

Milton is certainly in command of the pastoral mode—witness his use of the refrain, "Ite domum impasti, domino jam non vacat, agni" ("Go home unfed, you lambs, your master has no time for you"). It is facile to ask sardonic, disaffected questions of this line: why does the poet keep shooing them away; why do they not go away? The refrain is often simply part of the pattern. It marks off the verse paragraphs and, by its repetition, reminds us that the pastoral lament is notionally the "song" of a sheperd. Yet at times these minor but unobstructive virtues are imperiously transmuted by Milton. Thus, at line 65, because the preceding lines describe the sheep grieving at their master's grief, the refrain comes in freshly as the master's reply. It is an unfeeling reply, certainly, but we think of his preoccupying grief as the cause:

> Nec myrteta juvant; ovium quoque taedet, at illae
> Moerent, inque suum convertunt ora magistrum.
> Ite domum impasti, domino jam non vacat, agni.

[Nor are the myrtle groves any pleasure to me; I am tired of my sheep, too, and they grieve, turning their faces toward their master: only to be told, "Go home unfed."]

More commanding yet, Milton dismisses not the sheep but the refrain itself (203), by following its syntactic shape and verbally echoing its opening: "Ite procul lacrimae, purum colit aethera Damon" ("Begone far away, all tears, for Damon now lives in the pure air of heaven"). The dismissal of the grieving refrain is a most striking way to dismiss grief itself. In other words, in the use of pastoral just as in the use of Latin and the hexameter, Milton has absorbed the manner and motifs of the genre, but shows the power to spring from that footing up to moments of a more individual intensity.

The same alternation between zestful absorption of the generic and imperious new use of it meets us in the pastoral detail. Take, for instance, the description of high summer, the time of universal siesta:

Aut aestate, dies medio dum vertitur axe,
Cum Pan aesculea somnum capit abditus umbra,
Et repetunt sub aquis sibi nota sedilia nymphae,
Pastoresque latent, stertit sub sepe colonus.   (51–54)

[Or in the summer, while the day is at its summit and Pan sleeps hidden in the oak-tree shade, and the nymphs seek once more their accustomed haunts under the waters, the shepherds lie hidden from the heat and the farm-worker snores under the hedge.]

There is a loving artifice here, not only in the melodious d- and m-patterns of the first line, but in the invention, the rapid populating of the summer landscape with the appropriate mixture of pastoral beings— men, gods, and intermediate creatures. It is not so much a joy in words as a joy in what words can do; for instance, to depict the unlovely, antimasque grossness of the snoring farmworker. Yet the sentence is not simply one of joyful contemplation of the pastoral at its most idyllically lazy, for these clauses are subordinate to the renewed sense of having lost the friend in whose companionship these joys had once met and been heightened. The sentence goes on: "Quis mihi blanditiasque tuas, quis tum mihi risus, / Cecropiosque sales referet?" ("Who then will bring back for me your charm, your laughter, your elegant salty wit?").

But, what is more, nothing in the pastoral of the *Epitaphium* becomes it like the leaving of it. Whereas in *Lycidas* the poet returns in his quiet close to the pastoral world itself ("Tomorrow to fresh woods, and pastures new"), the *Epitaphium* closes on a different pastoral motif, to very different effect. This motif is pastoral's power to include the reaction against itself, to show the return from the pastoral scene to what exists outside it. I am thinking of pastorals which move to the regretful recognition that "Et in Arcadia ego" ("I, Death, am present even in Arcadia"), or which show a return from pastoral peace to a place of responsibility, or which even describe the smashing to pieces of all that fragile beauty by brigands, or conquerors, or impersonal historical forces. The common ground in this respect between Milton's two pastorals is the presence of death within the idyllic beauty. The difference between them is that where *Lycidas* turns aside for a time into political allegory, the religious and political evils which St. Peter denounces, our poem does not. Instead of turning aside en route, it turns upward at its close, rising to a sustained, ecstatic vision of the New Jerusalem to gain an effect which carries more weight than its counterpart in *Lycidas* (165–85). Milton does not, now, return to earth. He looks back down to it for a moment (208–11), but stays finally with the vision, that vision which his friend is enjoying and in which his own sight is submerged. So much, then, for comparison with *Lycidas*.

For the wider question of the use of pastoral, we seem to have the following major movement of thought. At first, Milton advances into a lovingly detailed picture of the pastoral world and a deepening realization of his loss of his friend—that is, into an imaginative possession of pastoral and a simultaneous alienation from it. Then, these simultaneous movements being contradictory, he advances beyond both pastoral and loss. And that concluding movement is not away, toward real life, but forward to contemplation of everlasting life.

The entry of transcendence into the pastoral I find to be the most powerful, the most authentically Miltonic feature of the poem, the clearest proof that it possesses its own excellence, not although, but because it is in Latin. The poem's concluding movement convinces me that its Latin, far from being an impediment or an excrescence, is fundamental to its thought and style.

To begin, I summarize the concluding movement, though I move into it from a slightly earlier point so as to convey how gradual is the intensifying of thought and mood. At line 113, Thyrsis chides himself for going to Italy; absent from his friend's death bed, he failed to do the last office of friendship and close Damon's eyes at death. And yet he will never forget Italy, and especially Tuscany, famous for pastoral beauty and talented poets, and beloved as the home of Damon's ancestors (125). While Thyrsis was there (140), he imagined himself talking about it all with Damon, hearing about Damon's work as a doctor and telling of his own plans for new poems conceived in Italy. One such poetic project was great and grand, indeed so much so that his shepherd's pipes broke with the force of it. He intended an epic of Britain, covering everything from Brut to Arthur, to be sung in a British way for a British—not a European—audience; that is, it was to be written in English. All these ideas he was keeping for Damon (180), along with two fine cups given him by the Italian humanist Manso. A description of the designs engraved on the cups, follows; then, the anticipated refrain being for once absent, we pass into a vision of heaven where Thyrsis imagines Damon in bliss among the company of heaven, sharing in the bacchanalia of Sion.

It is clear that the sequence contains very disparate materials, sudden, if not startling, transitions between them, and an ambitious finale. Doubts may be felt on all three points. Does not the poem lurch, for instance, between the pastoral and the epic prospectus or between Manso's cups and the heavenly vision? Indeed, is it not tasteless egotism thus to foist on the lament this talk of the epic? Again, are not some of the transitions strained by abruptness or arbitrariness? Is the finale not both out of key with the preceding pastoral and in itself bombastic? The sequence certainly raises such questions. Yet I agree with David Masson and A. S. P. Woodhouse that the poem overcomes such doubts (having first, perhaps deliberately, occasioned them), and I think it possible to add new grounds for supporting their approbation.[7]

The swings of subject matter can be defended quite meekly on the ground that they are not, after all, exceptional in a pastoral. It is an old subordinate motif of the genre for the elegist, as successor to the dead poet-shepherd, to digress concerning his own poetic aspirations.[8] Extended descriptions of prized cups occur prominently in Theocritus' first idyll and Virgil's third eclogue. By Milton's time there was precedent enough for pastoral to extend itself in various ways into the Christian frame of judgment.

Yet why defend Milton meekly when his thought and his control of it are so bold? The poem itself justifies its details and their placing. Thus the epic prospectus is given as Milton's side of an imagined dialogue, in which both friends talk about what each has done during the absence of Thyrsis. It is therefore appropriate enough to its place in the lament, and it gains as well the poignant irony that Thyrsis will never actually exchange news with Damon. Furthermore, those who find the prospectus egotistical may have misunderstood the text. As Thyrsis imagines himself talking with Damon, he interrupts the imagined conversation with a curse—from his present, lamenting moment—upon the arts of medicine which have failed to save the physician himself. After the two lines of present interjection (153–54), most editions imagine that Thyrsis continues, in the same present, to elaborate on his mighty theme and the hoped-for epic (155–78). His continuing in the present might indeed be thought intrusive, even hubristic. But the passage makes better sense if the imagined conversation with Damon resumes after the two-line interjection. So Thyrsis pours out the whole excited, somewhat conceited ("turgidulus") idea to his friend in the far country at a time when that friend is really dead, mute and deaf to the great self-discovery. This way, appropriateness is preserved and heightened by ironies. After the prospectus has ended, and only then, Thyrsis returns to the present moment of loss: 'Haec tibi servabam lenta sub cortice lauri," where "Haec" means "all these fond plans which I was keeping to share with Damon upon my return." The absence of speech marks in editions, or their mistaken insertion at lines 147 to 52, but not at 155 to 78, has obscured this commonsense expectation.

This interpretation also smooths the transition from the summary of the epic to the description of Manso's cups. In line 181, "Haec et plura simul, tum quae mihi pocula," joins the imagined conversation, and the epic as part of it, with the gifts: all, equally, Thyrsis thought to share joyfully with Damon upon his return. And yet the readers who have castigated the lines about the epic as intrusive or bombastic are not exactly mistaken, for the lines do alter the tone of the poem, its mood of expectation as it nears its end. But Milton is in full control of this alteration. Though the epic details belong within the prevailing pastoral as far as character and situation are concerned, they nonetheless elevate the diction and our expectation—surreptitiously, as it were, for until later we cannot see why the tone should become more exalted. Though the epic details relate backward to the pastoral situation in terms of narrative logic, they relate forward to the closing vision in terms of imaginative logic. We are being predisposed by this "false start" to absorb the coming, more decisive ascent above pastoral. This the description of the cups engineers.

The description of the cups, though no less a set piece than the description of the epic, has incurred less criticism. Yet it is in fact an even bolder way of moving the poem away from a pastoral to a celestial vision. The cups described at length by Theocritus and Virgil are a model from which Milton strikingly departs. He foregoes the aptness of embedding within his pastoral a pastoral object which depicts scenes of pastoral. Instead, he places on the cups many objects exotic to pastoral, and he describes them in a carefully controlled series, so that they accumulate into a Platonic ascent, or ladder of love. He moves the focus from the Red Sea and its spicy spring (185), which are already outside the Mediterranean ambience of pastoral, to the riches of fabled Arabia, and particularly to its divine bird, the phoenix (187–89). According to the climactic detail of its description, the phoenix looks back upon the dawn rising out of a glassy sea ("respicit," 189); so, the ascent has begun in earnest. Now comes mention of Olympus, home of the chief classical gods. Then, among the clouds above the top of that vast mountain appears Cupid, shooting his arrows of desire never downward, but "semper in erectum" (195): that is, either "upward" or "at the being of erected, high-aspiring mind"; most likely, Milton intends both meanings. Iconologically, then, these are the arrows of sacred, not profane love. The objects selected are moving us away from pastoral, through suggestions of the salvation-history of Israel and of the Resurrection, to classical myths which the Renaissance interpreted as emblems of divine love in man. The last word of the paragraph is "deorum" ("the gods"). It might have been followed by the refrain, but because Milton has now abandoned pastoral, he leaps still further forward. He takes what is now the quite easy leap into heaven itself. Thinking of Damon as just such a heroic, heaven-aspiring soul as Cupid's arrows would inflame, he imagines him indeed transported: "Tu quoque in his, nec me fallit spes lubrica, Damon, / Tu quoque in his certe es" (198–99) ("You too are now among these heaven-dwellers, Damon—it is no specious hope deceiving me—yes, you too are assuredly now among them"). And he says it twice over for emphasis. Then the rest of the last paragraph can go beyond those earthly prefigurings of heaven to direct vision of Sion. This vision uses images drawn direct from the natural source, the Revelation of St. John: the crowns, the special honors of those who died virgin, the wedding feast of the Lamb.[9] Now that Thyrsis sees his friend among the blaze of celestial beauty, he forgets his grief and no longer feels separated from him (207–11). The whole turning of the thought through the last two paragraphs is certainly a steep climb. Yet, partly because the previous two paragraphs have prepared the way, the final ascent is not strained, arbitrary, or abrupt.[10]

Doubters should consider how fully Milton prepares for the closing affirmation, in how many ways the vision, though different, arises from the pastoral preceding. Two more lines of argument must suffice, one concerned with the subject matter, the other with a point of style.

Immortality is a theme of the whole poem.[11] It is set beside death long before it becomes the triumphal theme of the ending. In lines 27 to 36, the first wave of grief ends on the thought that at least the dead shepherd will not be forgotten: the poet and the poem will perpetuate his memory. Humanly enough, Thyrsis is worse afflicted by his loss of Damon than by Damon's loss of life (37–123), and yet the thought of immortality enters even here. It comes in Thyrsis' thought of saying to Damon at the moment of dying, "vale, nostri memor ibis ad astra" (123) ("Goodbye, you will go now to the stars remembering me"). Such a hope is of course only hypothetical, in fact counterfactual, because Thyrsis was not at the bedside to say or hope anything. Consequently, the third and final turn toward immortality supervenes as the genuine completion of the previous, twice-thwarted aspiration. Thyrsis has not so much doubted of Damon's immortal life as he has questioned his own participation in his friend's further life (see, for instance, the powerful lines, 94–111, on fate's enmity to human friendship). This doubt, too, the poem's final movement answers.

I find a comparable change within consistency in a prominent feature of the style, Milton's use of names. When I traced their incidence and provenance through the poem, I seemed to find them occurring for the most part in little clusters, changing in evocation and impact. At first, the names of Theocritus' Sicily are coupled with those of Milton's Europe, as the collocation "Sicelicum Thamesina" (3) heralds. Soon after come names suggesting Virgil's Italy and his working-over of Theocritean materials: it is the Roman country gods, Pales and Faunus, who first confirm Thyrsis' vow to Damon (32). Since he next extends the reference to "Palladias artes," the common culture of Rome and Greece, I presume that Milton is making available to the field of his poem's suggestion *all* the sanctioned resources of nomenclature for the mixed landscape of pastoral. Lines 68 to 90 bring a flurry of pastoral names, mostly from Theocritus or Virgil, but latterly British as well; another flurry at lines 126 to 39 introduces places and people connected with the Italian journey. Now a change. After a passage with few names except two from Milton's own rural haunt near Horton (149), we are suddenly inundated with the British names of the epic prospectus (162–78). Some lines consist almost entirely of names: "Brennumque Arviragumque duces, priscumque Belinum" (164). The effect is of a grandiose march-past, of an exaltation set going in the poet by contemplating the story of Britain, and of an answering Spenser-like celebration of the names of British rivers. The reliance on names is not the least epic feature of the lines about epic. The choice of names suggests that pastoral is beginning to be set aside, and the exaltation prepares us emotionally for the greater exaltation to come.

The reliance upon names to create resonance and demarcate the conceptual range of the argument continues in the sequel; yet what it continues most is the *change* of resonance and reference. It would have been crude and probably ineffective to propel a second and greater wave of exaltation with a more direct bombardment of names. Playing a subordinate role, the names "Arabia" and "Aurora" (186 and 189), for example, support the suggestion of resurrection, but that is made more strongly by adjectives or adjectival phrases—by huge and splendid single adjectives like "odoriferum" and "diversicoloribus" or by the swelling majesty of the attributes of the phoenix:

> Has inter Phoenix divina avis, unica terris
> Caeruleum fulgens diversicoloribus alis
> Auroram vitreis surgentem respicit undis.

[Among these is the phoenix, the divine bird, the only one on earth, making a flash as bright as the blue of the sky with its diverse-colored wings; it is seen looking back on the dawn rising from the glass-clear waves.]

Similarly with the pictures of Olympus, the arrow-shooting Cupid (190–97), and the portrait of the holy city: the richness of effect and the exulting participation come from the things in themselves more than from their names; or perhaps they come from the sense of the god that, one and all, they point to.

Nonetheless, in two places the names do contribute strongly to the masterfulness of the finale. The name "Damon" itself is suddenly highlighted. Having been assumed (in all senses of that word) during most of the poem, it is now set aside (209–11). It is the name of the pastoral guise and that only, whereas "Diodotus" ("the one given by God" or "the one given to God") is both his name now, in heaven, and his real name all along, on earth (Charles Diodati). For a short while, then, it is as if the step out of the pastoral into the actual were indentical with the step into the celestial vision. If so, the poem gains double benefit from a single invention.

The other effect sought by using names comes in the last line of all; hence it is bolder:

> Ipse caput nitidum cinctus rutilante corona,
> Letaque frondentis gestans umbracula palmae
> Aeternum perages immortales hymenaeos:
> Cantus ubi, choreisque furit lyra mista beatis,
> Festa Sionaeo bacchantur et Orgia Thyrso.　　　　　(215–19)

[You yourself, my friend, have your shining head circled with a red-glowing garland, you carry the gladdening shade of a leaf-sprouting palm branch, and so you will be joining forever in performing the rites of the everlasting marriage ceremonies—there where the singing and the sound of the lyre rage among the dancing saints, and the festal orgies rave like Bacchic worshippers, but with the thyrsus of Sion.]

The climax of climaxes is here handed over to the startling conjunction of "Sionaeo" with "Thyrso." These are the adjective from "Sion," the New Jerusalem of the Christian Apocalypse, and the name of the wands carried by devotees of Bacchus (Dionysus). To make more plain the fusion of Bacchic with Christian elements, Milton takes the verb "bacchantur" and the subject "Orgia" from the terminology of the cult of Dionysus. Now the boldness here is not in any risk that we may facilely reduce the ecstasies of Sion to the joys of a booze-up, for as Milton would know from Euripides' *Bacchae*, Dionysus was a great and mighty power, a god whose power resides not only in wine but in many forms of life. What *is* risky is giving the poem's last word to ideas which come to

Milton from pagan antiquity with the very strong and vital connotation of an ecstasy of the senses: is it too forced, too assertive, this joining of the sexless nuptials of the Lamb with the very earthy, and not unsexual, ecstasy of Dionysus-worship? My guess is that Milton chose this concluding image precisely for its assertiveness. His whole ending has departed from his practice in *Lycidas* (and elsewhere) of closing quietly: he does it now noisily, downright corybantically. So, in the last particulars, likewise, he is ambitious. Does he not seek to marry things that are more usually contrasted and distinguished? The pagan with the Christian, the antique with the modern, the natural life of the country with the life of the redeemed city? A classical deity with the Son of God, the mystical initiations of Dionysus-worship with his friend's initiation into the dancing of Sion? The numinous which resides in wine because it belongs to Bacchus with the Christ whose blood is the wine of the Eucharist? If the last line is startling, well, it was meant to startle so that we should be startled into perceiving that, for this poem, it is the appropriate climax.[12]

All in all, therefore, Milton's concluding turn away from pastoral seems not only logical but controlled and persuasive. It is, moreover, and authoritative, characteristic way to close his poem. Indeed, looking back over the poem and this essay, I find that the ending and the whole use of Latin belong together; for, just as he wrote in Latin verse or more personal, intimate matters than he trusted to English, so Milton has expressed a more triumphant and explicit conviction at the close of this, his most ambitious Latin poem. Its unity of effect is epitomized for me by the majesty—of diction and thought, of rhythm and allusion—of its final line: "Festa Sionaeo bacchantur et Orgia Thyrso." Of course, the same thought could have come to him in English. But its Latin—for instance the sonority of the second word, or the symmetry of the paired nouns and adjectives, or the exultant dancing of the rhythm into, then out of, then again into, dactyls, or the resonant finality of its coinciding of accent with ictus after the previous six lines have had those rhythms in conflict—is the perfect medium of the thought, its living flesh.

These beauties, then, and many others in the poem, would not have been born except in, and by means of, Latin. They are this poem's best things. They are what most adequately fits the poem to its heartfelt occasion.

University of Otago

NOTES

1. The essay owes something to a group in which members of the English and Classics departments of Otago University meet to read medieval and later Latin; it owes a particular debt on points of detail to John Barsby, Doug Little, and Agathe Thornton.

2. All citations refer to *The Poetical Works of John Milton*, ed. Helen Darbishire (Oxford, 1955), II, pp. 278–83. The translations are my own.

3. *Milton* (London, 1930), p. 101.

4. *Mimesis: The Representation of Reality in Western Literature*, trans. Willard R. Trask (Princeton, N. J., 1953).

5. Roger Ascham, *The Schoolmaster*, in *Elizabethan Critical Essays*, ed. Gregory Smith (London, 1904), I, p. 8.

6. *Accentual Symmetry in Vergil* (Oxford, 1950.)

7. Masson, *The Poetical Works of John Milton* (London, 1874), II, p. 376; Woodhouse, "Milton's Pastoral Monodies," in *Studies in Honour of Gibert Norwood*, ed. Mary E. White (Toronto, 1952), pp. 261–78. I have also used points from Ralph W. Condee, "The Structure of Milton's 'Epitaphium Damonis,' " in *SP*, LXII (1965), 577–94. Adverse views of the poem include those of Tillyard, *Milton*, and Douglas Bush, in *A Variorum Commentary on the Poems of John Milton*, I, *The Latin and Greek Poems*, ed. Douglas Bush (London, 1970), pp. 284, 288–89.

8. This argument is mentioned, but set aside, by Bush, *A Variorum Commentary*, I, pp. 288–89.

9. Details ibid., p. 323.

10. Cf. Woodhouse, "Milton's Pastoral Monodies," pp. 270–72.

11. Ibid.

12. I have refrained from glossing the places in the *Epitaphium* where Milton anticipates *Paradise Lost* because I wish neither to overpraise the poem nor to borrow plumes for it. Yet my discussion suggests that there are such anticipations, and hence that the poem is both individual and characteristic. One such instance is the reliance at chosen moments on the sonority of names (cf. *PL*, I, 288–310). Another instance is the sensuality of the ecstasy imputed to the blessed in Sion, which seems consonant with Mitln's insistence in *Paradise Lost* that sex is prelapsarian or that angels enjoy food and coitus (IV, 741–75; V, 404–13; VIII, 618–29). The common factor is the wish to make heaven different from earth, certainly, but by extension from it rather than in contrast to it. Now this is done, perhaps, at the risk of overmaterializing beatitude. Yet what else does Dante do—what else can a poet do? In all these poems, the imagining of immortality prompts the finest, not the weakest, of the poet's flights.

MILTON AND THE DIVINE ART OF WEAPONRY: "THAT TWO-HANDED ENGINE" AND BUNYAN'S "NAMELESS TERRIBLE INSTRUMENT" AT MOUTHGATE

James F. Forrest

But that two-handed engine at the door
Stands ready to smite once, and smite no more.
—*Lycidas* (130–31)

INGENIOUS AS are the engines mounted to the assault on these lines of *Lycidas*, they seem fated more to perish through panache than prevail by persuasion—"over-politic fetches" Milton might well have called most of them. So are hapless scholars hoist with their own petards, as they struggle to identify and define something peculiarly recalcitrant to precise delineation. But why, it may be asked, should explicators be so eager to particularize what Milton, a poet who uses words exactly, must have intended to remain ambiguous? Even odder is that they should be so keen to denominate the artistically anonymous, to flesh it into substance and shape, when the preceding passage has poetically impugned horrendous carnality in images of the cynical bishops' rapacious greed and spiritual sloth. From any sympathetic reading, there ought surely to emerge from this movement of *Lycidas* a crucial antithesis, pointed by the adversative "But" at the start of line 130: a contrast between the grossness of a prelatical practice that lacks a sense of calling and the spirituality of the saints, which makes the climax nothing if not a vigorous demonstration of how the weak things of the world can ruin the mighty, even when the lordly "band themselves with the prevalent things of this world to overrun the weak things which Christ hath made chois to work by."[1] Recognition of this opposition alone may perhaps suggest that the "two-handed engine" is open to a less modishly outlandish interpretation, one which is immediately responsive to the poem itself and which can produce a richer reading than that usually offered; one, moreover, that can be illuminated by an inter-

131

esting allegorical detail in Bunyan, apparently never yet cited with reference to the crux.

In *The Holy War* (1682), his most ambitious and most neglected allegory, Bunyan takes up the ancient image of the five senses as portals of the soul, as it comes to him through such a writer as Richard Bernard, and conceives of Mansoul as a walled town with five gates, Eargate, Eyegate, Mouthgate, Nosegate, and Feelgate, "in at which to come, out at which to go," but which can "never be opened nor forced, but by the will and leave of those within."² The Mansoulians are seduced into admitting Diabolus and his rabble, misery ensues, the town petitions Shaddai for relief, and the mighty Prince Emanuel comes in glory to overthrow the tyrant and repair the damage. In an atmosphere of peace and love and joy, the town is then new-modelled and fortifications are set up to maintain its security:

There was also an instrument invented by *Emanuel*, that was to throw stones from the Castle of *Mansoul*, out at *Mouth-gate;* an instrument that could not be resisted, nor that would miss of execution; wherefore for the wonderful exploits that it did when used, it went without a name, and it was committed to the care of, and to be managed by the brave Captain, the Captain *Credence*, in case of war.³

From as early as Mason's edition (1782), editors have taken Mouthgate's "nameless terrible instrument" (to employ Bunyan's own marginal description) as "the prayer of faith." They adduce in support Matthew xxi, 22, and Mark xi, 23, on the miraculous power of prayer to move mountains, and Hebrews, chapter xi, that great text beloved of the Puritans, on the irrepressible impetus of faith.⁴ But also wholly apposite is Christ's significant comment on omnipotent prayer in Matthew xviii, 19–20, which is to be read as validation of the authority conferred on the Church to "bind and loose" (Matthew xviii, 18), and which might therefore be thought to invest Bunyan's "instrument" with the double potential of condemnation and commendation. The assumption is strengthened by Bunyan's subsequent designation of Mouthgate, not merely as an emplacement, but also as a "*Sally-port*" with two main uses: to "send their Petitions to *Emanuel*, their Prince," and to "play their slings at the enemies"; the latter imprecatory function is held so singularly efficacious as to constitute a major reason for Diabolus's seeking "to land up *Mouth-gate* with durt."⁵ And the relevance of Matthew xviii, 18–20, is further suggested by the congruity of Bunyan's assertion in *The Barren Fig-Tree* (1673) that fruitless professors may be laid as low by the Church's censure as by the axe.⁶

As a clue to the appreciation of Milton's lines, this extract consequently invites close attention. First, it ought to be observed that the
allegory's generality is itself part of the import, for what beggars description of Mouthgate's "instrument" is precisely its infinite capacity for
"wonderful exploits," which issue from a resource "wonderful beyond
description," so that "no name can sufficiently describe the use and
power of prayer."[7] This awesome force, moreover, is irresistible and
infallible, its successful application preveniently ensured, simply because it is "invented by *Emanuel*." Since it cannot be thwarted, the sole
bulwark against it (as Diabolus becomes dreadfully aware) lies in fore-
stalling its deployment by blocking up Mouthgate with silt; doubtless it
is to prevent such an occurrence that its care is entrusted to "Captain
Credence," who is also to manage it "in case of war." The device is thus
a means divinely sent, but its operation is given into other hands, controlled by confidence in its use. Such an arrangement exhibits Bunyan's
characteristic preservation of the human bailiwick, and it perhaps explains his sophisticated election here of the substantive "instrument"
rather than "engine," which he uses elsewhere: "instrument" (*instruere*,
"to equip") implies merely a contribution toward the goal's attainment
and therefore serves to point the synergistic nature of the interplay
between God and man. Altogether, the spiritual artillery so depicted fits
well with what Milton recommends, in *The Reason of Church-Government* (1641), as "the approved way which the Gospell prescribes" to
bring apostates to heel; and with what (quoting Paul) he extols as "*the
spirituall weapons of holy censure*, and ministeriall *warfare, not carnall,
but mighty through God to the pulling down of strong holds, casting
down imaginations, and every high thing that exalteth it selfe against the
knowledge of God, and bringeth into captivity every thought to the
obedience of Christ*."[8]

To concede that Bunyan here offers a suggestive parallel to Milton
need thus involve no blunting of critical acumen. Demonstrably, the
two lines in *Lycidas* constitute great poetry of an urgent intensity and a
density that far exceed the relaxed virtue of Bunyan's limpid prose.
They have the ambiguity of compressed metaphor, without the progres-
sive disclosure of sustained allegory; nor do they bear, as do Bunyan's
passages, marginal authorial gloss to clarify the import or underline an
emphasis. But as often in Bunyan the merest item is quite significantly
revealing, so this brief allegorical excerpt can inspire a sense of the illim-
itable Christian resource that similarly informs the compacted vision of
Milton's lines.

At the very least it may indicate a common linguistic concern.

While Bunyan's difficulty alone is voiced, Milton's is no less real. Milton's engine image has the concreteness that poetry demands, but its darkness continues visible; and no amount of scholarly dredging or drudging can render totally palpable what must remain essentially obscure. Yet if we conceive of the lines as having something to do with the omnipotent force of believers' prayer, we can readily perceive why the poetic image is formally uncircumscribed and ambiguous: constrained to represent an arcane and supernal power, the poet appropriately responds with the plain conciseness of imprecision. This constraint, rather than any crude desire to enhance the mystery, explains one element in Milton's judgment. But his choice of metaphor is loaded as well by other considerations, including the well-established association of the ordinance of prayer with weaponry.

Such an analogy may derive from Ecclesiasticus xxxv, 17: "The prayer of him that humbleth him self, goeth thorowe the cloudes, and ceaseth not til it come nere, and will not departe til the most High have respect thereunto." The figure appears in English among the proverbs quoted by Tilley—"Prayers like petards break open heaven gate"—and in Shakespeare: "And my ending is despair, / Unless I be reliev'd by prayer, / Which pierces so, that it assaults / Mercy itself, and frees all faults."[9] After Erasmus in his *Enchiridion* had distinguished prayer as a very special weapon of the Christian soldier, seventeenth-century divines like Jeremy Taylor discovered afresh the "holy violence" implicit in prayer, and the image accorded with the cultural temper of the period to become common stock.[10] Thus, Herbert conceives of prayer not only as "the Churches banquet," but also as an "Engine against th' Almightie, sinners towre, / Reversed thunder, Christ-side-piercing spear," while Donne likewise dallies with the notion, invoking patristic and other sources:

Wee threaten God in Prayer; as *Gregory Nazianzen* adventures to expresse it . . . Prayer hath the nature of Violence; In the publique Prayers of the Congregation, we besiege God, saies *Tertullian*. . . . The words of man, in the mouth of a faithfull man, of *Abraham*, are a Canon against God himselfe, and batter down all his severe and heavy purposes for Judgments . . . yea, God charges, and discharges the Canon himself upon himselfe.[11]

According to the popular Benjamin Keach, "*Luther* ascribed to Prayer a kind of Omnipotency. . . . There is none of the battering Rams, or Artillery of Hell can stand against it. 'Tis like an Engine (as one observes) that makes the Persecutors tremble; and woe to them that are the Buts and Marks that it is levell'd at, when it is fired with the Fire of the Spirit, and discharged in the Strength of Faith."[12] Absolute trust in the efficacy of this divinely fashioned ordnance of prayer sanctions Bunyan's allegory as it also justifies Bishop Henry Hammond's parallel description of "binding and loosing" as "only an engine of *Christ's* invention to make a battery and an impression on the obdurate sinner."[13] So affecting is the figure, so replete with excited recognition of prayer as a paradoxically gracious and coercive power beyond man's power to tell, that Thomas Harrison, doughty major-general in the New Model Army, feels moved to write thus to Cromwell on the eve of battle in 1650:

My lord bee carefull for nothing, but praie with thanksgiving (to witt in faith), Phill. 4. 6, 7. I doubt not your successe, but I thinke Faith and Praier must bee the cheife engines, as heretofore the ancient Worthies through Faith subdued Kingdomes, out of weakness were made strong, waxed valiaunt in fight, and turned to flight the armies of the Aliens. Oh that a spirit of Faith and Supplication maie bee poured forth on you and your Armie! There is more to bee had in this poore simple waie then even most Saints expect.[14]

Echoing Paul's letter to the Hebrews, these remarks from one who was himself heroically engaged in "the Lord's battells" not only help to substantiate our reading of Milton, but also reinforce it by making us feel on our pulses the devastatingly corporeal potency of faithful prayer in the Christian arsenal.

Although Harrison's separation of faith and prayer may seem a sufficient answer to the enigmatical "two-handed" power of Milton's single "engine," the image's rich ambiguity naturally admits other cognate solutions. Apart from alluding to the hands clasped in the usual posture of prayer, the image may appear as an almost literal representation of the two-handedness of prayer such as that offered by the blessed John Fisher, who in a Latin treatise (c. 1530) summons up Homer's golden chain, an ancient symbol of concord and necessity, to portray prayer's consummation, the perfect freedom of the soul enslaved by God:

Prayer is like to a certeine golden rope or chaine lett downe from heaven, by which we endeavour to draw God to vs whereas in deed we are more truly drawne by Him. For so it is as if one standing in a higher place and wold draw another from below he letteth downe some cord or line vnto him, on which he laying hould, and with all his forces drawing is att last elevated to the topp. This rope or golden chaine holy S. Dionisius calleth prayer. . . . what other thing doth it, but elevates the mind above all things created, soe that att last it is made one spirit with God, fast bound vnto him with this golden line or chaine of prayer.[15]

More consonant with the sense of the passage in Matthew, 18, the engine's two-handedness may serve to epitomize the marriage of Christ and the Church, joined hand-in-hand in the formidable, cooperative enterprise which constitutes the Church's disciplinary procedure. While initiative in that undertaking rests with the gathered, no matter how few, these are assured that they never act alone, but that their faithful and prayerful handling of problems ensures for their corrective decisions simultaneous ratification in heaven: the endorsement is possible only because the saints are themselves the body within which Christ dwells. Indeed, so complete is this union that it might seem to tell against the use of "two-handed"; but to feel the force of the attribution is merely to apprehend the imaginative deliberateness of Milton's intent, which rather argues for his determination of a double agency to express the prior need of human choice. Milton's solicitude in reserving room for the individual to act is here patently no less eloquent than Bunyan's. Like Bunyan's "instrument," Milton's "engine" is a something given, an antidote once dispensed and forever available (hence, "stands ready"), which depends for its salutary effect only upon an original exercise of faith in taking it. It is likewise "two-handed" in that it is a restorative doubly virtuous: it has power to "bind" and "loose," absolve and condemn, admonish and reprove, all with the aim of reformation, but more immediately to the end of inducing shame and terror, which, though "invisible," Milton takes to be among the most puissant "Serjeants or maces" to the arrest, castigation, and recovery of the recreant soul.[16] Its cure being prompt and total, it entails no regimen, exacts no repetition: that is why it need "smite" but once.[17] Most wonderful of all, it is not unfamiliar (as Milton's use of the demonstrative "that" confirms); it involves no seeking abroad, but is conveniently to hand "at the door," by which phrase on Hammond's authority (though not on his alone), we may understand "[within] the Church."[18]

But even this cannot contain the poetic mind's astonishing fecundity. Within the same metaphoric context, further association adds strength to the lines. Mysteriously linked as the "two-handed engine" is to the superior force of fervent prayer, it may indeed quite naturally relate also to the human tongue, by which faith is articulated and prayer ejaculated. (Popular literary precedent for the usage of "engine" as "tongue" is provided by Shakespeare: "O, that delightful engine of her thoughts / That blabb'd them with such pleasing eloquence.")[19] So denoted, the "engine" is rendered "two-handed" in a double sense. As Solomon insists, the tongue holds the power of death and life, "and that," according to Richard Allestree, "not only directly in regard of the good or ill we may do to others, but reflexively also, in respect of what may rebound to our selves." The fire-hallowed organ is also gloriously versatile, as were the Pentecostal tongues, which manifested themselves as cloven "to be the more diffusive of good," whereas "those that are *fired from Hell* are forked James 3.6 to be the more impressive of mischief."[20] Moreover, that the tongue is anatomically singular, but "a little member" (James iii, 5), merely points the prodigious strength it wields when it is spiritually grown. This strength fascinates Thomas Adams, who contrasts the magnanimity of the man whose tongue is tamed by the altar coal with the small-minded niggardliness of that other: "They can fill him with Scripture sentences, but they send him away with a hungry stomach; whereas the good man's hand is as ready to give as his tongue to speak. . . . Words run like Asahel; but good works, like the cripple, come lagging after."[21] If this phenomenological concept is relevant to the passage under discussion, the phrase "at the door" becomes in this instance very precisely located by analogy with Bunyan's "Mouthgate," or, indeed, with what Milton himself elsewhere refers to as the "ports and passages" of the senses.[22] Not only so, but that relationship is sustained and enriched, when one recalls that Renaissance mythographers and poets commonly equated doorkeepers/gatekeepers (or porters) with genii, an association provoked by an interesting etymology that also links "engine" and "genius" and which lends even more support to the identification of Milton's image with what Spenser calls a "celestiall powre."[23] The fact is that within the figurative setting, as we have conceived it, there is no rift that cannot be mined for ore; and to be alive to this is to be aware of something far beyond the totally tangible, whose virtue is all-inclusiveness.

Ultimately, what is at stake in a determination of Milton's "two-handed engine" is the measure of our apprehension of eternal providence. To accept the image as an instrument of retributive justice alone, as it is so commonly received, is surely to limit ourselves to a partial view and to overlook the healing miracle revealed in the kissing of justice and mercy that seals the union of earth and heaven at this most difficult juncture of reconciliation within the lyric. Dread as the poetic voice may be in urging that God will not be mocked, the remedial action indicated is still in line with "the approved way which the Gospel prescribes," being no less than "a kind of saving by undoing."[24] The disciplinary rule of the Church, when conscientiously invoked, is invariably genial, a kindness, whereas (as Hammond points out) the dereliction of the negligent bishop, "his not-performing his office of *excision*," is rather a means of leaving the sinner "*remedilesse* unto it (his *binding* being indeed such a *remedy*, if it be made use of)."[25] Lines 130–31 of *Lycidas* thus play Miltonic to the very essence; they do not merely state, but poetically enact the priest's proper role in the saving of souls. As Jeremy Taylor sees it, that office is a categorical imperative of the Christian tongue:

"we must reprove" our sinning brother; "for the wounds of a friend are better than the kisses of an enemy," saith Solomon: we imitate the office of "the great Shepherd and Bishop of souls," if we go "to seek and save that which was lost"; and it is a fearful thing to see a friend go to hell undisturbed, when the arresting him in his horrid progress may possibly make him to return; this is a course that will change our vile itch of judging and censuring others, into an act of charity; it will alter slander into piety, detraction into counsel, revenge into friendly and most useful offices, that the viper's flesh may become Mithridate, and the devil be defeated in his malicious employment of our language.[26]

By the same course does Milton commend his cause to charity. Having for seventeen lines inveighed against the temporal preoccupation of the unconcerned and fruitless clergy, he abruptly turns the tables by prescribing to their immediate discomfiture the assured remedy for ultimately regaining such forfeited souls as theirs: that elemental pastoral duty, here demonstrated, is what the bishops in their willful blindness have themselves not seen fit to perform. Yet that duty is what most truly defines the spiritual awesomeness of the shepherd's traffic, the meaning of what it is to be a priest, to imitate "the great Shepherd and Bishop of souls." It is a superbly ironic stroke, this setting the ass to play the dragon among them, to show how the diligent meek, whom these unprofessional ministers ("blind mouths" landed up "with durt") slight and despise, confound them by the faithful exercise of the "herdman's art."

That art, of course, belongs also to the poet, who in resorting to the sacred weaponry of priestly discipline manifests not only a genuine concern for the welfare of his flock, but also the right conduct of one who, moved by such a benign hope as Paul had, and by a vital sense of vocation in mediating God's will to man, nicely employs "great plainness of speech" to remove the veil and unblind the mind.[27] For Captain Credence is indeed the glad genius of his tongue, and he tunes its use to judgement in a manner fit to outsing the bootless burdens that escape the choked mouths of Diabolus's captive advocates. With his divine instrument Apollo did not more artfully put down Marsyas.

University of Alberta

NOTES

1. *The Reason of Church-Government*, in *Complete Prose Works of John Milton*, ed. Don M. Wolfe et al. (New Haven, 1953–), I, p. 830. This edition is cited hereafter as YP.

2. Ed. Roger Sharrock and James F. Forrest (Oxford, 1980), pp. 8–9.

3. Ibid., p. 117.

4. Annotation of this edition is attributed by the B. M. Catalogue to Samuel Adams, who might have appended 2 Chronicles xxvi, 15, as source of the allegory's literal sense.

5. *The Holy War*, p. 195. A weighty detail, which by analogy supports J. A. Himes's argument from Strabo that Milton's "blind mouths" implies "shallowness" and "impeded utterance." See "Some Interpretations of Milton," *MLN*, XXXV (1920), 441.

6. *The Barren Fig-tree* (London, 1673), p. 91.

7. *The Holy War*, ed. George Burder (London, 1803), p. 177 n.

8. YP, I, p. 848.

9. Ecclesiasticus cited from the Geneva Bible; M. P. Tilley, *A Dictionary of the Proverbs in England in the Sixteenth and Seventeenth Centuries* (Ann Arbor, 1950), p. 554; Shakespeare, *The Tempest*, Epilogue. Ecclesiasticus xxxv, 20, has been claimed as a source also of Portia's simile of mercy as rain.

10. *The Enchiridion of Erasmus*, trans. and ed. Raymond Himelick (Bloomington, Ind., 1963), p. 47; *Holy Living and Holy Dying*, in *The Whole Works*, ed. R. Heber, rev. C. P. Eden, 10 vols. (London, 1850–59), III p. 181. See also Richard Sibbes, *Works*, ed. A. B. Grosart, 7 vols. (Edinburgh, 1863), II, p. 303, and VI, p. 194; Thomas Manton, *A Practical Exposition of the Lord's Prayer* (London, 1864), p. 9; Thomas Brookes, *The Privie Key of Heaven; or Twenty Arguments for Closet-Prayer* (London, 1665), pp. 67–68; Christopher Nesse, *A Christians Walk and Work on Earth Until he attain to Heaven* (London, 1678), p. 66; George Swinnock, *Works* (London, 1665), p. 502; David Clarkson, *Practical Works*, 3 vols. (Edinburgh, 1864), I p. 226, and II, p. 184; and especially William Gurnall, *The Christian in Compleat Armour: or, a treatise of the Saint's War Against the devil* (1655–62), intro. J. C. Ryle, 2 vols. (London, 1864–65), II, pp. 297 f., 304, 392, 409, 420,f., 499.

11. Herbert, "Prayer (1)," in *Works*, ed. F. E. Hutchinson (Oxford, 1945), p. 51; Donne, *Sermons*, ed. G. R. Potter and E. M. Simpson, 10 vols. (Berkeley, 1953–62), V, pp. 364–65, and III, pp. 152–53. Herbert's "Artillerie" develops the same figure: cf. Crashaw, "On a prayer booke sent to Mrs. M. R."

12. *Troposchemalogia:Tropes and Figures; or, a Treatise of the Metaphors, Allegories and express Similitudes, &c. contained in the Bible of the Old and New Testament* (London, 1682), p. 161.

13. *Of the Power of the Keyes: or, of Binding and Loosing* (London, 1647), p. 86.

14. H[enry] E[llis], *Original Letters, illustrative of English History*, 3 vols. (London, 1824), II, p. 354.

15. *A Treatise of Prayer and of the Fruits and Manner of Prayer*, trans. R. A. B.[att] (Paris, 1640), pp. 10–12. (Cf. Tennyson, "The Passing of Arthur": "For so the whole round earth is every way / Bound by gold chains about the feet of God.") This view of prayer incidentally adds dimension to Milton's exploitation in *Paradise Lost* (II, 1051; III, 510–17) of the great traditions associated with the Homeric golden chain and Jacob's ladder, and it is surely not without interest that Dante, employing the latter figure in the *Paradiso* (XXI) to formulate the prayerful life of the contemplative, should use the occasion to pronounce

through St. Peter Damian his own judgment on greedy and corrupt prelates who disgrace the Church. For comparable illustrations of the synergistic ("two-handed") aspect of faithful prayer, see Jeremiah Burroughs, *Gospel-Worship: or, The Right manner of Sanctifying the Name of God in generall* (London, 1647), pp. 290–91; Richard Baxter, *A Christian Directory* (London, 1673), p. 587; Thomas Brookes, *Precious Remedies Against Satans Devices*, 2nd ed. (London, 1653), p. 339; Gurnall, *The Christian in Compleat Armour*, p. 405.

16. YP, I, p. 832. Clarkson's description of prayer as a restorative is surely suggestive of the *Lycidas* passage: "It is an universal expedient . . . a ready way, always at hand. . . . He that can pray . . . has the key in his hand which can open all the treasures of heaven. . . . The violence of men may take estates away from you, but . . . they cannot shut you out from access to God by prayer. . . . Prayer is an expedient ready at all times, on all occasions, to bring you in what supply and relief you need. . . . Such an admirable engine is prayer, never used in vain" (*Pray for Everything*, in *Practical Works*, II, pp. 182–84).

17. In "Milton's Two-Handed Engine," *MLN*, LXVIII (1953), 229–31, J. Milton French cites from Scripture some metaphorical uses of "smite," but ignores what is perhaps the most apposite, Jeremiah xviii, 18: "Come, and let us smite him with the tongue."

18. *Of the Power of the Keyes*, p. 104. Hammond's elaboration of the metaphor suggests another apposite proverb: "Prayer should be the key of the day and the lock of the night." Also see Tilley, *A Dictionary*, p. 554; Gurnall, *The Christian in Compleat Armour*, II, pp. 353, 361. Herbert changed the title of one of his "Prayer" poems (Williams MS) to "Church-lock and key." Cf. Arthur Dent: "Prayer is as a Bunch of Keyes, wherewith Gods children doe open all the doores of heauen, and enter into euery closet." *A Learned and Fruitful Exposition vpon the Lords Prayer* (London, 1612), sig. A6. And Donne: "So therefore prayer is our first entry, for when it is said, *Ask and it shall be given*, it is also said, *Knock and it shall be opened*, showing that by prayer our entrance is. And not the entry onely, but the whole house: *My house is the house of prayer*" (*Sermons*, V, p. 232). See also William Secker, *The Nonsuch Professor in His Meridian Splendor, or the Singular Actions of Sanctified Christians* (London, 1660), p. 481; Brookes, *The Privie Key*, p. 68; Clarkson, *Practical Works*, I, p. 215.

19. *Venus and Adonis*, 367. See also *Titus Andronicus*, III, i, 82–83.

20. *The Government of the Tongue* (Oxford, 1674), p. 223.

21. *The Taming of the Tongue* (1629?), in *The Three Divine Sisters*, ed. W. H. Stowell (London, 1847), p. 273.

22. YP, I, p. 831.

23. *The Faerie Queene*, II, xii, 48. On the concept of the genius, see D. T. Starnes, "The Figure Genius in the Renaissance," *Studies in the Renaissance*, II (1964), 234–44; Michael J. B. Allen, "Macbeth's Genial Porter," *English Literary Renaissance*, IV (1974), 326–36.

24. YP, I, pp. 848, 847.

25. Hammond, *Of the Power of the Keyes*, pp. 130–31.

26. *The Duties of the Tongue* (1653), in *Works*, IV, p. 315.

27. See 2 Corinthians iii, 12, to iv, 4.

GARLANDING THE DEAD:
THE EPICEDIAL GARLAND IN *LYCIDAS*

Charlotte F. Otten

I T IS November 1637 in England. A young man has been asked to
contribute a poem to mourn the death of a young Cambridge
scholar drowned in August at the age of twenty-five in the Irish Seas,
cut off before his prime. The young mourner, John Milton, plucks the
berries of three plants—laurel, myrtle, and ivy—which have for centuries been used for burial:

> Yet once more, O ye Laurels, and once more
> Ye Myrtles brown, with Ivy never sere,
> I come to pluck your Berries harsh and crude,
> And with forc'd fingers rude,
> Shatter your leaves before the mellowing year.[1]   (1–5)

The difference is that these berries are unripe in England in November,
as unripe as Edward King is for death and the poet is for writing a
"funebrial" monody. The young poet's "forc'd fingers rude" lack the
deftness that comes with practice in weaving funerary garlands into
epicedial poetry. It is the old who are ripe for weaving funerary garlands
for the old; and, although the young are occasionally called upon to
weave a funerary garland for one of their peers, there is something
inexperienced, unnatural, poignantly clumsy about the young burying
the young. This young poet/garland-weaver is no more ready to construct an epicedial wreath than his drowned friend is to receive one. We
notice that the poet is weaving an epicedial garland in the opening lines
of his monody, and not the garland of poetic laureation.[2]

These garland plants—laurel, myrtle, and ivy—have long been regarded by critics as plants that symbolize poetic fame—for either Edward King, or Milton, or both—and the garland has long been seen as
the garland of poetic laureation. Brooks and Hardy, for example, insist
that "the laurel is a symbol of poetic fame"; Rosemond Tuve, through
research into the cultural history of plants, concludes that "it is Lycidas'
garland, which, like his poetic promise, is cut while it is still harsh and
unready. . . . I do not read in Milton's first lines the note of apology for

141

his own unripe verses familiarly referred to in commentary and criticism"; and J. B. Trapp, by examining the poetic laureation of three major poets of the Middle Ages (Dante, Mussato, and Petrarch), suggests that Milton is giving "botanical expression of his modesty" as a poet, not crowning Edward King's poetic achievement.[3]

These interpretations (and variations on them) fail, however, to recognize the inappropriateness of poetic laureation for either Edward King or for Milton himself. The "lofty rhyme" (11) which King had built was occasional poetry celebrating the birth of princesses, the king's recovery from smallpox, and the king's safe return from Scotland—"a few scraps of Latin verse, scattered through those volumes of encomiastic poetry which the University had published during his connexion with it."[4] And it would seem unbecoming that a young poet self-consciously denigrating his own obscure attempts should publicly place himself in the illustrious Petrarchan tradition of poetic laureation.

It is important to remember that the monody in which Milton "bewails a learned Friend, unfortunately drown'd," appeared in a volume of poetry expressly designed to mourn the death of a mutual friend. This kind of volume participated in the funerary tradition of memorializing the dead. Funerary traditions and burial customs, as Peter Brown observes, "are among the most notoriously stable aspects of most cultures. . . . the customs surrounding the care of the dead were experienced by those who practiced them to be no more than part and parcel of being human. As a sixth-century Egyptian lady declared, such arrangements were duties which she had to discharge as a human being. . . ."[5] The funerary garland was in Milton's day one of the cultural burial elements that had remained stable.

In Milton's England there were garlands for almost all occasions—weddings, births, military victories, sports, poetic achievements, burials—as there had been in antiquity, although today's readers of the commentary on the opening lines of *Lycidas* may think that only the poetic garland remained in use. Sir Thomas Browne's gentle reproof to his readers may be as apt today as it was in the seventeenth century: "flowry Crowns and Garlands is of not slender Antiquity, and higher than I conceive you apprehend it. For, besides the old Greeks and Romans, the AEgyptians made use hereof . . . in Gestatory, Portatory, Suspensory, Depository" form, for "convivial, festival, sacrificial, nuptial, honorary, funebrial" purposes.[6] Of all the garlands, the epicedial or "funebrial" was the most ancient and long lived: actual and symbolic garlands (the actual and the symbolic frequently intertwining) had been used for centuries. And they continued to be used. On his travels late in the nineteeth century, for example, James Henry observed that garlands kept the story of Héloïse and Abélard alive: "Throughout continental Europe at the present day, the making of wreaths and garlands for tombs gives employment to a vast number of persons, those wreaths and garlands being periodically renewed during a long series of years by the affection of relatives or friends, or even of strangers. The fresh wreath still hangs on the ancient monument of Abelard and Heloise in the cemetery of Père la Chaise at Paris."[7] The epicedial garland could be found in history, poetry, and manuals on the preparation for death; it appears, for example, with a typical, laurel-crowned skeleton on the title page of James Cole's *Of Death A True Description* (1629). It could be found in churches, catacombs, and forums; on sarcophagi, monuments, and tombstones: the stone placed in 1776 for Susannah Jayne in Marblehead, Massachusetts, for example, displays an elaborately carved skeleton crowned with a laurel wreath.[8] Since the epicedial garland has received only passing notice by commentators on *Lycidas*, this study will show that Lycidas' garland belongs in the "funebrial" tradition, that the laurel, myrtle, and ivy participate in the ceremonial rites of pagan burial and in the eschatology of Christian burial, and that the Christian eschatology of these plants helps to fuse Milton's poem with the Christian affirmation of paradise, where "*Lycidas* . . . is not dead" (166).

The epicedial garland was a garland with a long history. In ancient drama the funerary garland was essential to proper burial. In Euripides' *The Women of Troy* (1143–44) Talthybios tells Hecabe how Andromache has pleaded with the Greek Neoptolemos for Astyanax to be given a proper burial—that is, that he be laid on Hector's shield, rather than in a cedar or stone coffin, and put in Hecabe's arms "so that she would wrap the corpse with funeral robes and garlands" (1143–44).[9] In the elegiac tradition, the shade of Cynthia, Propertius' mistress, reproaches him for not giving her a proper funeral; it is her old servant, Petale, who has correctly observed her death by bringing garlands to the sepulcher.[10] In earliest times, the garland was placed on the head of the dead person by a close relative or dearest friend: Pericles himself placed a funerary garland on the head of his dead son.[11] Sometimes, perhaps to symbolize the depth of the anguish, the funerary garland was placed awry on the head: "et stygio sum sparsa lacu, nec recta capillis uitta data est" ("I was sprinkled with water from the pool of the Styx, and the headband was improperly placed on my head"). Even the bark which conveyed the shades across the Styx was wreathed: "ecce coronato pars altera rapta phaselo" ("But observe! the other sort is carried off on a garlanded bark").[12] In that same spirit, Herrick, sailing to the haven of eternal life, asked that his bark be garlanded: "MY wearied Barke, O Let it now be Crown'd! / The Haven reacht to which I first was bound."[13]

As archaeological evidence has shown, the garlanding of the dead also played a major part in Judaic burial rites. Antonius J. Brekelmans calls special attention to a votive picture on a mosque column immured at Djamiel-Kebir in Gaza, where a Hebrew inscription is flanked by a palm, and the garland consists of laurel leaves and a band of ivy leaves.[14] Edwin R. Goodenough observes that "wreaths were . . . commonly used on synagogues and graves by Jews and Christians, as well as pagans, to intensify the symbolic value for immortality."[15] In paleo-Christianity, the eschatological garland often figured in the context of martyrdom and death. A now lost funerary inscription from the Via Salaria says of Liberalis, a former Roman consul: "gratia cui trabeas dederat, dedit ira coronam" ("To the person on whom favor conferred the robe of the consulship, the wrath [of the persecutors] presented the garland [of martyrdom]").[16]

That sixteenth- and seventeenth-century England continued the practice of garlanding the dead is evident from a letter published in *The Gentleman's Magazine* of 1747:

In this nation . . . by the abundant zeal of our ancestors, virginity was held in great estimation; insomuch that those which died in that state were rewarded, at their deaths, with a garland or crown on their heads, denoting their triumphant victory over the lusts of the flesh. . . . And, in the year, 1733, the present clerk of the parish church of *Bromley* in *Kent*, by his digging a grave in that churchyard, close to the east end of the chancel wall, dug up one of these crowns, in filagree work with gold and silver wire, in resemblance of myrtle (with which plant the funebrial garlands of the ancients were compos'd.). . . .

Besides these crowns, the ancients had also their depository garlands, the use of which were continued even till of late years (and perhaps are still retain'd in many parts of this nation, for my own knowledge of these matters extends not above 20 or 30 miles round *London*) which garlands, at the funerals of the deceas'd, were carried solemnly before the corps by two maids, and afterward hung up in some conspicuous place within the church, in memorial of the departed person. . . .

About 40 years ago these garlands grew much out of repute, and were thought, by many, as very unbecoming decorations for so sacred a place as the church; and at the reparation, or new beautifying several churches, where I have been concern'd, I was oblig'd, by order of the minister and church-wardens, to take the garlands down, and the inhabitants strictly forbid to hang up any more for the future. Yet notwithstanding, several people, unwilling to forsake their ancient and delightful custom, continued still the making of them, and they were carried at the funerals, as before, to the grave, and put therein, upon the coffin, over the face of the dead; this I have seen done in many places.[17]

In the eyes of the eminent seventeenth-century gardener John Rea, a funerary garland was a "guerdon"—a reward, a recompense. In the poem at the end of his gardening book, he craves flowers for his grave and "one sprig of Bays" for his hearse:

> And for my guerdon this is all I crave,
> Some gentle hand with Flowers may strew my Grave,
> And with one sprig of Bays my Herse befriend,
> When as my Life, as now my Book, doth End.[18]

Even empty tombs were garlanded. According to John Weever, the Renaissance historian of ancient and contemporary burial practices, a cenotaph was erected for those whose bodies had perished, leaving no physical remains for burial:

A Cenotaph is an emptie Funerall Monument or Tombe, erected for the honour of the dead, wherein neither the corps, nor reliques of any defunct, are deposited, in imitation of which our Hearses here in England are set vp in Churches, during the continuance of a yeare, or for the space of certaine moneths. . . . The second kinde of Cenotaphs were made *Religionis causa*, to the memory of such whose carcases, or dispersed reliques, were in no wise to be found, for example, of such as perished by shipwracke. . . . To these *inania busta*, or *vacua Sepulchra*, friends of the defunct would yearely repaire. . . . [19]

The "*Religionis causa* . . . carcases . . . in no wise to be found . . . of such as perished by shipwracke . . . the *vacua Sepulchra*"—these phrases haunt the memory of Edward King and are echoed in *Lycidas:* "sad occasion dear . . . bones are hurl'd . . . the remorseless deep . . . the wat'ry bier . . . the Laureate Hearse where *Lycid* lies." The garland of laurel, myrtle, and ivy that Milton weaves in epicedial poetry is not the kind that was banned from churches, or from the hearts of those who knew that grief is more than a series of steps in the mourning process, and that sorrow channeled through the proper ritual of bringing funebrial plants for burial can give way to singing "in the blest Kingdoms meek of joy and love" (177).

The first clue to the funerary function of laurel, myrtle, and ivy is in the opening phrase, "Yet once more," an allusion both universal and personal. The funerary garland is "yet once more" marking the universality of mortality; and, personally, Milton is "yet once more" weaving a funeral garland in poetry. The adverbial phrase refers not to Milton's early poem *Comus*, but, far more appropriately, to two previous deaths, both young and untimely, for which Milton had to write a tribute: for the "Fair Infant Dying of a Cough" and for the Marchioness of Winchester. For the marchioness he brought a garland: "some Flowers and some Bays / For thy Hearse to strew the ways" (57–58). The flowers and bays, "Devoted to [her] virtuous name" (60), function eschatologically, leading straight to the "bright Saint" sitting high in glory (61). Later, in *Mansus*, Milton prayed for a friend to give him a proper burial with the epicedial myrtle and laurel:

> Tandem ubi non tacitae permensus tempora vitae,
> Annorumque satur, cineri sua iura relinquam,
> Ille mihi lecto madidis astaret ocellis,
> Astanti sat erit si dicam, "Sim tibi curae."
> Ille meos artus, liventi morte solutos,
> Curaret parva componi molliter urna.
> Forsitan et nostros ducat de marmore vultus,
> Nectens aut Paphia myrti aut Parnasside lauri
> Fronde comas, at ego secura pace quiescam. (85–93)

[And at last, after I shall have lived though the span of no silent career, and when, full of years, I shall pay to the ashes their due, that friend would stand with tears in his eyes beside my bed. I should be content if I might say to him as he stood there, "Take me into your care." He would see to it that, when livid death had relaxed them, my limbs were gently bestowed in a little urn. Perhaps he might even cause my features to take form in marble and wreathe my locks with Paphian myrtle and Parnassian laurel. So I should rest in perfect peace.] (Hughes, p. 130)

Still later, Milton referred to the garland of virginity, martyrdom, and immortality in *Epitaphium Damonis:*

> Ipse, caput nitidum cinctus rutilante corona,
> Laetaque frondentis gestans umbracula palmae,
> Aeternum perages immortales hymenaeos. (215–17)

[Your glorious head shall be bound with a shining crown and with shadowing fronds of joyous palms in your hands you shall enact your part eternally in the immortal marriage.] (Hughes, p. 139)

The botanic description of laurel by a contemporary herbalist confirms Milton's description in *Lycidas:* "In English the laurel is also called the Wild Bay Tree; while the fruit of this tree ripens in October in warm climates, such as Portugal, it does not flower in England until December, January, and February, if the winter is neither too early nor too extreme. All are evergreen."[20] Used for centuries in magic, folklore, medicine, and pharmacy, long known as a symbol of victory, salvation, and rescue,[21] laurel was still used in funerary garlands of Milton's day:

[Laurel will] serue both for pleasure and profit, both for ornament and for vse, both for honest Ciuill vses, and for Physicke, yea both for the sicke and for the sound, both for the liuing and for the dead: And so much might be said of this one tree, that if it were all told, would as well weary the Reader, as the Relater: but to explaine my selfe; It serueth to adorne the house of God as well as of man . . . to crowne or encircle as with a garland, the heads of the liuing, and to sticke and decke forth the bodies of the dead: so that from the cradle to the graue we have still vse of it, we have still neede of it.[22]

Laurel shaded the tomb of King Bebryx at the harbor of Amycus.[23] Manoa vows to plant it at the grave of Milton's Samson: " . . . and plant it round with shade / Of Laurel ever green" (*SA*, 1734–35). Emperor Haile Selassie of Ethiopia placed a wreath of laurel on the tomb of the unknown soldier in Rome.[24] Writing "To Laurels," Herrick chooses the tree to assure him of personal immortality:

> A Funerall stone,
> Or Verse I covet none;
> But onely crave
> Of you, that I may have
> A sacred Laurel springing from my grave:
> Which being seen,
> Blest with perpetuall greene,
> May grow to be
> Not so much call'd a tree,
> As the eternall monument of me.[25]

Laurel's eschatological context is most apparent in the post-Apostolic age, where it appears on the Passion Sarcophagi. The most famous of these tombs can be seen in the Lateran Museum; the left of this Sarcophagus shows "Simon of Cyrene carrying the Cross and the 'crowning' of Our Lord with the wreath of victory; the crown of thorns is replaced by one of laurel. In the central niche the focal point is the cross-monogram of Christ; the wreath hangs from the beak of an eagle. . . . The sarcophagus dates from about 350. The motif of the 'Trophy of the Cross' was adopted into the liturgy and also into the preaching. . . . It is still heard during Holy Week in the hymns of Venantius Fortunatus on the Cross."[26] In the garland of the laureled Christ is visible evidence of victory over death and the promise of life everlasting: "Today shalt thou be with me in Paradise."

The botanic description of myrtle by contemporary herbalists sheds light on Milton's "Myrtles brown" and "Berries harsh and crude":

myrtles are evergreen, are "couered with a browne bark," and in "England they neuer beare any fruit."[27] Myrtle was a ubiquitous plant. It was used in wedding garlands, in cultic religious ceremonies, in purifications, in wreaths of ovation, in festive garlands at circuses.[28] It also adorned graves. Euripides' Electra bewails the absence of myrtle at Agamemnon's tomb: "And Agamemnon's tomb is set at naught: / Drink-offerings never yet nor myrtle-spray / Had it, a grave all bare of ornament." Later she is comforted by the myrtle sprays that an old man has placed on the tomb: "There kneeling, for its desolation wept, / Poured a drink-offering from the skin I bare / Thy guests, and crowned the tomb with myrtle-sprays."[29] In the context of Elysium, the poet Suckling recalls the appropriateness of myrtle; he asks for bays "or myrtle bough" for the "noble Martyrs here."[30] And we remember that, in 1733, a myrtle garland was dug up in a churchyard grave in Kent, "most artificially wrought in filagree work with gold and silver wire."

"Ivy never sere," according to the herbalists, produces leaves "abiding fresh and greene Winter and Summer," but does not flower in England until July. Its "berries are not ripe usually untill about Christmas."[31] Ivy leaves were painted on vases as early as the Mycenaean epoch and continued to appear in later ancient art adorning vases, drinking cups, columns, statues, sarcophagi. Archaeologists have discovered this funerary plant on an ivy-decorated mask in an Etruscan grave; in still another grave, they have found a metal ivy wreath with leaves and berries.[32] In the elegiac tradition, the shade of Cynthia pleads with her survivor, Propertius, to plant ivy on her tomb: "pone hederam tumulo, mihi quae praegnante corymbo / mollis contortis alliget ossa comis"[33] ("Plant ivy on my grave so that as its cluster swells it may bind my bones with its gently twisting tresses."). Ivy's eschatological uses were so widespread in the Greco-Roman world that ivy leaves became a part of the symbolic vocabulary of artisans. A glance at sarcophagi reveals the omnipresence of ivy as a symbol of immortality:

Toutes les essences à feuillage persistant, qui restent verdoyantes quand la nature se meurt, comme le pin, le cyprès, le laurier sont . . . devenus des plantes funéraires. . . . A Vence . . . , un cyprès se dresse de chaque côté du croissant. Pareillement le lierre, dont le feuillage n'est point caduc, et qui appartient à Bacchus, dieu d'une religion de salut, semblait doué d'un pouvoir de renouveau, qui faisait triompher du trépas. . . .[34]

[All the species which retain their leaves and remain green in the autumn, species such as the pine, cypress, and the laurel, became funeral plants. At Vence a cypress is set up on either side of a crescent. Similarly, the ivy, which retains its foliage and is associated with Bacchus, a redeemer god, was regarded as endowed with the power of renewal, bringing triumph over death.]

Jewish symbols of the Greco-Roman period abound in affirmations of the afterlife. Goodenough's statement that "Pagan motifs in Jewish synagogues and the graves have already led us to suspect that Jews used them to express faith in heaven, in the love of God, in coming victory," is supported by his studies of the paintings of the Dura Europas synagogue. What art historians had at first regarded as decorative borrowings from the pagan world emerged, upon investigation, as a full set of symbols to express confidence in the existence of a life after death. Bacchus, dolphins, and ivy on Christian sarcophagi, Goodenough concludes, "refer to hope of life after death . . . refer, that is, to heaven."[35]

Rising from the opening lines of *Lycidas*, then, is the image of a premature death and burial, of an immature epicedial poet/garland-weaver, and of three ancient funerary plants whose berries are unripe in November. This nature imagery is more profound and more inspiring than proponents of poetic laureation have imagined. The garland of poetic laureation, a purely honorary decoration, could have only a superficial relevance for Milton's monody. Rooted in laurel, myrtle, and ivy is the mortality in which all creation participates; emanating from these plants is the immortality to whose reality funerary garlands attest.

Funerary garlands, as we have seen, paid respect to the dead and brought comfort to their givers by alleviating the harshness and pain of death; witnessed to personal immortality; and functioned eschatologically, symbolizing the victory over death by the laureled Christ and the hope of heaven through his death and resurrection. The consolation and affirmation in the garland bear the marks of the traditional biblical passage used in the burial of the dead: "So also is the resurrection of the dead. It is sown in Corruption; it is raised in incorruption: It is sown in dishonour; it is raised in glory: it is sown in weakness; it is raised in power: It is sown a natural body; it is raised a spirtual body. There is a natural body, and there is a spiritual body" (1 Corinthians xv, 42–44, Authorized Version). The epicedial garland in *Lycidas* is a natural-spiritual garland leading the mourners from the sad image of the young body hurled to "the bottom of the monstrous world" (158) to the triumphal vision of Lycidas "mounted high . . . / In the blest Kingdoms meek of joy and love" (172, 177). The strains of the opening dirge are replaced by the resonances of the solemn and victorious song: "Yet once more" is counterpointed by "Weep no more." In the funerary garland is the preparation for celebration. The process of mourning will be turned into the litany of singing:

There entertain him all the Saints above,
In solemn troops, and sweet Societies
That sing, and singing in their glory move,
And wipe the tears for ever from his eyes.   (178–81)

Calvin College

NOTES

1. *John Milton: Complete Poems and Major Prose*, ed. Merritt Y. Hughes (New York, 1957). This edition is cited throughout.
2. For a summary of the arguments, see *A Variorum Commentary on the Poems of John Milton*, ed. A. S. P. Woodhouse and Douglas Bush (New York, 1972), II, ii, pp. 639–40. If we recognize that "shatter" is an agricultural term meaning "to cause (seed, leaves, etc.) to fall or be shed," Milton's metaphor is intensified; see Conrad Heresbach, *The Whole Art and Trade of Husbandry*, trans. Barnaby Googe (London, 1586), I, p. 32.
3. Cleanth Brooks and John Edward Hardy, "Essays in Analysis: *Lycidas*," in *"Lycidas": The Tradition and the Poem*, ed. C. A. Patrides (New York, 1961), p. 137; Rosemond Tuve, "Theme, Pattern and Imagery in *Lycidas*," in ibid., p. 180; J. B. Trapp, "The Owl's Ivy and the Poet's Bays: An Enquiry into Poetic Garlands," *Journal of the Warburg and Courtauld Institutes*, XXI (1958), 255.
4. David Masson, *The Life of John Milton* (New York, 1946), I, pp. 647–48.
5. *The Cult of the Saints* (Chicago, 1981), p. 24.
6. "Of Garlands and Coronary or Garland-Plants," *The Works of Sir Thomas Browne*, ed. Geoffrey Keynes (London, 1928), III, pp. 49–50. For a recent study of seventeenth-century attitudes toward wreaths, see Judy Z. Kronenfeld, "Herbert's 'A Wreath' and Devotional Aesthetics: Imperfect Efforts Redeemed by Grace," *ELH*, XLVIII (Summer 1981), 290–309.
7. *Aeneidea* (Dublin, 1878), II, pp. 376–77.
8. Allan I. Ludwig, *Graven Images* (Middletown, Conn. 1966), plate 6, p. 78. See also Frederick Burgess, *English Churchyard Memorials* (London, 1963); J. M. C. Toynbee, *Death and Burial in the Roman World* (London, 1971); and J. M. Gesnerus, *De coronis mortuorum* (Göttingen, 1748).
9. See August F. von Pauly and George Wissowa, *Pauly's Real-Encyclopädie der Classischen Altertumswissenschaft* (Stuttgart, 1893–1956), XI, 2, 1595, 1604; hereafter designated as *PW*.
10. *Elegies: Book IV*, ed. W. A. Camps (Cambridge, 1965), vii, 43–44.
11. Plutarch, *Pericles*, 36; *PW*, XI, 2, 1596.
12. Propertius, *Elegies: Book IV*, *iii*, 15–16, *and vii*, 59. The translations, except where noted, are my own.
13. *The Complete Poetry of Robert Herrick*, ed. J. Max Patrick (New York, 1968), *H-1127*. All citations are from this edition.
14. *Martyrerkranz* (Rome, 1965), pp. 10–11.
15. *Jewish Symbols in the Greco-Roman Period* (New York, 1964), IX, p. 53.
16. Brekelmans, *Martyrerkranz*, p. 116, n. 35.

17. XVII (June 1747), pp. 264–65.

18. *Flora: Seu de florum cultura* (London, 1665), p. 239.

19. *Ancient Fvnerall Monvments* (London, 1631), p. 41. Weever gives a long list of empty tombs in the ancient world and an elaborate, detailed description of monuments in various dioceses in England (Canterbury, London, Norwich).

20. John Parkinson, *Theatrum botanicum* (London, 1640), pp. 206–07. See also John Gerard, *The Herball, or Generall Historie of Plantes* (London, 1597), enlarged and amended by Thomas Johnson in 1633 and 1636; all references cite the 1633 edition. For the description of laurel, see pp. 1405–10.

21. *PW*, XIII, 2, 1432–42. See also M. B. Ogle, "Laurel in Ancient Religion and Folklore," *AJP*, XXXI (1910), 287–311; Josef Murr, *Die Pflanzenwelt in der Griechischen Mythologie* (Innsbruck, 1890; Groningen, 1969), p. 93.

22. John Parkinson, *Paradisi in sole paradisus terrestris* (London, 1629), pp. 598–99.

23. Pliny, *Naturalis historia*, trans. W. H. S. Jones, Loeb Classical Library (London, 1956), XVI, 239.

24. 7 November 1970.

25. *H-89*.

26. F. van der Meer and Christine Mohrmann, *Atlas of the Early Christian World* (London, 1958), p. 143. For further studies of the "Trophy-of-the-Cross" motif, see H. von Campenhausen, "Die Passionssarkophage," *Marb. Jahrb. f. Kunstwiss.*, V (1929), 39–85; F. W. Deichmann and T. Klauser, *Frühchristliche Sarchophage* (Basel, 1966), cf. tafel 16. See also *The Works of Michael Drayton*, ed. J. W. Hebel (Oxford, 1961), "sixth Eglog": "Upon thy toombe shall spring a Lawrell tree, / Whose sacred shade shall serve thee for a hearse" (145–46).

27. Gerard, *The Herball*, pp. 1411–13; Parkinson, *Paradisus*, pp. 427–28. See also Charlotte F. Otten, "Milton's Myrtles," *Essays in Criticism*, XXIV (January 1974), 105.

28. *PW*, XVI, 1, 1179–83; Pliny, XV, 119–26.

29. *Electra*, trans. Arthur S. Way, Loeb Classical Library (New York, 1924). See lines 323–25 and 510–12.

30. *The Works of Sir John Suckling*, ed. Thomas Clayton (Oxford, 1971), *Sonnet III* (29–32).

31. Parkinson, *Theatrum*, pp. 678–81; Gerard, *The Herball*, pp. 857–58.

32. *PW*, V, 2, 2839–46 and 2845–46.

33. Propertius, *Elegies: Book IV*, vii, 79–80; see Camps, p. 123n. Whether one reads *pone* with Sandbach or prefers to read *pelle*, the sense is clear: ivy was considered an appropriate grave plant.

34. Franz Cumont, *Recherches sur le symbolisme funéraire des Romains* (Paris, 1966), pp. 11, 219–20.

35. *Jewish Symbols*, IX, pp. 7, 54. See also *Reallexikon für Antike und Christentum* (Stuttgart, 1954), II, 29. The paradise motif is so common an early Christian funeral symbol that a whole group of sarcophagi have been gathered under the rubric "Paradeisossarkophage." For a comprehensive study of the paradisal eschatology of plants in poems, see my forthcoming book, *"Environ'd with Eternity": God, Poems, and Plants in Sixteenth- and Seventeenth-Century England*.

WORDS, WORDS, WORDS, AND THE WORD: MILTON'S *OF PRELATICAL EPISCOPACY*

Thomas Kranidas

T HERE IS in Milton's polemical writing a kind of systole of grandeur and meanness. Always, the vision of some kind of radiant community, but within it, or opposed to it, modes of carping, of harsh, sometimes near arrogant dispatching and punishment. This punishment is necessary; the success of an argument is tied as much to the strength as to the virtue of the speaker. Milton is solidly enough in this world, and in his rhetorical tradition, to want to make his enemies look foolish or evil.

Of Prelatical Episcopacy[1] is the least of Milton's antiprelatical tracts, it is the shortest, and it is the smallest in rhetorical spirit and, on the surface at least, in intellectual ambition. Yet even here there are passages of power and, more rarely, beauty, usually in the condemnation of spurious authority or in the praise of Scripture. And even here, there is an impression of success, of Milton's having used the piece as he intended. It should be instructive, then, to follow the argument closely, observing the structure of oppositions as they unfold. In analyzing the oppositions, the distances and tensions between, it may be necessary to identify or stabilize certain details of the piece within the polemical context of the early 1640s.

The tract is essentially devoted to discrediting, with considerable sophistication, the authority of the Fathers, especially as they are cited by Bishop Hall in *Episcopacie by Divine Right Asserted* (1640), by Peloni Almoni in *A Compendious Dicourse, Proving Episcopacie to be of Apostolical and Consequently of Divine Institution* (1642), and by James Ussher, archbishop of Armagh, in *The Judgement of Doctor Reignolds Concerning Episcopacy, more largely confirmed out of antiquity* (May 1641, after an earlier edition of *The Judgement*, also published in 1641). Ussher, a scholar and theologian whom the Puritans had once admired and considered one of their own, is the most important antagonist. Milton puts Ussher's name on the title page and concentrates on his argument. Hall, though not mentioned by name, appears to be directly answered in at least one passage, and the pseudonymous and still unidentified Almoni receives no specific attention.[2] In addressing his foes, Milton is anonymous but by no means characterless. The fervent dedication of the fledgling poet-prophet is muted here—in respite after *Of Reformation*. But the assurance has grown; perhaps Milton has discovered that the opposition is simply not that formidable.

Milton seems, for one thing, to fight with one hand tied behind his back—a very different stance from that of writing with the left hand. Milton is fully committed to his argument, but the task at hand, one deduces, does not use all his faculties:

it came into my thoughts to perswade my selfe, setting all distances, and nice respects aside, that I could do Religion, and my Country no better service for the time then doing my utmost endeavour to recall the people of GOD from this vaine forraging after straw, and to reduce them to their firme stations under the standard of the Gospell: by making appeare to them, first the insufficiency, next the inconvenience, and lastly the impiety of these gay testimonies, that their great Doctors would bring them to dote on. And in performing this I shall not strive to be more exact in Methode, then as their citations lead mee. (627)

Despite "my utmost endeavour," the tone is almost patronizing; the speaker puts aside "nice respects" and "for the time" devotes himself to an argument in which his intellectual energies seem circumscribed: "I shall not strive to be more exact in Methode, then as their citations lead mee." The speaker of *Of Reformation* and of *The Reason of Church-Government* is also unwilling, but he is hardly casual; there the personal stakes are much higher, imagery and rhythms suggest an eschatological argument in language for more passionate. Here the speaker is a proud Englishman, "being borne free, and in the Mistresse Iland of all the *British*" (624), but the nationalism, the sense of English moment and momentum, is not so strong as in the other tracts. Concern shrinks to the problem at hand. We are in a present with little of the prophetic and proleptic identity of the best of the Puritan writing. The speaker is here to dispatch—logically, briskly, really quite easily—"the broken reed of *tradition*," "that indigested heap, and frie of Authors, which they call Antiquity," "fragments of old *Martyrologies*, and *legends*," "these gay testimonies" (624–27).

The battle is won in the first twenty lines. Episcopacy is either of divine constitution or human. If only of human, we can take it or leave it. If of divine, the only authority is Scripture. But nowhere in Scripture, "either by plaine Text, or solid reasoning" is there found "any difference betweene a Bishop, and a Presbyter" (625). Ergo, we can leave it.

The business of this tract is to discredit not the great doctors themselves, but their evidence. Milton is the leader who would "recall the people of GOD" and "reduce them," lead them back, "to their firme stations under the standard of the Gospell." He would show the "insufficiency . . . inconvenience . . . impiety of these gay testimonies" (627). The categories overlap; they are often indistinguishable. And though Milton technically observes his outline, the emphases (as in *Of Reformation*) are very disproportionate. The tract pretty much restates Milton's hostility to a tradition which prides itself on mere age and mass, unexamined sanctities and repetitions, "*Martyrologies,* and *legends*"—the contempt is obvious. Milton throughout his career hates the use of regular compendia of borrowed knowledge: "*quodlibets,*" "alphabetical servility," commonplace books (yes, he has one), the yellowing notes of dormant educations. His persistent charge against his scholarly foes implies his own strenuous, continual rethinking of controversial positions, his insistence on the continuous erection of mind and will on earth, in Paradise, in Heaven.

The details and context of Milton's historical arguments are most conveniently discussed in W. R. Parker's biography, in J. Max Patrick's notes to the Yale edition, and especially in the general introduction to the same volume (YP, I, pp. 114–23). I should like here to comment briefly on what Milton finds spurious or disturbing in the evidence summoned by Hall, Ussher, and Almoni and on what programmatic use he makes of this occasion. In opposing their uses of evidence, Milton uses common sense and a kind of rustic suspicion. The one just man may be admirable in action, the oral witness to truth in the hostile arena, but the single witness in history is not enough; the evidence of "an obscure, and single witnesse" (627) is "this bare Testimony" (628). Faith in titles is disparaged: "Councells" are as suspect as present day "Convocations" for containing "some bad and slippery men" (628). Written records have been falsified "both anciently by other *Heretiks,* and modernly by Papists . . . whence Canons, Acts, and whole spurious Councels are thrust upon us" (628–29). The argument repeats *Of Reformation* (YP, I, p. 553). Spurious, fabricated tradition joins the accidental which we have already seen in the extraordinary image of the Fathers: "Whatsoever time, or the heedlesse hand of blind chance, hath drawne down from of old to this present, in her huge dragnet, whether Fish, or Sea-weed, Shells, or Shrubbs, unpickt, unchosen, those are the Fathers" (626). Those who aspire plunge: "ungodly Prelatisme . . . so farre plung'd into worldly ambition" (629) leaps into a threatening and debris-filled sea of "authorities" to seek endorsement, to hide, to feed away from the light. One remembers the richer statement in *Of Reformation:*

they feare the plain field of the Scriptures, the chase is too hot; they seek the dark, the bushie, the tangled Forrest, they would imbosk: they feel themselvs strook in the transparent streams of divine Truth, they would plunge, and tumble, and thinke to ly hid in the foul weeds, and muddy waters, where no plummet can reach the bottome. (YP, I, p. 569)

Carnal and ambitious, these "blind Judges of things before their eyes" (629) operate as often as not "from reason of State" (630). A council "beginning in the Spirit, ended thus in the flesh," gives us little hope even if the records of it are authentic (630).

Antiquity itself—at least the better voices of it —"turn'd over the controversie to that sovran Book which we had fondly straggl'd from" (631; cf. *Of Reformation,* YP, I, pp. 541, 553). Eusebius, a famous writer, finds it difficult to establish who were appointed bishops by the Apostles; Leontius, "an obscure Bishop speaking beyond his own Diocesse," is therefore to be doubted (631). Milton urges utmost care in the use of extrascriptural evidence, no matter how early, and a rigorous common sense ministers to that care—a rule of evidence to be observed throughout Milton's writings on church history and doctrine. The end of this tract will in fact give us a quite startling statement on the uses of theological writing.

The sufficiency of Scripture is complemented and confirmed by its simplicity (632; cf. *Of Reformation,* YP, I, p. 569), and the inadequacy of antiquity is confirmed by its complexity, for example, the creation of "a new Lexicon to name themselves by . . . προεστως or *Antistes* . . . Gnostick . . . Sacerdos" (632). Again, Scripture is the original, the simple, the sufficient. Tradition is, paradoxically, "new-fangled" "innovation."[3] Invented words and titles, like logic-chopping and obscurity, are in Milton's eyes characteristic of the authority cited by the prelatical party. Authority is in fact carelessly or selectively cited. Photius, for example, upon whose testimony the tradition of Timothy's martyrdom is based, follows that topic with the Martyrdom of the Seven Sleepers of Ephesus (633); Milton's contempt does not have to be made explicit. But the main point of the tract is not mere contempt at unnecessary complexity, at innovation and foolishness. The chief purpose of the tract becomes the rigorous examination of evidence. *Of Prelatical Episcopacy* is, in a very real sense, a methodological treatise on Christian polemic.

To this point the opposition, indeed English prelacy itself, has suffered little of the astonishing abuse that Milton has demonstrated so brilliantly in *Of Reformation*. Is it perhaps the figure of the archbishop of Armagh that temporarily blunts the Puritan invective? Milton was to address himself yet once more to Ussher in *The Reason of Church-government*, and there too one notes a "comparative mildness." Ralph Haug suggests that "Ussher was an old man, with a European reputation for integrity and learning. Moreover, Ussher was not particularly high church in his doctrines; his compromise of the summer of 1641 was notably tolerant" (YP, I, p. 739). But Bishop Hall was a moderate too and, if not so learned, at least "literary"; Hall is about to get it in spades. Though archbishop and a pleader for the hated Strafford's life, Ussher was highly thought of by the Puritans, not only as a moderate but as a former member of their party.

There is indeed a small legendry about Ussher, including a moderately Puritanical sermon falsely ascribed to him in December 1641.[4] In July 1645, the anonymous writer of *The Copy of A Most Pithy and Pious Letter . . . to James Usher* [sic] *to persuade our King to return to His Parliament* singled him out because "you have formerly given to the truly Godly and Religious party in these Kingdoms (both by your life and doctrine) that you are one of them" (p. i). Ussher was said to have "Ebb'd so far from his Archiepiscopall dignity, as to turn Lecturer, and so brought himselfe into a possibility of Heaven, till the old man began to dote upon the World again."[5] At the false news of his death in December 1645, there appeared a series of announcements about the once honorable, since defected, great scholar:

That unhappy and unholy *Neuter* or ambo-dexter, Dr. Usher *[sic]* Arch-Prelate of Armagh, resident at Oxford, a man once, I confesse, of good, yea of great esteem . . . ; but at length, whose last days (hitherto) have proved his worst days.[6]

The True Informer informs:

hee was much admired and reverenced for his learning and parts, and honoured for a shew of Pietie and Devotion but his adhering unto the Popish partie lost his repute and will eclipse that glorie which would have otherwise been ascribed unto him by this Age.[7]

The Scotish Dove comments:

surely many excellent parts died with him (the best before him) for he was a brave Scholar and an excellent Preacher; had he not been poysoned with the office of a Bishop, and sullyed by the vices of a Courtier, he had been one of ten thousand: but ambition and timeritie lost his Nobilitie, and his good name went to the Grave before him; it is my sorrow, that such a man should staine his vertues, and in so great oblivion goe into the chambers of death.[8]

I cite these statements not as immediate sources of Milton's modest deference (the news accounts are dated 1645), but as indications that the Puritans—Milton included—had a range of opinions on the bishops, that they did not apply "such abuse indiscriminately,"[9] and that Milton adjusted his decorum scrupulously to the problem at hand. What he does to Hall in *Animadversions*, published only a few weeks later, is vastly different from what he does to Ussher in this tract. Here it is Anglican methodology and consequently the evidence derived from the Fathers which is at stake.

When, in sifting the evidence, Milton does not find logical imprecision, he finds "judaical," papist, or pagan taints (634–38), signalized by suspicious references that imply sacrifice. Nearness to a known corrupt passage makes a passage suspect. In a brisk analysis of Ignatius' *To the Smyrnaeans*, he finds that "all those short Epistles must either be adulterat or else *Ignatius* was not *Ignatius*, nor a Martyr, but most adulterate, and corrupt himselfe" (639). After the quite strenuous scholarly analysis, Milton concludes:

Had *God* ever intended that we should have sought any part of usefull instruction frō *Ignatius*, doubtles he would not have so ill provided for our knowledge, as to send him to our hands in this broken and disjoynted plight; and if he intended no such thing, we doe injuriously in thinking to tast better the pure Euangelick Manna by seasoning our mouths with the tainted scraps, and fragments of an unknown table; and searching among the verminous, and polluted rags dropt overworn from the toyling shoulders of Time, with these deformedly to quilt, and interlace the intire, the spotlesse, and undecaying robe of Truth, the daughter not of Time, but of Heaven, only bred up heer below in Christian hearts, between two grave & holy nurses the Doctrine, and Discipline of the Gospel. (639)

The records of history are part of God's plan for our education. Our analysis of those records against the standard of Scripture is an essential part of the experience of revelation. The Word of God is food; to season it with "the tainted scraps and fragments, of an unknown table," is an injury to God. But not all words of man are tainted and fragmented; the reason must strive to identify the truth as it has come down to us through God's will. Reason and common sense are the necessary human elements.

The double metaphor of food and clothing is typical of Milton's continuous synthesizing. Both figures, the true "Evangelick Manna" and

Truth in her undecaying robe, are daughters "not of Time, but of Heaven"; yet, crucially, both are "bred up heer below in Christian hearts, between two grave & holy nurses the Doctrine, and Discipline of the Gospel." Faith and reason, revelation and study—we are not very far from *Christian Doctrine*. Milton is hooting at the specious uses of human learning and analysis, but he is at the same time insisting on the necessity of the proper uses of the human reason. He is not antirational or mystical. The "two grave & holy nurses" are hardly seraphs with fire-tipped arrows.

Though Milton sometimes defends his youth in the face of age and experience, here he dismisses the testimony of Irenaeus, bishop of Lyons, because it depended on memories from childhood. The problem is quite delicate because the testimony criticized is embedded in a powerful passage of Eusebius, one which follows a touching injunction to "keep those truly saintly men of an earlier generation in mind, as a splendid example of meticulous accuracy."[10] Yet Milton firmly denies that one could properly "conclude a distinct, and superior order from the young observation of *Irenaeus*" (640).

Despite steady debunking of the Fathers, Milton expresses firm admiration for the primitive church. Anglicans and Puritans alike cited the primitive church, but for the latter it was of much briefer duration. For Milton, the golden age of Christianity endured scarcely a generation—through the mature days of the Messiah and the lives of his Apostles; decay followed almost immediately: "They which came after these Apostolick men being lesse in merit, but bigger in ambition, strove to invade those priviledges by intrusion and plea of right, which *Polycarpus*, and others like him possest from the voluntary surrender of men subdu'd by the excellencie of their heavenly gifts" (640–41). The corruption of the church was the movement into carnality, a fall recorded in language which falls away from the truth of Scripture. Monitoring that fall from truth, measuring the distance we have fallen, is one of the primary purposes of theology.

In *Of Reformation*, the speaker had defended zeal against the charges of Lord Digby (YP, I, p. 601). The speaker in this later tract now accuses Irenaeus of being "so rash as to take unexamin'd opinions from an Author [Papias] of so small capacity," and ascribes the spread of idle traditions to "the inconsiderate zeal of the next age, that heeded more the person, then the Doctrine" (641). There is no contradiction here. Both Anglicans and Puritans knew St. Paul's distinction in Romans x, 2—"For I hear them record that they have a zeal of God, but not according to knowledge"—and they regularly cite Saul's persecution of the church as an example of "inconsiderate zeal" (Philippians iii, 6; Galatians i, 14).[11] Inconsiderate zeal is further linked to the anecdotal, the personal, perhaps even to the cult of personality, true zeal to strict observance of scriptural injunction and example. So, in a shrewd passage, Milton describes how

the exercise of right instructing was chang'd into the curiosity of impertinent fabling: where the mind was to be edified with solid *Doctrine*, there the fancy was sooth'd with solemne stories: with less fervency was studied what Saint *Paul*, or Saint *Iohn* had written then was listen'd to one that could say here hee taught, here he stood, this was his stature, and thus he went habited, and O happy this house that harbour'd him, and that cold stone whereon he rested, this Village wherein he wrought such a miracle, and that pavement bedew'd with the warme effusion of his last blood, that sprouted up into eternall Roses to crowne his Martyrdome. (641–42)

The sarcasm is aimed directly at Irenaeus, but one is tempted to see baroque art itself, perhaps even the Ignatian meditative process, as the target. The polemical point, however, is both more precise and more important. Sentimental concerns for personality obscure the essentiality of Scripture:

Thus while all their thoughts were powr'd out upon circumstances, and the gazing after such men as had sate at table with the *Apostles* (many of which *Christ* hath profest, yea though they had cast out Divells in his name, he will not know at the last day) by this meanes they lost their time, and truanted in the fundamentall grounds of saving knowledge, as was seene shortly by their writings. (642)

Milton's cardinal tenet is: keep your eye on the text. When the eye strays, when the mind falters, error creeps in. The need for intellectual rigor is perpetual. Irenaeus faltered so badly as to call Mary the advocate of Eve (642), a serious lapse toward Mariolatry, which for the Puritans meant the supplanting of Christ as mediator.

An important and rather surprising statement has been made. The Word speaks, but having spoken it is written down and confirmed. Christ and the Apostles aside, oral tradition—including talk about religion—has been disparaged. One remembers the passage in *Of Reformation:* "doubtlesse that which led the good men into fraud and error was, that they attended more to the neer tradition of what they heard the Apostles sometimes did, then to what they had left written" (YP, I, p. 550). Truth is printed, not spoken. I am convinced that Milton's considerable emphasis on the specious oral traditions of the early church is a sign of his increasing insistence on having the word in hand, where it can be perused by the human reason. This increasing emphasis would account for the number of times Milton makes the printed word an autonomous body, most notably in the beautiful passage of *Areopagitica:* "a good Booke is the pretious life-blood of a master spirit, imbalm'd and treasur'd up on purpose to a life beyond life" (YP, II, p. 493). The life of the spoken word in Milton then, needs some more investigation. On the one hand, the spoken word is holy when it comes from Christ's lips, when it comes from one whose lips are touched and purified by God's seraphim "with the hallow'd fire of his Altar" (*The Reason of Church-Government*, YP, I, p. 821),[12] and when it is preached fervently, intelligently, from the pulpits of the nation. Inspired speech is the highest virtue of the godly preacher, silence the vice and sin of the "dumb dog," the ultimate villain of Puritan politics, the unpreaching minister— "Blinde Mouthes." But the Puritan revolutionary ministry is about to become the preaching establishment. And here are the signs that Milton is beginning, consciously or not, to describe an oral tradition that is not as responsible to the reason as is the written word. By 1649, in *The Tenure of Kings and Magistrates*, the real villains of the piece will be the venal preachers, including Stephen Marshall himself. The beginnings of that critique are here, and so is the recognition that zeal can move too easily into "inconsiderate zeal."

Rhetorical zeal is an energy essential to the early stages of a revolution. As the movement matures and assumes power the possibilities of corruption of that zeal increase; the need for rational control becomes greater. For Milton, the emblem and mode of rational truth is the perused, printed word. There is, of course, no hint of doubt of Scripture's simple and obvious veracity. But the holiness of the Word must be checked out in every dependent instance. This may seem a contradiction to us; it is not for Milton. As in the *Christian Doctrine*, the absolute veracity of Scripture and the absolute need to confirm that veracity will stand together:

On the one hand, having taken the grounds of my faith from divine revelation alone, and on the other, having neglected nothing which depended on my own industry, I thought fit to scrutinize and ascertain for myself.

I deemed it therefore safest and most advisable to compile for myself, by my own labour and study, some original treatise which should be always at hand, derived solely from the word of God itself, and executed with all possible fidelity.

The offers of God were all directed, not to an indolent credulity, but to constant diligence, and to an unwearied search after truth.

Since we are ordered *to prove all things*, and since the daily progress of the light of truth is productive far less of disturbance to the Church, than of illumination and edification. . . .

It is my particular advice that every one should suspend his opinion on whatever points he may not feel himself fully satisfied, till the evidence of Scripture prevail, and persuade his reason into assent and faith.

Neither adopt my sentiments, nor reject them, unless every doubt has been removed from your belief by the clear testimony of revelation.[13]

In the antiprelatical tracts, Milton establishes the symbiotic relationship of reason and faith. He sustains his belief in that relationship throughout his career—in the *Christian Doctrine* and in the three great last poems.

As part of his methodological inquiry in *Of Prelatical Episcopacy*, Milton analyzes the creation of legends. In *Of Reformation*, the focus was on legends that grew into myths of considerable political power: the myth of Beckett, the myth of the Prelate-Martyrs, the myth of No Bishop, No King. These issues were treated as the dangerously forceful political issues that Anglican apologetic had made of them. Here, in the later tract, the legends are easily patronized; Milton attacks them for fostering habits of mind, not for themselves, but as representatives of methodologies and traditions that are dangerous to the exercise of reason and the pursuit of truth. Milton credits "the great honour, and affection" (642) which the brethren bore Polycarpus, [14] but the stories of his miraculous death must be coolly dismantled and dispatched. Polycarpus foretold his death by fire, but, at the stake, the fire will not consume him. He is stabbed, "at which wound such abundance of bloud gusht forth as quencht the fire. By all this relation it appeares not, how the fire was guilty of his death, and then how can his prophesie bee fulfill'd?" (643). Indignation has given way to rather sophisticated dryness. "We grant them Bishops, we grant them worthy men"; we do not grant that the Apostles "alterd their owne decree set downe by St. *Paul,* and made all the *Presbyters* underlings to one Bishop" (644–45). Heresy (645) and foolish legends (646) contributed to making "the tradition of the Church . . . ridiculous . . . disconsenting from the Doctrine of the *Apostles*" (646). The "cloud" or "petty-fog of witnesses, with which Episcopall men would cast a mist before us" (648), has been dispatched. But the war is not over, for "it be the wonted shift of errour, and fond Opinion, when they find themselves outlaw'd by the Bible, and forsaken of sound reason, to betake them with all speed to their old starting hole of tradition, and that wild, and overgrowne Covert of antiquity" (648). "That wild, and overgrowne Covert" is like the rubbish "drawne down from of old to this present" (626) and "the dark, the bushie, the tangled Forrest" (YP, I, p. 569); it is an emblem of error in tradition, disordered and congested.[15] Almost throughout *Of Prelatical Episcopacy*, Milton insists that tradition is suspect; at the very least the tract argues that the good Christian should maintain a defensive alertness when evaluating theological materials outside of Scripture.

There is a correct use of the Fathers, in whose volumes all good scholars should, of course, have read. The Fathers are a measure of the distance from truth! We should read them "not hereby to controule, and new fangle the Scripture, *God* forbid, but to marke how corruption, and *Apostacy* crept in by degrees, and to gather up, where ever wee find the remaining sparks of Originall truth, wherewith to stop the mouthes of our adversaries" (650). We must "take the good which wee light on in the Fathers, and set it to oppose the evill which other men seek from them." We must not "turne this our discreet, and wary usage of them into a blind devotion towards them"; we must "hold to the Scriptures against all antiquity" (650). Few would have disagreed with this last statement. But almost no one would have insisted on the Fathers as a text from which to learn how error has crept into the Christian tradition. It is not, therefore, enough to say that Milton calls for the proper uses of tradition and decries the wrong ones. His suspicions and hostility are too pronounced. The whole, elsewhere nearly sacred, corpus of traditional writings on the doctrine and discipline of Christianity is to be approached with a caution born of the conviction that much of that corpus is spurious, superficial, or just plain wrong.

There is little of Milton's customary spaciousness in *Of Prelatical Episcopacy*. The confident debater moves briskly through his self-appointed tasks, and the tract closes quickly and simply. It issues one last warning, that the acceptance of episcopacy logically implies the acceptance of Roman Catholicism. The admission of one nonscriptural tenet opens "a broad passage for a multitude of Doctrines that have no ground in Scripture, to break in upon us" (651). The Gospel mentions only two ecclesiastical orders, bishops (presbyters) and deacons. To deny this is to oppose "the offals, and sweepings of antiquity" to "the sacred verity of Saint *Paul*" (651). Christ's Word is not to be denied or altered. In a final stout dismissal of authorities often and reverently invoked by the prelatical party, Milton celebrates the Word against words, words, words:

And this shall bee our *righteousnes*, our ample warrant, and strong assurance both now, and at the last day never to be asham'd of, against all the heaped names of Angells, and Martyrs, Councells, and Fathers urg'd upon us, if we have given our selves up to be taught by the pure, and living precept of *Gods* word onely, which without more additions, nay with a forbidding of them hath within it selfe the promise of eternall life, the end of all our wearisome labours, and all our sustaining hopes. But if any shall strive to set up his *Ephod*, and *Teraphim* of Antiquity against the brightnesse, and perfection of the *Gospell*, let him feare lest he and his *Baal* be turn'd into *Bosheth*. And thus much may suffice to shew that the pretended *Episcopacy* cannot be deduc't from the *Apostolicall* TIMES.

And the tract ends, its salient polemical point restated simply in the last sentence. But the larger issues of methodology, of the strenuous evaluation of evidence, of inconsiderate zeal, sentimentality, greed, stupidity in the misreading of texts—in effect of the relationship of all knowledge to Scripture—have informed this tract, one of the least attractive and, on the surface at least, one of the least resonant of Milton's prose pieces.

But we pause before final judgment; and we realize that a powerful statement has been made. All theology is a measure of our distance from Scripture. All right doctrine and discipline should return us to Scripture, where we confront the exemplary life and teaching of Christ. Nothing hindering that return is acceptable. Man's role as a thinking, acting creature is to examine, forcefully and unsentimentally, the records of our decay in order to return to the health of Scripture, to repair the ruins of our first parents. There is no substitute for the process, no mystical or mediated way outside Christ. The process itself is not to be distorted into an idolatrous view of the materials or the actors in that process: "let him feare lest he and his *Baal* be turn'd into *Bosheth*." Even here, the apparently shallow image has resonance. As Patrick reminds us, "the Hebrew *Baal* (Lord) in the names of Saul's family was superseded by the contemptuous *bosheth* (shame)" (652, n. 93). Behind that lordship is the idol of the Old Testament, perhaps most obviously the Baal of Jezebel. The passage has contemporary significance. Archbishop Laud is sitting in the Tower, his lordship–idol-derived, idol-directed—has been turned to shame, and will end in his execution. There is a real threat here. More subtle is the glancing reference to Queen Henrietta Marie, who is at this time coming under increasing attack as the "strange woman," the Jezebel who brings false gods into the very palace of the king.[16]

The transformation of *Baal* into *Bosheth* is a final demonstration of the vitality and danger of language.[17] One word literally changes into another: *Esh-baal* becomes *Ishbasheth* (652, n. 93). Lordship based on idolatry becomes shame, archbishops fall, and queens—perhaps—face threats for importing false gods. Under the surface bluster is an ominous density.

In much of Milton's early English prose, there is a present and promised joy at the imminent return to scriptural truth. This aspiring motion upward crosses and braces and in fact reinforces the strong horizontal thrust toward Apocalypse. The overall movement throughout *Of Reformation* is toward the emblem of revelation in the final paragraphs. In Milton's second tract, the joy and the surging forward and upward movement are severely muted; the major motion is the more localized search for method. *Of Prelatical Episcopacy* offers a demonstration of rigorous rational humanity—the search for the way back. Neither frivolous contention nor the contemplation of blood-roses is rational or appropiate or useful to the good Christian. Our reason— which *is* our God-given humanity—is properly engaged in the study of God's Word, the rigorous study of our fall from that Word, and the ways of our return.

State University of New York, Stony Brook

NOTES

An abbreviated version of this paper was delivered at the section on Milton's prose during the MLA meetings in Houston, 30 December 1980.

1. Throughout this essay, I cite J. Max Patrick's edition of the tract, in *Complete Prose Works of John Milton*, ed. Don M. Wolfe et al. (New Haven, 1953–), I, pp. 618–52. The text specifies page numbers for quotations. It refers to other prose works in the Yale edition (YP) with volume number and page.
2. This is curious, since only Almoni specifically attacked Milton as "the late unworthy Authour of a book entitaled *Of Reformation*" (sig. A4). Almoni's pomposity, his adjuration to Milton to check Fevardentius (ibid.), and his claim to the advantage of being older (sig. B4), all seem to me incitements to which Milton would normally have responded. Is it time to reopen G. W. Whiting's hypothesis that Almoni was answering *Of Prelatical Episcopacy?* See *Milton's Literary Milieu* (Chapel Hill, 1939), pp. 293–94; and J. Max Patrick's comments (YP, I, p. 619).
3. At this time, both words were used chiefly to describe Laudian ceremony. Among other examples of language commandeered for polemical uses are, on the Anglican side: "precisian," "fanatic," "enthusiast"; on the Puritan side, we find "firebrand," "incediary," "scandal."
4. *Vox Hibernae or Rather the voyce of the Lord from Ireland in A Sermon Preached in St. Peters Westminster 22 Dec. 1641.* Thomason's manuscript in the British Library copy: "a disavowed and most false coppie."
5. *The Character Of An Oxford Incendiary* ([26 April] 1645), p. 4.
6. John Vicars, *Gods Arke Overtopping the Worlds Wares, Or the Third Part of the Parliamentary Chronicle* ([Dec.] 1645), p. 153.
7. No. 34 (6–13 December 1645), p. 271.

8. No. 113 (10–17 December 1645), p.895.

9. Don M. Wolfe and William Alfred, *Of Reformation*, YP, I, p. 617 n.

10. Eusebius, *The History of the Church* (Baltimore, 1967), p. 227 (bk. V, chap. xx, sec. 2 and 3).

11. See, for example, L. Wemocke, *Beaten Oyle for the Lamps of the Sanctuarie* . . . (1641), sig. B; Richard Hooker, *Of the Laws of Ecclesiastical Polity*, 2 vols. (London, 1907), II, 21–22 (bk. V, chap 3).

12. Cf. the Nativity ode, line 28. Behind the image is, of course, the great passage from Isaiah vi, 1–13.

13. All quotations of the preface to the *Christian Doctrine* derive from *John Milton: Complete Poetry and Major Prose*, ed. Merritt Y. Huges (New York, 1957), pp. 900–02.

14. A gesture toward the passage cited above from *The History of the Church*, p. 227.

15. Cf. George Herbert's "dark and shadie grove" in "H. Baptism" and the "bushie grove" in "Faith." See *The Works of George Herbert*, ed. F. E. Hutchinson (Oxford, 1959), pp. 43, 51. Spenser's Error is of course relevant.

16. J. P. Kenyon notes that in this period Roman Catholic activity in the king's own household was considerable: "Priests celebrated mass daily without the least pretense of concealment, while the Jesuits, the bogeymen of all honest Protestants, were particularly active. . . . Laud warned Charles of the danger from 'the queen's party', but short of repudiating his wife there was little he could do." *The Stuarts* (London, 1973), p. 79. After 1641 the queen's influence on policy grew and so did the opposition to her.

17. My colleague Carole Kessner has pointed out to me the quite sophisticated verbal play. In the Old Testament, *Bosheth* means: shame, blushing; ignominy; an idol (*Hebrew-English Lexicon of the Bible* [New York, 1975], p. 34). The idol is humiliated and yet becomes what it always was.

ALLEGORICAL POETRY
IN MILTON'S LUDLOW MASK

Kathleen M. Swaim

M ILTON'S *Mask Presented at Ludlow Castle* is allegorical poetry, and in important ways it is about allegorical poetry. It makes available definitions, guidelines, and processes of its literary modes, poetry and allegory, and has built into it the bases of its own poetic which also imposes upon readers the special ways in which it must be read. *Comus* provides at once a special and unique Miltonic performance and also evidence to support generalizations about Milton's continuing poetic practice.

I am using *allegory* in its normal handbook sense of a narrative in which abstractions are given concrete forms in order to make a moral or other thesis interesting and persuasive. Like other allegories and other masques, *Comus* is a highly episodic sequence of events, and the individual episodes recapitulate the elements of a core idea and device. Allegorical settings, agents, and actions (both general and particular) invite interpretation on the horizontal lines of continued metaphor and on a vertical scale of concretion and abstraction. Individual details are sometimes charmingly specific, sometimes soaringly general and spiritual, but regularly multiple. There is a continuing mutually vitalizing rhythm of interaction of higher and lower possibilities whose process as well as goal is didactic and edifying.

I am also using *allegory* as Michael Murrin has defined it to include the Renaissance equation of allegory with poetry itself.[1] The poet translates inexpressible truth received through divine inspiration and his own exercises in learning, contemplation, and memory into tropological figures. Through tropes the poet forces his audience to cooperate in the creation of invisible moral standards. By the analogy of poetry as man's myth and the universe (Logos) as God's myth, the poet can be simultaneously precise in his images and mystical in his themes; his fictions address the most comprehensive truths. Two of the poet's principal functions are as a repository of his society's memory and as a prophet who, on the basis of his remembered vision, chides and guides future conduct. The audi-

167

ence re-creates the poet's truth in themselves and themselves in truth—
hence poetry's soaring and provocative self-definition and moral reformation. The creative act, the verbal structure, the cooperative exegesis, the
universe itself are radically allegorical. In these terms allegory equates
with poetry itself; and against a background of such implications, Milton
can speak of making himself "a true poem" in *Apology for Smectymnuus*.
Scores of passages from Milton's poetry and prose demonstrate that this
theory speaks directly to Milton's sense of his poetic creations and poetic
role. It is my purpose to examine the ways in which that theory and its
practice are figured forth in *Comus*.

I am concerned throughout the following study with the overlap-
ping of poetry and allegory. *Poetry* is defined as the verbal processes
and structures which interrelate the fictional givens and images with the
themes they carry and provoke or entice readers to explore and articulate. Poetry for Milton may be described as an incarnational action
interrelating images and themes, just as literary imagination—both in
the author's making and in the reader's receiving and remaking of
poetry—suggests its spiritual analogue. Poetry and imagination are inseparable from Logos and grace, which they variously figure forth. A
central theme in Milton's early as well as late poems is thus the nature
of poetry itself.

Robert Adams has voiced the distress of a number of readers of
Comus criticism, if not of *Comus* itself, when he complains of critical
overreading, of "overloading the allegory, probing too deeply into the
background of the imagery, and enlarging upon the incidental implications of secondary concepts at the expense of the work's total structure."[2]
The present study seeks to relieve such distress by addressing the "total
structure" as focused on the theme of poetry/allegory. Keeping the varied
evidence within a duly proportioned design, it recognizes that Adams's
overloading, probing, and enlarging are audience actions inseparable
from the theme of the masque and even one kind of testimony to the
effectiveness of Milton's structure of layered ideas and the questing implicit in such a structure. C. L. Barber seems to me on more productive
ground than Adams and than the critics Adams takes to task (A. S. P.
Woodhouse, Cleanth Brooks and John Enward Hardy, D. C. Allen) when
he calls attention to an opening-up or reaching quality of *Comus*'s artistry
and to "the systematic grids of Renaissance thinkers" which "the masque
keeps moving in and out of."[3] The allegorical grids and the Platonic
opening up provide the foundations of the present examination of allegorical poetry in *Comus*.

I

We must begin with simple matters, with Barber's grids, and specifically with the givens of the masque genre and the masque occasion, and therefore also with allegory as it is understood in the rhetorical tradition. At its most basic, allegory is an exercise in mediating between levels of concretion and abstraction, emphasizing now one, now the other, suggesting and illuminating now one, now the other, in order to present both with sufficient simultaneity to allow the audience to transcend and thereby redeem their own immediate concrete experience and rootedness in the experiential and to ratify the abstract claims of their minds and spirits, the aspirations of their imagination and faith. Rosemond Tuve has put the matter well in terms of the operation of the images when she speaks of "the constantly possible double reference of two equally but differently real worlds." She notes further that these images do not offer description or argument, but revelation: "the Lady does not represent but presents Virtue."[4]

The textual givens of the masque occasion provide the foundation of an allegorical continuum whose layers build into the experience of *Comus* a process of questing for thematic equivalents that is the audience's analogue of the masque's main action or hinge, what Barber calls "opening up." We cannot receive this (or any) masque rightly without the appropriate factual, geographical, historical information. In this case, we must know that the earl of Bridgewater is being installed as lord president of Wales, that Wales is (or was) largely woodland, that Ludlow Castle shines as a palace of light against that background, that the earl has at least three children of particular sexes and ages, and that Henry Lawes is in the employ of the earl's household. Once such matters are in hand we may proceed to "read" with thematic resonances. Henry Lawes then layers into music maker, music teacher, teacher, guide, friend of poets; thus, as our interpretations climb the ladder into higher and older literary, mythic, and spiritual rungs, Lawes becomes simultaneously shepherd-pastor, Orpheus, Hermes, attendant spirit, agent of the divine, mediator between human and divine and between earth and heaven. When the Second Brother identifies Thyrsis as "my father's Shepherd sure"(493),[5] the audience must respond to the implicit layering with acknowledgment of the charming artfulness. The lines which follow confirm and explore the resonances of the figure more fully:

Elder Brother: Thyrsis? Whose artful strains have oft delay'd
The huddling brook to hear his madrigal,

And sweeten'd every musk rose of the dale.
How cam'st thou here good Swain? hath any ram
Slipt from the fold or young Kid lost his dam,
Or straggling wether the pent flock forsook?
How couldst thou find this dark sequester'd nook?
Spirit: O my lov'd master's heir and his next joy,
I came not here on such a trivial toy
As a stray'd Ewe, or to pursue the stealth
Of pilfering Wolf; not all the fleecy wealth
That doth enrich these Downs, is worth a thought
To this my errand, and the care it brought.

(494–506)

The "artful strains" of Lawes as Orpheus in Shropshire lead into a series of variations on pastoral motifs and possibilities that make both immediate and transcendent what pastoral has traditionally incorporated. If we do not equate the dramatis personae with the ram, young kid, dam, and straggling wether of the Elder Brother's speech, we must do so when the Attendant Spirit speaks, despite his denials. That difference in interpretation is the key to the role of the Attendant Spirit: he leads his immediate flock's and the audience's interpretations into literary and otherwise higher prospects and thereby redeems their minds and their experience through the exercise of imagination and memory. Thyrsis is precisely in quest of the strayed ewe that is Alice Egerton and the stealthy, pilfering wolf that is Comus. Such interpretative actions variously gratify the audience, rewarding participation in the processes of the art with intellectual satisfaction—wonder, exercised ingenuity, and "getting the point"— with aesthetic (which is also spiritual) satisfaction, an exercise in the play and joy of artful, soaring complexity. As tutelary daemon, the Attendant Spirit specializes in teaching allegorical methods and ends.

Two of the mythological analogues of the Attendant Spirit, Orpheus and Hermes, deserve further notice as amplifying the role and theme of poetry in A Mask. Orpheus, son of the Muse Calliope, provides the archetypal pattern of the poet; his wondrous and legendary song could control nature, persuade even deity, and defy mortality. In the lines just cited, Thyrsis has affected the huddling brook and the musk rose; he is one "Who with his soft Pipe and smooth-dittied Song / Well knows to still the wild winds when they roar, / And hush the waving Woods" (86–88). Thyrsis' role in the narrative also derives variously from Hermes in The Odyssey and in Greek mythology. Hermes is Zeus' herald, protector of divine property, speaker of truth (but not necessarily the whole truth), maker of treaties, promoter of commerce, maintainer of travelers' ways on all the world's roads, and inventor of the lyre, the reed pipe, fire, astronomy, the musical scale, and certain forms of divination.[6] Edgar Wind supplies a concise commentary on Hermes' roles as viewed by the Neoplatonists:

Not only was Mercury the shrewdest and swiftest of the gods, the god of eloquence, the skimmer of clouds, the psychopompos, the leader of the Graces, the mediator between mortals and gods bridging the distance between earth and heaven; to humanists Mercury was above all the "ingenious" god of the probing intellect, sacred to grammarians and metaphysicians, the patron of lettered inquiry and interpretation to which he had lent his very name . . . , the revealer of secret or "Hermetic" knowledge, of which his magical staff became a symbol. In a word, Hermes was the divine mystagogue.[7]

Virtually every detail in these two lists may serve as an entree to interpretation of the Attendant Spirit and his functions within the themes and narrative of *Comus*.

Several of the Attendant Spirit's roles are available to the audience of *Comus* in costuming alone, for at the conclusion of the first scene he exchanges his "sky robes spun out of *Iris'* Woof" for "the Weeds and likeness of a Swain / That to the service of this house belongs" (84–85). He is both musician and "Mountain watch" (89). He can assume mortal forms or invisibility, a "viewlessness" that serves both the masque's change of scenes and his mediation of abstract themes. Comus assumes a carefully paralleled pastoral disguise in the following scene—Comus is characteristically an imitator—with this crucial difference: although the Attendant Spirit is really capable of varied forms, Comus only appears to be a shepherd to eyes that have been cheated and bleared by his illusionary art. It is Comus' nature to exert constant pressure downward and toward things at the expense of spirit. Even his art has physical form as dust or confetti. The Attendant Spirit is the true pastor, and assumes form in order to present truth and to guide others to transcend experience and form; he is also true poet, true teacher, both muser and Muse. Comus is the deceiver who imitates true forms, true vision, true art. He bemuses and amuses. He insists on the validity of mere forms and unredeemed experience.

A wide array of evidence from *Comus* could be cited to demonstrate that the allegorical continuum or the pattern of layered grids of interpretation dominates its data and its imagery. Layered domains of "several government" (25) enforce the continuum between mythological and human from the Attendant Spirit's first words, moving downward from

"*Jove's* Court" (1)—"where those immortal shapes / Of bright aerial Spirits live inspher'd" (2–3)—to Neptune's sway (18), to the "new-entrusted
Scepter" (36) of "A noble Peer of mickle trust and power" (31), the earl of
Bridgewater. There is a layering of light in the stars and candle of lines
97–98, and a hierarchy of sound in lines 547–60. "Hidden strength" is of
heaven and of the chaste person (417–20). "Another country" contrasts
with "this soil" (631–32), and the sword with "Far other arms" (611–12).
The shepherds' dance gives way to Mercury's between 957 and 958.
Instances are varied and constant, the more so because *Comus* is a
masque in which the poetry, more than the props, is multimedial.

A further extended example, this time from setting rather than character, will make the same and additional points. The woods of *A Mask*
point now to Welsh groves and now to Spenserian forests of delusive and
entangling moral and spiritual pilgrimage. As the goal of such a journey,
the great hall of Ludlow Castle with its festive assembly points both to
parental home and to heavenly mansions, both to the inaugural celebration and to participation in the supernal community of realized virtue.
The setting is chiefly rural and natural. It is the western reaches of the
western isle, Wales and Shropshire, where pastures and woodlands shift
from fact to poetry: pastures supply grounding for the varied pastoral
possibilities; woodlands suggest and are measured by the woods of Error
in Spenser's *Faerie Queene* (I, i) and Dante's "*selva selvaggia*" (*Inferno*, I,
5). Cited in numerous epithets early in the masque, such woods become a
metaphor (or inherit the metaphor they are) for human life, the earthly,
mortal condition. Woods and mortality are primarily dark and darkly
viewed, but the geography is not without its healing liquid element,
factually and mythically represented in Severn/Sabrina, whose layering,
like that of Comus/woods/error, conflates setting and character. We may
if we wish read Severn/Sabrina/healing liquid as explicitly Christian baptism, but we must not neglect the natural facts, a nature that redeems and
is redeemed. In daylight and in company the Lady perceives "the kind
hospitable woods" (187), but alone and at night she experiences "the blind
mazes of this tangl'd wood" (181). The difference between the two perceptions is light, and light is what the Attendant Spirit mediates, as his
light in a different sense (his vision, memory, literary resources, and
ability to transcend experience) makes possible the call to Sabrina for
rescue. Setting, character, and theme participate in the allegorical continuum. A certain moral ambivalence is inseparable from the things of experience by their very physical nature. As one who is alive, the Lady cannot
avoid being a traveler in the woods and thus cannot avoid encounters with
Comus, who represents experience and the pressures that experience be

accepted as an end in itself. Rightly apprehended, such experiences are (as ever) tests of faith, tests that must be passed for graduation to a higher class—to redemptive vision, to faith, to allegorical-poetic perception. As the Attendant Spirit points out, "some there be that by due steps aspire / To lay their just hands on that Golden Key / That opes the Palace of Eternity" (12–14). Setting in *Comus* participates in a spatial continuum and in a temporal continuum. It looks from earth to heaven and from heaven to earth; it looks backward to the literary tradition, its golden age and golden social and moral norms, and it looks forward to eternity, when such ideals can be fully and transcendently realized. It exercises memory and judgment to perceive the comparative alignments and to assess contrasts as a basis for moral and spiritual choice. As we shall see more fully below, such continua embody the roles, processes, and lessons of the allegorical poet; memory and judgment are especially important both within and without the masque, both in the narrative and in the audience's experience of it.

A closer look at Ludlow Castle will anticipate several later observations. Ludlow Castle supplies the setting which contrasts with the rural scene. Moral choice is obviated when the Attendant Spirit makes the contrast of geography and theme explicit between "this cursed place" (939) and "holier ground" (943):

> I shall be your faithful guide
> Through this gloomy covert wide,
> And not many furlongs thence
> Is your Father's residence.   (944–47)

The final phrase here deserves comparison with Milton's conflation of the houses of Manoa and God in *Samson Agonistes* and the resonating contrast between the temple at Jerusalem ("thy Father's house," IV, 552) and the Son's "Mother's house" (IV, 639) in *Paradise Regained*. When a latter-day audience recalls the biblical basis of Milton's later poetry, it follows the memory model which the Attendant Spirit inculcates in his Bridgewater pupils. *Comus* carefullly eschews the explicitly biblical tradition in favor of the classical, but the purport is the same. It may be that at the climax of *Comus* the earl of Bridgwater's Ludlow residence is more immediate to the audience's consciousness than the palace of eternity as the place of safety, rescue, celebration, joy, and reunion, but in giving temporal and spatial form to the larger meaning, Ludlow Castle also tests and rewards the audience's success in processing the allegorical continuum that the *Mask* has so carefully built to unify abstract masque theme and concrete masque occasion.

II

The allegorical continuum exercises in its audience that facet of poetry that may be variously labeled as imagination, playfulness, openness or receptiveness to possibilities of interpretation beyond the obvious. It is invitational, provocative, creative. Comus and Comus' awareness function at the bottom of (or even outside of) such a laddered continuum; indeed, his raison d'être is a denial that such a continuum exists, a denial of allegory and true poetry. His function within the masque is to allow the Lady—as outside the masque it is to allow the audience—to define and explore the inexhaustible alternative to himself and his lack of vision. We measure his lies against a standard of truth that we at once remember and create; we measure the liar against the aspirant toward truth, and ourselves become successful aspirants. Such measurement exercises the judgment of the audience. Judgment operates to explore and thus go beyond the poet's tropes and analogues; it operates within the allegorical continuum to sort out the varied layers as lower or higher, less or more inclusive, more or less tangible or mundane. The structures that invite judgment are part of the subtle equipment through which the poet compels the audience to cooperate in the creation of moral norms and therefore also of spiritual aspiration. The largest figures of contrast and the principal focus of judgment are Comus and the Lady. Verbal and stylistic evidence of this dichotomy of character should repair some faults previous commentators have found with the art of A Mask and add insight into the nature and operations of the central theme of allegorical poetry.

Since the eighteenth century, a number of critics have echoed all or part of Thomas Warton's evaluation: "Comus is a suite of Speeches, not interesting by discrimination of character; not conveying a variety of incidents, nor gradually exciting curiosity; but perpetually attracting attention by sublime sentiment, by fanciful imagery of the richest vein, by an exuberance of picturesque description, poetic allusion, and ornamental expression."[8] I shall not undertake to argue the absolute individuality of each of the speakers in A Mask, but it is necessary to take issue on the very artful, and indeed highly "interesting," discrimination between the characters of the Lady and Comus. The former attracts attention with "sublime sentiment," he with "fanciful imagery," rich, exuberant, and picturesque. Most of the textual evidence speaks to this contrast: the two differ nearly as much in their views and voices as in the moral positions underlying their language. To illustrate their divergence in large and small matters, I shall linger on two comprehensive patterns of imagery, speech, and attitude: the contrasts explicit in frequent citations of light and nature.

Both Comus and the Lady speak repeatedly of the facts and forms and sources of light. Light is a matter of theme, setting, character, dramaturgy, and even plot. For Comus, "daylight . . . makes sin" (126); the "telltale" sun (141) is a "blabbing Eastern scout" (138). Comus voices "welcome" to "Joy and Feast, / Midnight shout and revelry, / Tipsy dance and Jollity" (102–04). Such dance contrasts dramatically and thematically with the Bridgewater's stately inaugural ball late in the masque, as the early "riotous and unruly noise" (92–93) of Comus and his rout contrasts with the Lady's song to Echo. Closely paralleling Comus' line 102, the Lady exclaims her "welcome" to "pure-ey'd Faith, white-handed Hope . . . And thou unblemish't form of Chastity" (213–15). In a parody of religion and a reversal of moral daylight, Comus is one of the "vow'd Priests" (136) of the "Goddess of Nocturnal sport" (128). He speaks of night as the time "when the Dragon womb / Of *Stygian* darkness spits her thickest gloom, / And makes one blot of all the air" (131–33). In Comus' speech and vision, the world of things dominates, especially as minutely apprehended by the senses. He is often artful, but his art relies on gay wit, tinkling alliteration, and detailed sensuous imagery. His language is characteristically and charmingly specific and experientially alive. He is a realist, a sensualist, and a parodist.

The Lady's view of night contrasts with Comus' in tone and psychological tenor. Where Comus is visual and tactile, the Lady is visionary and sublime. Where his heaven is near and low and closed, hers opens, soars, beckons. She speaks of "the grey-hood'd Ev'n" which "Like a sad Votarist in Palmer's weed / Rose from the hindmost wheels of *Phoebus'* wain" (188–90). In contrast to her apprehensions of light, darkness is "envious" (194), night thievish (195) and threatening. Her accusations against darkness reverse Comus' complaints against light:

> Why shouldst thou, but for some felonious end,
> In thy dark lantern thus close up the Stars,
> That nature hung in Heav'n, and fill'd their Lamps
> With everlasting oil, to give due light
> To the misled and lonely Traveller?   (196–200)

To Comus, night is "empty-vaulted" (250); to the Lady, night, like the Echo it contains, resounds heaven's harmonies (243). When Comus claims, "We that are of purer fire / Imitate the Starry choir" (111–12), he means only and quite literally that both groups come out at night to mark or pass the time. Comus' later image of light makes the point well. He judges ore and gems as "all-worshipt" (719) and illustrates nature's bounty with the prospect that

> th' unsought diamonds
> Would so emblaze the forehead of the Deep,
> And so bestud with Stars, that they below
> Would grow inur'd to light, and come at last
> To gaze upon the Sun with shameless brows.   (732–36)

The Lady's inexhaustible light source is quite differently based and apprehended. She is a votarist of "the Sun-clad power of Chastity" (782), an investiture that speaks for both her worship and her vision or light. The virtuous Lady is herself a form and source of light and an analogue that transcends mere cosmic equivalents. She can see "By her own radiant light, though Sun and Moon / Were in the flat Sea sunk" (374–75). The Elder Brother indirectly explains her difference from Comus:

> He that has light within his own clear breast
> May sit i' th' center, and enjoy bright day.
> But he that hides a dark soul and foul thoughts
> Benight'd walks under the midday Sun;
> Himself is his own dungeon.   (380–84)

The Lady is able to say, "I see ye visibly," to faith, hope, and chastity; such vision confirms her belief in "the Supreme good" and its ministering guardians. Through a sudden change in dramaturgical lighting, the masque's cosmos ratifies the Lady's faith: "I did not err, there does a sable cloud / Turn forth her silver lining on the night" (223–24).

Comus and the Lady also provide radically contrasting views of nature, both as Natura and as human traits and possibilities. To the Lady, nature is "most innocent" (762) and a "good cateress" of "Nature's full blessings" (764, 772). To Comus, nature is merely "the unexempt condition / By which all mortal frailty must subsist" (685–86). He appeals to weariness and refreshment, the Lady to "truth and honesty" (691). To Comus nature is bounteous (710), equated with plant, animal, and even mineral life. He would have the Lady worship his "nature," but such service, even as he defines it, means enslavement to surcharged fertility. To Comus, the highest good "Consists in mutual and partak'n bliss" (741), but this the Lady assesses as slavery to youth, flesh, and time. Comus claims that without such service as he proposes, "Th' all-giver would be / Unthank't, would be unprais'd" (723), but the Lady's hierarchical judgment teaches her how "the giver would be better thank't, / His praise due paid" (775–76). Her hierarchy is cosmic as well as moral, spatial as well as religious:

> for swinish gluttony
> Ne'er looks to Heav'n amidst his gorgeous feast,
> But with besotted base ingratitude
> Crams and blasphemes his feeder.   (776–79)

She measures his low, closed way of seeing; she judges his horizontal measurement against her own vertical one. Comus advises the Lady to think about the meaning of nature and of her beauty and gifts; she does, but comes to conclusions quite different from his. Because he sees and values only immediate nature, he is unable to judge even that soundly. He misreads (as have some critics) the Lady's active virtue and rejection of the merely sensuous as cold, passive insensitivity. He misreads liberty, that clarion call of all Milton's verse and prose, as license and licentiousness. He challenges her patience, the supreme Miltonic and Christian virtue, with an insistence upon the priority of easy convenience here and now. His nature is rife and ready; her human nature aspires to the divine it incorporates. Both would have the external form reflect the internal will, spirit, and mind; but for Comus this is signified by the brute form charactered in the face, whereas for the Lady the body may at last turn all to spirit.

The voices of Comus and the Lady necessarily differ radically. Morally and epistemologically it could not be otherwise when their uses of language and their views of nature and creation are so irreconcilable. The textual evidence regularly links Comus with the perversion of reason that is caused by (and in turn causes) idolatry of the experiential. He excels his mother Circe by transforming the minds of his victims even more than their outward forms and by destroying their capacity to see themselves and to remember their "native home." He is an intellectual juggler who can bolt vicious arguments (760), charm judgment, and obtrude false rules (757–59). He has the "power to cheat the eye with blear illusion, / And give it false presentments" (155–56); he speaks 'well-plac't words of glozing courtesy, / Baited with reasons not unplausible" (161–62). He has, as Thyrsis says, "Many baits and guileful spells / To inveigle and invite the unwary sense / Of them that pass unweeting by the way" (537–39). Comus represents rationalization, self-interest, dependence upon experience that looks by definition to the past rather than forward and upward; he expresses the sensuality, passivity, and despair that attend such vision. Comus' experience conduces to unconsciousness as surely as the Lady's faith aspires to heightened consciousness. He argues from and for the rational and experiential; his is the school of hard knocks. The text has much to say of his oblivion and her spiritual ecstasy.

Critics who have found *Comus* wanting as mimetic drama have been answered in recent studies recognizing the demands of the masque genre. Some critics have faulted the style of *Comus* on the same and different grounds. D. C. Allen, for example, finds that *Comus* fails in what he calls "the higher compromise" of sources, artistry, and themes; it is to him aesthetically unsatisfying, "a patchwork of styles," "a melange of various tendencies and styles that never merge into anything intensely organic."[9] E. M. W. Tillyard has complained of *Comus* as a sequence of poetical experiments; he objects to both "the mixture of styles" and "the fluctuations of style."[10] Tillyard measures by his own emotional reactions and by the norms of contemporary drama. If we assume that individual textual units are to be measured by the governing themes of the whole and that a central theme of *Comus* is the nature and process of poetry itself, an examination of style or styles becomes telling evidence in support of the masque's unity.

A later section of this essay fully examines true poetry and the roles of the true poet. For the present, we should note that Comus takes on the shape of what Murrin calls the pseudopoet, that is, the versifier who exploits the commonplaces of his own day and ignores his poem's and his audience's relationship to past and future and his own roles relative to memory and prophecy. The traditional carpe diem song on Comus's lips is thus a multiple definition of his character: In Murrin's words: "True poetry combines *sophia* and *techne*, wisdom and art; false poetry has only *techne*, images without vision, art without inspiration. It is not the child of Mnemosyne" (p. 93). Such phrases describe the quality of Comus' mode precisely and measure it against the appropriate moral and Platonic standard. It is not accident or futile experiment that Comus is, in Tillyard's words, "the livest character in the masque," or that his speech is full, opulent, and hyperbolic (p. 69). Nor is it chance, that, as Allen obseves, "the Lady has most of the metaphors" (p. 39), or that Tillyard can at once praise and fault the Lady for "the exquisite circumlocutions of the pastoral," "a delightful conceit," "lines which in their beauty can be detached with no loss of value from their histrionic setting," and "rapturous meditation" (pp. 68–69). These terms precisely describe the characters' modes and roles. The problem lies in these critics' failure to recognize that such evidence supports the masque's coherence of art and theme. Experience is often lovely, enchanting, vitalizing, but it should not be allowed to exhaust or confine the human condition and human possibilities. As exclusive vehicle of perception it embodies and embrutes and becomes "the unexempt condition / By which all mortal frailty must subsist" (685–86).

C. L. Barber looks more closely at the text and design, but errs also in misconstruing what is an artistic feat of no small skill. He finds "a failure of rhythm" in Comus' speeches:

Much of his part seems too shallow rhythmically for the impact it should have, too stilted, as though Milton's auditory imagination could not risk getting more deeply involved. Milton certainly had a genuine artistic problem here; his whole design would not admit of Comus' capturing our imagination fully. His solution, so far as he does solve the difficulty, is to allow his god to revel, to begin each speech strongly, often beautifully, with appeals to the traditional sanctions, youth, feast, and nature's vital dance. Then he spoils it. (P. 61)

If Comus and what he represents were to capture our imaginations fully, we would be damned. The risk of full involvement with him is our spiritual challenge, not Milton's artistic faltering. Milton does not "spoil" his characterization; he serves his didactic themes. He deliberately makes Comus an anticlimactic character. Anticlimax is the inevitable rhythm of unredeemed experience. As an immortal, Comus has one thing to do and he keeps doing it again and again. But the human condition is dynamic for all but those who embrace the bestial alternative and abjure pilgrimage to "their native home." Comus and his adherents give up their claims to humanity and to the spiritual and poetic exercises of judgment and memory. By contrast, the Lady engages in creative, not merely imitative, acts and verbal acts. She creates song and vision, not mere noise and wit. Within the flux of experience she achieves self-definition that is at once dynamic and transcendent and that ratifies human access to the divinity it can incarnate.

III

The role of the true poet in *A Mask* is shared by the Lady and the Attendant Spirit. Poetry is, as its Greek etymology makes inescapable, a process of making. That making occurs through a combination of artistic craftsmanship and meditation. To meditate the Muse describes the process in *Lycidas;* to meditate one's rural minstrelsy is the equivalent in *Comus*. Meditation facilitates responsiveness to external stimuli, including nature, the cosmos, and the Muses; meditation makes possible the recognition and representation of the universe and its order. The two halves of the word *uni-verse* nicely combine both oneness and craftsmanship. The higher one climbs on the Neoplatonic ladder of perception, the more clearly the oneness emerges and the less hidden and distorted the idea by the matter in which it inheres. The meditation that gives access to oneness and vision is, among other things, a chronological process, a stepping outside time's flow which provides a perspective on time and, sometimes, access to the eternal. Its antithesis is the impatient, insistent immediacy that characterizes Milton's masque tempter.

Thyrsis describes to the brothers his meditative process of poetry-making in characteristic pastoral terms. He has learned of Comus and his Homeric Circean background, he says, while and through "Tending my flocks hard by i' th' hilly crofts" (530–31). On the evening in question, when his flocks had been safely enfolded, he recalls:

> I sat me down to watch upon a bank
> With Ivy canopied, and interwove
> With flaunting Honeysuckle, and began,
> Wrapt in a pleasing fit of melancholy,
> To meditate my rural minstrelsy,
> Till fancy had her fill.   (543–48)

Il Penseroso has taught us how to read aright the creative energy and vision of such melancholy; it is an emotion and a condition beyond the awareness of Comus, who can only parody and dismiss it along with "mere moral babble" (807) when he faults the Lady's equivalent as "the lees / And settlings of a melancholy blood" (809–10). Comus assesses the role of fancy in characteristically erotic terms when he proffers the Lady "all the pleasures / That Fancy can beget on youthful thoughts, / When the fresh blood grows lively" (668–70). The Second Brother speaks of "musing meditation" that "most affects / The pensive secrecy of desert cell" (386–87), in reply to the Elder Brother's fuller account of the process:

> And Wisdom's self
> Oft seeks to sweet retired Solitude,
> Where with her best nurse Contemplation
> She plumes her feathers, and lets grow her wings
> That in the various bustle of resort
> Were all to-ruffl'd, and sometimes impair'd.   (375–80)

The final two lines nicely capture a view of experience and its effects; the whole presents a miniature of the masque's themes and major conflict. These related citations illustrate the verbal echoing that gives the masque coherence and exercises the audience's judgment and artistic participation.

More important, they examine in theory what we see in practice as the Lady's poetry-making process in the Echo song. Our first view of the Lady at line 170 finds her in isolation and entangled in the confusion of the woods, a woods rugged enough in themselves but made more rugged and confusing through Comus' imposition of his "Magic dust" (165). In the nocturnal absence of light, the Lady follows her ear as "best guide now" (171) and goes through a process of ratiocination that climbs above real and imposed experiential delusions to issue in her song to Echo. She assesses the misguidedness of the rude worshippers of "bounteous *Pan*," but asks, "O where else / Shall I inform my unacquainted feet / In the blind mazes of this tangl'd Wood?" (179–80). Her phrasing nicely captures the fact and threat of experience. She rightly reconstructs the cause of her separation from her brothers and measures the apparently "thievish Night" (195) against cosmic moral norms which she affirms. At line 205, Comus' magic dust begins to take effect and intrudes a parody of poetic meditation:

> What might this be? A thousand fantasies
> Begin to throng into my memory,
> Of calling shapes and beck'ning shadows dire,
> And airy tongues that syllable men's names
> On Sands and Shores and desert Wildernesses.   (205–09)

Comus' spells intrude upon her processes of intellection, specifically her memory, and seek to substitute experiential fear for transcendent faith. Such thoughts startle but do not astound the Lady, however, and her virtuous mind transcends the threatening occasion to affirm a yet more clarified vision of faith, hope, and chastity and to find increased assurance of "a glist'ring Guardian" (219). Her ratification of faith is confirmed by an access of light from the cosmos dispelling the clouds. Her spirits "new enliv'n'd" (228), she ventures into song. The action is poetic in variously telling ways. Remembering Echo, she shows memory in wholesome, rather than deluded form, for it is a recollection of the literary and mythological past brought to bear upon the present experience in order to transcend it for a future goal and good. It shows a rising above present time and place that puts the rememberer in touch with what is constant in humanity and the cosmos. Echo is a particularly rich agency to invoke for dramaturgical as well as mythological purposes.[11] Like the Lady, that nymph was lost and wandering, and her experience too was translated into transcendent resonance. The Lady's invocation is both an act of memory and hope and an act of self-actualization and faith. In Barber's words, "The act of singing is an exercise of the Lady's integrity; she is internally related, beyond the darkness, to what she looks to and realizes in the song" (p. 53). The call to Echo layers allegorically beyond Echo to the literary and mythological tradition and to the Attendant Spirit and the court of Jove whose ambassador he is. The invocation of Echo will have its counterpart later in the invocation of Sabrina. The link between Echo and the nightingale (234) is recalled when the Attendant Spirit alludes to the Lady herself as "poor hapless Nightingale" (566). All the female figures are in fact forms of the same psyche—Psyche herself (1005) is the final one—and figure forth the Lady's psyche as masques and allegories generally represent ideas and spiritual action.[12] Such fractionating of character is a special kind of echo that reinforces merely verbal interations and further evidences the nature and operations of both poetry and allegory. In its aspiration, elocution, awareness of cosmic resonances, appeal for spiritual ratification and rewarded vision, the Lady's song to Echo is a paradigm of the poet's creative act.

The iterative structural sequence of A Mask provides two later responses to the Lady's act of song that show the moral, poetic, epistemological conflict of the masque and demonstrate the resonant layerings of Echo within the masque's action. Comus' comments immediately following the Lady's song call attention to the religious impression it makes—"Divine" (245), "holy" (246), "sacred" (262), "blest" (268)—but that religion is confined by his linking the goddesslike Lady with Pan (268), by his libidinous vocabulary ("enchanting ravishment," 245; "raptures," 247; "bliss," 263), and by his citation of Circe and the Sirens' music that "would take the prison'd soul, / And lap it in Elysium" (256–57) as "they in pleasing slumber lull'd the sense, / And in sweet madness robb'd it of itself" (260–61). The Lady, though in extreme shift, is not susceptible to Comus' flattery. She does put herself under his guidance, however, when he echoes her reconstruction of her brothers' absence and parodies her own vision in an imitation which also parodies the central quest of the masque. The Lady trusts "the sure guess" of his "well-practic'd feet" (310); she is obliged to accede to the claims of experience. Like the first parents in Paradise Lost (IX, 919, 807–08), the Lady seems to submit to what seems remediless and accepts experience as best guide. Comus' lines are these:

> Their port was more than human, as they stood;
> I took it for a faery vision
> Of some gay creatures of the element
> That in the colors of the Rainbow live
> And play i' th' plighted clouds. I was awe-struck,

And as I past, I worshipt; if those you seek,
It were a journey like the path to Heav'n
To help you find them.   (297–304)

Barber has pointed out that the lines embody "the delight of perfect
imaginative freedom," the more so because the speech is "a downright
lie" (pp. 49–50): "It is as though Comus gave the Lady a subliminal dose
of his potion." Barber goes on to say that "Comus' fabrication opens an
exquisite vista, exactly in the manner of the masque. It is his supreme
moment as a tempter, because a sight of her brothers is just what the
Lady, prisoned from them in darkness, most desires" (p. 50). The temptations and style of Comus are designedly imitative and feed on the
Lady's psyche which they realize and parody, as they are designedly
anticlimactic. Comus is closer to success here in pretending awe than in
asserting his own opportunistic claims in the argument at his palace.
Here he is acting out an echo, and echoes are by definition repetitious
fragments unless, in the hopeful words of the Lady's song, they are
"translated to the skies" (242).

The Lady's song to Echo resonates also to a more distant hillside
where the "glist'ring guardian" Thyrsis meditates his pastoral minstrelsy. From him the Lady's call for help finds a true response that will
eventuate in her salvation. The Attendant Spirit is, even in merely
topographical terms, higher than Comus. Barber has praised the skillful
design of the episode between Thyrsis and the brothers: "It repeats the
movement the Lady has been through from isolation in darkness to an
encounter opening out the situation toward a world of pastoral generosity; but the succor offered the Brothers is real, not Comus' "glozing
Courtesy." We re-experience the threat of intemperance from the perspective of high lawns, in language which cues an active response" (p.
57). The "real" aid to the brothers will become real to the Lady also. If
the assistance the Lady calls for comes indirectly, through agencies
other than those initially posited, it is because this is an occasion of
grace, even of strictly theological grace as described by the Son's question in Book III of *Paradise Lost:*

> man shall find grace;
> And shall grace not find means, that finds her way,
> The speediest of thy winged messengers,
> To visit all thy creatures, and to all
> Comes unprevented, unimplor'd, unsought?   (227–31)

As Comus has judged the Lady's song, so she judges his. Overhear-
ing the rout's "Riot and ill-manag'd Merriment," "wanton dance," and

"swill'd insolence" (172, 176, 178), she assesses the revelry as praise of "the bounteous *Pan*" (176), worship through which "loose unletter'd Hinds" (174) "thank the gods amiss" (177). The gods are wrong, the goals wrong, the worship wrong. The misguidedness lies in Bacchic revelry and worship and in confining the perception of nature to its goat-footed "Panic" form. The error lies in preferring chaos and fecundity (Pan) to order and higher life (Apollo). Pan's pipe creates monochromatic music, enchanting perhaps, but overly simple. Apollo's lyre provides an alternative, polychromatic music. When the Attendant Spirit later describes the revelry to the brothers, he contrasts the woods' "wonted roar" and "barbarous dissonance" (549, 550) with the "sudden silence" (552) and "solemn-breathing sound" (555) of the Lady's song, which

> stole upon the Air, that even Silence
> Was took ere she was ware, and wish't she might
> Deny her nature, and be never more,
> Still to be so displac't. I was all ear,
> And took in strains that might create a soul
> Under the ribs of Death.   (557–62)

Nature's denial of nature in favor of music and poetry keys the moral theme and the definition of poetry, as does the view that poetry is capable of creating a soul in defiance of mortality and the experiential.

The Lady's poetry is clarified and extended in the dialogue with Comus, where she exercises her transcendent speech even as she claims to check its energies:

> Yet should I try, the uncontrolled worth
> Of this pure cause would kindle my rapt spirits
> To such a flame of sacred vehemence,
> That dumb things would be mov'd to sympathize,
> And the brute Earth would lend her nerves, and shake,
> Till all thy magic structures rear'd so high,
> Were shatter'd into heaps o'er thy false head.   (793–99)

The Lady's poetry is muse-begotten and Orphic. The Orpheus image she shares with the Attendant Spirit nicely suggests many points about the role of poetry, especially about the relationship of poetry to nature— Comus' nature in particular. Like Orpheus the Lady controls nature, especially her own human nature. Her poetry equates with "sacred vehemence" as Comus' does with "magic structures." Comus acknowledges the Lady's "superior power . . . not mortal" (801–02), but retreats to dissembling and caviling at her "mere moral babble" (807). He retreats to nature as merely "drooping spirits" (812) to be cured by his potion and "delight / Beyond the bliss of dreams" (812-13). In the words of the Elder Brother, when such erotic dreaming, or its realization,

> Lets in defilement to the inward parts,
> The soul grows clotted by contagion,
> Imbodies and imbrutes, till she quite lose
> The divine property of her first being.   (466–69)

The Elder Brother presents also the alternative to such dreaming— "clear dream and solemn vision" (457)—a matter of morality and spirituality as well as the visionary, and a further articulation of the pattern of poetry-making. Poetry for the Lady is the meditation of rural minstrelsy, an affirmation and rediscovery of "the divine property" within herself, and the mediation of divine idea, order, and harmony. The sincerely chaste soul is doubly served by muselike liveried angels who ward and drive off sin and guilt and who also

> Tell her of things that no gross ear can hear,
> Till oft converse with heav'nly habitants
> Begin to cast a beam on th' outward shape,
> The unpolluted temple of the mind,
> And turns it by degrees to the soul's essence,
> Till all be made immortal.   (458–63)

Converse with the mysteries of the Muses realizes the soul's climb; matter redounds, the soul transcends. The contrast here, as throughout *Comus*, is between the Lady and Comus, beauty and "bold incontinence" (393, 397), the "soul's essence" and "carnal sensualty" (474), between chastity and lewdness, faith and experience, transcendent theme and merely sensuous image, responsive freedom and the tyranny of selfishness and self-servingness. The *Symposium's* and the Neoplatonists' model of aspiration is a figure for poetry as well as for philosophy and religion.

The poetry-making process in *A Mask* consists of an interrelated series of ingredients, including craftsmanship, aspiration, meditation, vision, and translation of vision into experience and experience into vision. The vision admits both echoing and unity/union. Vision descends into matter and, ascending, translates the things of experience into images that include the possibility of their own transcendence. The images of true poets frequently participate in myths remembered from the past and applied to the present. Poetry is thus the recognition of and the making of allegorical continua. The exercise of judgment leads from knowable experience toward the unknowable transcendent. To Milton and others, poetry is the highest model for human growth, which is why the poet is the highest form of the heroic. The poet encompasses culture and leads it to new growth. The Lady in *Comus* figures forth poetry in action. The Attendant Spirit guides the audience securely to the apprehension of and interpretation of the meanings implicit in, but transcending, plot and spectacle. From his long introductory speech to his extended epilogue, the Attendant Spirit guides the audience to a recognition of the moral, philosophical, and spiritual-poetic distinctions between earth and the higher realms from which he comes and to which he returns. Judgment, which is presumed as well as developed in the audience, condemns and rejects Comus and the experiential and affirms and aspires to the transcendent vision the Attendant Spirit shares with the Lady. That moral judgment and consequent choice have not succeeded with critics who succumb to Comus' appeals needs no belaboring. The fault may lie with the unfamiliarity of the masque genre and its ways of presenting, rather than representing, its themes. It may lie with modern attitudes toward memory and the literary tradition, or with modern ears alert to the Siren songs of experience but deaf to the music of the spheres and faith, or with a scientific preference for the evidence of things seen minutely over "the righteousness of God revealed from faith to faith" (Romans i, 17).

IV

Among the functions poets inherit from Homer is the moral education of the audience. Modern students are indebted to Frances Yates as Milton's contemporaries were indebted to Peter Ramus for the recognition that Renaissance education was largely memory training. In making and interpreting allegory, the poet and audience draw on memory to connect abstract ideas and concrete images; the two kinds of meditation put them in newly enlivened touch with ancient values. Significantly, in Hesiod's myth, the Muses are the daughters of Memory (Mnemosyne). In Murrin's words, memory is "the medium of moral value" (p. 86), poetry "a kind of moral and social mnemonics" (p. 77): "Through memory the poet breaks out of the world of time into a kind of extratemporal viewpoint, from which past and future are seen to form different parts of a common human pattern" (p. 84). Memory is thus variously a pedagogical matter, and the textual evidence of *Comus* variously renders it as such. But memory is simultaneously a crucial religious matter; the Hebrew word for faith also means memory, and Christian teaching enjoins the faithful to remember, in particular to remember the promises. Like Bunyan's Christian on the Hill of Difficulty, one can go forward only by going backward to retrieve the scroll on which the promises are written. The paradox of past and future time patterns recurs in the spiritual as in the poetic-rhetorical tradition, recalling the similarly paradoxical interrelationship of type and antitype. Typology is God's allegory, as poetry is man's. God is the poet of the Logos; the human poet is the interpreter and translator between temporal and eternal languages as between images and ideas or between earth and the heavenly equivalents here incarnate. The cosmos in God's image and imagery, as the poetic microcosm is man's imagery and man's answer to the divine patterns of making.

When we turn to *Comus* for evidence of the teaching value of memory, theorizing takes simpler, more direct and telling forms. Looking ahead in summary: the Attendant Spirit teaches the brothers—in fiction as in fact—to understand the process and the rewards of memory through lessons that center on literary texts. A miniature of such instruction occurs when the Elder Brother turns pedagogue to the younger. Since book learning feeds memory and thus vision and faith, it is no accident that Comus consorts with "unlettered hinds." Though regularly given to charming verbal expressions, Comus is the pseudopoet or antipoet who is too impatient and too consumed in sensory immediacy to meditate, to look to the past, to interrelate past and future in a temporal and literary perspective transcending the present.

As noted earlier, each episode of *Comus* reenacts the central themes and illuminates the poetic process in a fashion characteristic of masques and allegoricial poetry. A suggestive instance occurs in the theoretical discussion between the two brothers about their sister's plight, before the Attendant Spirit arrives to focus their energies on the practical realities of Comus and the woods. The Elder Brother seeks a solution through the eyes and therefore light; the younger through ears and therefore sound/music. The younger is more frightened for his sister's safety; the elder is more optimistic. The younger is more aware of and frightened by experience, the elder more informed about the alternative. The Elder Brother chastises his junior's excessive specificity— "Be not over-exquisite / To cast the fashion of uncertain evils" (359– 60)—because too much attention to experience leads to "false alarms of Fear" and "self-delusion" (364–65). "Over-exquisite" nicely describes Comus' threats and mode of speech. Evil and experience are "uncertain," frightening, and delusive unless measured against higher certainties. Like his sister's, the Elder Brother's primary resources are internal; as she relies on spiritual, he depends on educational resources. He apprehends the "hidden strengths" of heaven and the incarnate heavenly (chastity) and presents his case by remembering (re-citing) the fictional analogues of his sister's state, at first in general ("a quiver'd

Nymph," 422), then in specific reference ("the huntress *Dian*," 441, and "that wise *Minerva*," 448). The former is called "fair silver-shafted Queen" (442) and "queen o' th' woods" (446), the latter "unconquer'd Virgin" (448). The Elder Brother calls (re-calls) "Antiquity from the old Schools of *Greece* / To testify the arms of Chastity" (439–40). He seeks to understand the present in terms of the past, in light of the unalterables in the human condition as these are available through memory, education, and poetry. His vision and his delivery soar to Neoplatonic heights of "the soul's essence" (462) and Christian assurance of "A Thousand liveried Angels" (445). His innocence shows through his theorizing—at age twelve, his own wrestlings with the threats of the tangled woods of experience have not yet shadowed and defiled his inward parts—but the process of seeking solutions to immediate problems through inner resources and memory is what the masque as a whole recommends. The Elder Brother's personal process is also pedagogical, and his rightly instructed Younger Brother responds to the lesson as the Ludlow and reading audiences should repond to the inaugural entertainment:

> How charming is divine Philosophy!
> Not harsh and crabbed as dull fools suppose,
> But musical as is *Apollo's* lute,
> And a perpetual feast of nectar'd sweets,
> Where no crude surfeit reigns.   (476–79)

A Mask is charming, divine, musical, perpetually sweet. Those in its audience who fail to respond to its Apollonian resonances and varied orders condemn themselves as dull, foolish, unrefined, and unrefinable. The Elder Brother has recourse to his learning also at lines 341–42 and 604–06. Having delivered and responded to the soaring vision of chastity, the brothers receive direct superhuman assistance and access to further information from the appearance of the liveried Attendant Spirit ("habited like a Shepherd"). The scene reenacts their sister's analogous Echo song.

The Attendant Spirit's arrival presents the brothers and the audience with additional information on the problem and its solution, information which emphasizes the remembered literary tradition, specifically Homer. The problem is Comus. Among others, Rosemond Tuve has spoken with particular eloquence on Comus as Circe's Renaissance son and on the operations and appropriateness of that figure within Milton's masque. Without rehearsing familiar material, I would like to cite several points quickly. As the Attendant Spirit has described him to the

Ludlow audience, Comus "Excels his Mother at her mighty Art" (63) by bestializing victims' "human count'nance, / Th' express resemblance of the gods" (68–69), and rendering them ignorant, vain, and forgetful of their "native home" (cf. "Father's residence" and memory). When the Attendant Spirit later reviews Comus' background for the Egerton brothers, the vocabulary shifts slightly—"weary Traveller" (64) becomes "thirsty wanderer" (524), and "human count'nance" (68) becomes "reason's mintage / Character'd in the face" (529–30). More important, the source of this new information is the poetic tradition of the Greek Homer and such Roman heirs as Ovid and Virgil. The audience has a double access to the memory process in remembering the literary tradition and also in recalling the Attendant Spirit's initial presentation of it 460 lines earlier. The Spirit says to the brothers:

> 'tis not vain or fabulous,
> (Though so esteem'd by shallow ignorance)
> What the sage Poets taught by th' heav'nly Muse
> Storied of old in high immortal verse
> Of dire *Chimeras* and enchanted Isles,
> And rifted Rocks whose entrance leads to hell,
> For such there be, but unbelief is blind.   (513–19)

Verse is high and immortal, its source heavenly, its maker sage, its audience those who can or will believe. In sum, it serves and gives access to remembered truth; it rejects and is rejected by shallow ignorance and blind unbelief.

A *Mask* makes explicit its debt to and radical difference from the Homeric text when the Attendant Spirit cites Moly/Haemony, one solution to the problem of Comus. The Attendant Spirit describes Haemony, that "small unsightly root" "of divine effect" (629–30), "of sovran use / 'Gainst all enchantments" (639–40). Enchantment is throughout the masque the medium of Comus and experience. Haemony is "yet more med'cinal . . . than that *Moly* / That *Hermes* once to wise *Ulysses* gave" (636–37). It is unknown and unvalued "in this soil" (633)–the Shropshire woods, the earth—but true and precious "in another Country" (632), that geography to which the Attendant Spirit and "a certain Shepherd Lad" (619) have access. A Spenserian link of Haemony with Thessaly has led some to conjecture that, in *Comus*, Haemony represents pastoral, as opposed to epic, poetry;[13] in Barber's words, "haemony is made the highest fruit of pastoral learning, the knowledge of simples" (p. 56). Access to health, to safety, to weaponry to "quell the might of hellish charms" (613), to truth, is again via poetry. The Attendant Spirit remembers.

> Care and the utmost shifts
> How to secure the Lady from Surprisal,
> Brought to my mind a certain Shepherd Lad
> Of small regard to see to, yet well skill'd
> In every virtuous plant and healing herb
> That spreads her verdant leaf to th' morning ray.
> He lov'd me well, and oft would beg me sing,
> Which when I did, he on the tender grass
> Would sit, and hearken even to ecstasy,
> And in requital ope his leathern scrip,
> And show me simples of a thousand names,
> Telling their strange and vigorous faculties.   (617–28)

"A certain Shepherd Lad" and the vegetative landscape, the pastoral at its most basic, invoke all the hills and shades where for centuries book-filtered shepherd-poets have sat one with another, making verse that apprehends civilized complexity through the artifice of rustic simplicity. Poetry is radically and well defined as "a knowledge of simples." We know something of the relationship between Milton and Lawes from *Sonnet XIII*, where Milton cites him as "the Priest of *Phoebus'* Choir" (10). Given the economy, even the opportunism, of masque resources for this Ludlow occasion, I would suggest, as others have, that Milton himself is the "certain Shepherd Lad."[14] Translating downward on the scale of abstraction, I would hint that the shepherd's leathern scrip with its thousand simples, suggests something like the poet's commonplace book, researched to answer to (requite) the musical settings supplied by the Bridgewater Thyrsis. But we need not credit such historical speculations to take the larger point, that here as elsewhere, when *Comus'* dramatis personae encounter difficulties that defy solution by ordinary means, they seek and find relief in recourse to poetic means; they turn to the poet, maker of song and verse and heir and mediator of the poetry and learning of the past.

A second occasion for poetic remembering arises when the Attendant Spirit seeks the means to release the motionless Lady from her "stony fetters" (819). He says to the brothers:

> Yet stay, be not disturb'd, now I bethink me,
> Some other means I have which may be us'd,
> Which once of *Meliboeus* old I learnt
> The soothest Shepherd that ere pip't on plains.   (820–23)

"The soothest Shepherd" is cited as "the old Swain" (852) later in the account. The invocation of Spenser is doubly evidenced through that poet's self-styling in the February eclogue of *The Shepheardes Calendar* and through the content imported from *The Faerie Queene* (II, x, 19). The layerings are various and multiple, especially in the literary domain. Milton cites Spenser as Meliboeus, as Spenser had cited himself as Meliboeus and Chaucer as Tityrus, and as Virgil cited himself as Tityrus in conversation with his Meliboeus in his first eclogue. Milton inherits and appropriates Spenser's Sabrina, but probably not without consciousness of Geoffrey of Monmouth, Michael Drayton, and Phineas Fletcher the Elder. The inclusion of these individual names and others suggested in the *Variorum* may raise a critical eyebrow, but the overall thrust calls for concurrence. The poetic realm and tradition are available to the memories of the dramatis personae as to the author and to all of us; poetry is a continuing resource, recourse to which saves us from the difficulties we mortal shepherds and travelers must regularly meet, at moments of special trial or in ordinary striving "to keep up a frail and Feverish being" (8) amid "the rank vapors of this Sin-worn mold" (17).

The audience's memory is exercised in small details within the text as well as in the larger figures and episodes of *A Mask*, not least in the regular processing of individual words, as we have seen, to clarify distinctions between the styles and epistemologies of the major characters in the masque's conflict. The Attendant Spirit's memory, exercised for the brothers' benefit, makes important points about the literary tradition, memory, and imagination. When the Attendant Spirit promises to tell the Ludlow audience "What never yet was heard in Tale or Song / From old or modern Bard, in Hall or Bow'r" (44–45), and proceeds to introduce Comus' parentage, he makes another, similar point for the benefit of the larger audience of Bridgewater celebrants and readers. That point is that the present literary occasion is now to be a part of the audience's memory and memory equipment, a resource when we face our own trials with moral self-definition in defiance of the pressures and delusions of experiential challenges to faith and integrity.

Meliboeus is remembered in order to focus the classical literary tradition upon the immediate problem, but remembering Sabrina also redirects the time dimensions of the action and poetry. Besides the citation of contemporary poetry, the Sabrina figure shifts awareness to what abides—the eternal. Barber addresses the special aptness of Sabrina:

Closer to the Lady's actual condition, and crucial in her rescue, is the figure of Sabrina, perhaps the most remarkable inspiration or revelation of the whole masque. Sabrina is, of course, exactly the sort of local genius looked for in noble entertainments; but Milton's mythopoetic power created almost all her particular qualities, qualities that are exactly, deeply right. (P. 62)

Sabrina is the "guiltless damsel" (829) who "Commended her fair innocence to the flood" (831); she is the Severn and its water nymph. Like Lycidas, who became the "Genius of the Shore," Sabrina "underwent a quick immortal change and was / Made Goddess of the River" (841–42); she dispenses precious healing liquors and carols at shepherds' festivals (847–49): "She can unlock / The clasping charm and thaw the numbing spell, / If she be right invok't in warbled Song" (852–54). Poetry relieves the burden of experience; its charm and spell ease the "hard-besetting need" (857) of mortality. Such comforting means the Attendant Spirit undertakes: "This will I try / And add the power of some adjuring verse" (857–58). To poetry as Orphic and poetry as memory, the Attendant Spirit adds poetry as incantation, thus moving from the past to the present and future. He intones: "Listen and save" (866); "Listen and appear to us" (867); "Listen and save" (889). Within his conjuration the Attendant Spirit invokes several sirens (Parthenope and Ligea) which translate Comus' sirens (253). The poetic strategy of such translation will be examined more fully in the next section of this essay.

It has not previously been emphasized that Milton's mythopoetic power here includes the positing of Sabrina as a present and future mythological figure, a new element in the audience's memory bank, or that the basis of the poetry here shifts to incantation, or that Sabrina's action allows for a representation of nature as redeemed as well as redeeming. The time evidence attached to Sabrina clarifies the point and the pattern. Having answered the invocation to "Listen and save," Sabrina rises and sings. Like so much of the action and themes in *Comus*, she rises out of the natural, even geographical context. Poetically, like so much else in the masque, her listening is transformed into her song, recalling previous meditation and poetic aspiration. Her announced presence, her affirmed identity ("I am here," 901), and her music break the spell of the experiential Comus. When she steps from her "sliding Chariot" (892), her footsteps are "printless" (897). Her form is at once a natural emanation and an ethereal effect. She represents nature and nature transcended.[15] Spatially, when Sabrina again descends, the Lady reenacts her previous movement by rising to show that what Sabrina signifies has been incarnated in the Lady. Sabrina is invoked through incantation and dismissed in blessing. The dismissal incorporates an annual natural cycle also blessed: the "brimmed waves" (924) of spring that follow the melting of winter snows (927), "Summer drouth" (928), and the mud of "wet *October's* torrent flood" (930). As in the Attendant Spirit's epilogue, the scene moves through a sequence of natural and chronological details, redeeming and looking beyond nature and time, in this case toward the "Groves of myrrh and cinnamon" (937). The Lady's nature too is redeemed and transcended through the encounter with Sabrina. As Barber says of the episode: "Such is the power of the masque, in Milton's hands, to reach out and find, transformed, what, if embraced, is already there" (p. 63). Barber observes elsewhere that Milton here

presents the possibility of destructive [sexual] release, and meets it by another sort of release, the release of the imagination carried by rhythm out and up to other objects of love. This alternative release is in its way physical, and so can work to counter that which Comus offers. For poetry and song *are* physical. (P. 60)

In the wake of Sabrina's appearance and through the guidance of the Attendant Spirit, the Bridgewater children are redeemed and transcend the "cursed place" (939) in favor of the "holier ground" (943) of their "Father's residence" (947). "While Heaven lends us grace" (938) specifies the Christian context in which the action is to be read. We find ourselves in the allegorical continuum. The country dancers at Ludlow Castle enact the harmony of redeemed nature that counters the earlier antimasque of Comus' rout of monsters. Their rustic dance gives way to the courtly dancing first devised by Mercury (963), then to the Bridgewater children who "triumph in victorious dance / O'er sensual Folly and Intemperance" (974–75). The inaugural ball ends with the Attendant Spirit's epilogue and transcendence.

Nature and nature redeemed are the terms on which *A Mask* concludes, and nature is redeemed through acts of memory and imagination. Nature as so often in literature and philosophy, grounds art. In a context where grace is possible, nature places and replaces Comus' idol, nature as experience. The masque offers clarified, undeluded, human and poetic vision and teaches its audience to see—to look, for example, at a local river and apprehend not geography and topography, but resonance, personification, the mythopoetic. Sabrina is an analogue of the genius of the shore in *Lycidas;* if the audience will accept the opportunity, they can know and incarnate memory, imagination, and grace. They need weep no more, if they will meditate the Muse.

V

The Attendant Spirit begins by descending and concludes by reascending, and the spatial pattern is from divine to human, heavenly to earthly, idea to matter, transcendence to experience—followed by the reversals of these pairings. It is a ladder also of music and light. As the Attendant Spirit answers Spenser's question—"And is there care in heaven?" (*The Faerie Queene*, II, viii, 1)—so the Lady figures forth the test of mortal consent to aspiration that is also spiritual self-definition. The Attendant Spirit's epilogue confirms the pattern of aspiration and imaginative spiritual exercise for the audience and the audience's thematic and artistic interpretation of the masque. In the process he recurs to a verbal pattern that deserves special notice as a characteristically Miltonic poetic strategy. That pattern may be labeled "translation," by which I mean both the idea of transcendence and the transfer of a basic concept from one verbal medium to another. The conclusion of the Lady's song to Echo plays directly and indirectly upon the two denotations: "Sweet Queen of Parley, Daughter of the Sphere, / So mayst thou be translated to the skies, / And give resounding grace to all Heav'n's Harmonies" (241–43).[16] Such translation epitomizes the artistic practice and the thematic interpretation of *A Mask* and thus conclusively defines the roles of poet and audience.

The Attendant Spirit enacts and describes a concluding sequence of nature redeemed. He departs to those realms "Where day never shuts his eye" (978), to the element of "liquid air" (980)—not just elemental, geographical water—to the gardens of "jocund Spring" (985) and "eternal Summer" (988) where true "bounties" (987) translate Comus' misguided fertility, to the "bow'd welkin" (1015) which, like the Attendant Spirit dressed again in Iris' woof, bends to join heaven and earth at the western horizon, "the green earth's end" (1014). The Attendant Spirit thus represents his climb to the highest describable rung of the allegorical continuum and looks beyond it.

As the Attendant Spirit withdraws from the "pinfold" of earth to the Platonic realms of Ocean, "Gardens fair / Of *Hesperus*" (981–82) where "eternal Summer dwells" (988), he parenthetically reminds the audience to heighten its imagination to apprehend the poetry that rewards with truth: "(List mortals, if your ears be true)" (997). The line is a marginal insertion in the Trinity manuscript and, as Carey notes, a "warning that the following lines are not to be taken as mere mythological decoration" (p. 227). The Attendant Spirit proceeds through a series of images and echoes that confirm the distinction between Comus' proposals and his own, those of *A Mask* itself, and that again exercise the audience's judgment and allegiance. Concern with place shifts to concern with persons and their relationship:

> Beds of *Hyacinth* and Roses
> Where young *Adonis* oft reposes,
> Waxing well of his deep wound

> In slumber soft, and on the ground
> Sadly sits th' *Assyrian* Queen.   (998–1002)

Venus/Aphrodite is invoked by an epithet whose connotations transcend earthly passion. Comparing Milton's scene with Spenser's Garden of Adonis, A. S. P. Woodhouse concisely sets forth the hierarchical dimensions of the figure: "In classic myth and its elaborations one recognizes three different roles assigned to Venus: she is the goddess of wanton love . . . she is the great mother, a principle of generation in all things; and she is the celestial Venus, the symbol of intellectual or spiritual love."[17] Like other figures in *A Mask*, Venus participates in an allegorical continuum. Here that continuum invites, even demands, audience recognition of the possibility of translation, one of several tests of audience participation in and realization of the matter the masque has presented. Dismissing the Ludlow audience to its Shropshire rest, the allusion emphasizes healing, quietude, sobriety. The deity and her context reverse Comus' earlier introductory rouse: "What hath night to do with sleep? / Night hath better sweets to prove, / *Venus* now wakes, and wak'ns Love" (122–24). The masque has brought the audience to participate in the Attendant Spirit's translation, in his vision soaring above experience into the realm of faith. But it simultaneously has recognized the fact, the necessity, the limitations, and the poetic usefulness of interrelating fiction and themes. Such translation and poetic participation are also acts of moral choice and spiritual definition, of mediated vision, of poetry.

A similar reversal, though more direct and more expansive, occurs in the image with which the Attendant Spirit continues his epilogue:

> But far above in spangled sheen
> Celestial *Cupid* her fam'd son advanc't,
> Holds his dear *Psyche* sweet entranc't
> After her wand'ring labors long,
> Till free consent the gods among
> Make her his eternal Bride,
> And from her fair unspotted side
> Two blissful twins are to be born,
> Youth and Joy; so *Jove* hath sworn.   (1003–11)

That the Attendant Spirit's Cupid is as "celestial" as an earlier Cupid was "frivolous" (445) concisely stresses the point of translation and contrasting epistemologies. Similarly, the Attendant Spirit's invocation of bliss contrasts with Comus' phrases—"in mutual and partak'n bliss" (741) and "Beyond the bliss of dreams" (813). Coming as it does at the conclusion of a carefully structured allegorical continuum, the invocation of Psyche cannot fail to include the Lady of the masque, whose wandering and trial and ceremonial reward and reunion have supplied the action/ passion of the dramatic performance just witnessed. Apuleius' Psyche bore the daughter Pleasure. Milton bifurcates Psyche's offspring into "Youth and Joy," precisely the basis of Comus' repeated appeals, but here translated into the redeemed language of innocence, virtue, aspiration, transcendence. An unpersonified Psyche and Cupid and twins occur in Milton's *Apology for Smectymnuus*—a generally accepted prose gloss on *A Mask*—when he speaks of learning lessons "of chastity and love . . . and how the first and chiefest office of love begins and ends in the soul, producing those happy twins of her divine generation, knowledge and virtue" (Hughes, p. 694). Love, knowledge, and virtue are crucially misunderstood and misrepresented on Comus' lips. When Comus speaks of "the virtue of this Magic dust" (165), he describes virtue shorn of its numinosity; for Comus love is what is wakened with Venus (124), and chastity is merely the target for his art and glozing. The Attendant Spirit's translation includes the audience's memory of both the literary-mythological tradition and the preceding text of *A Mask*.

In the *Apology for Smectymnuus*, a reference to Circe makes explicit the contrasting realms that the Attendant Spirit mediates and translates for his audience. Speaking parenthetically of chastity and love, Milton asserts: "I mean that which is truly so, whose charming cup is only virtue, which she bears in her hand to those who are worthy—the rest are cheated with a thick intoxicating potion which a certain sorceress, the abuser of love's name, carries about" (Hughes, p. 694). The Lady in *Comus* is among the worthy who drink of virtue's cup, as the angels in *Paradise Lost* "Quaff immortality and joy." She is not among "the rest" who are cheated and abused, for she does not accept confinement to the "pinfold" of experience and mere physical nature, at the expense of faith, memory, and imagination. *Castitas* and *caritas* are the names for love when it is not abused.

Virtue is the note on which *A Mask* ends and is its principal lesson. The word itself asserts verbal disjunction when measured against Comus' usage (165). It also reintroduces the allegorical continuum:

> Mortals that would follow me,
> Love virtue, she alone is free,
> She can teach ye how to climb
> Higher than the Sphery chime;

Or if Virtue feeble were,
Heav'n itself would stoop to her.   (1018–23)

"Stoop" in the final line of *A Mask* takes us back to the Attendant Spirit's and *A Mask's* opening line, reemphasizing the rhythm of the descent of grace and the ascent of the worthy, the "graceful." In Tuve's words:

We have imaged before us in the entire piece the greater beauty, superior reasonableness, and the naturalness, of all that we can lodge within the insufficient word *Virtue* . . . and imaged also all the dark perversions that can betray it—disorder, intemperance, voluptuous self-love, *libertin* naturalism, the beast in its relation to the beauty. 'Imaged'—that is, we see what things look like; and see the real not behind the apparent but in the apparent. [18]

"Virtue" in line 1019 is that principle, spiritual quality, and agency whose cup the Lady in *A Mask* and the worthy in *Smectymnuus* have drunk and whose refreshment is edification, aspiration, freedom, spiritual community and reward. But "virtue" in line 1022 is these principles and processes as embodied in the fragile, mortal traveler whose trial the audience has witnessed and shared—to the extent, that is, that we too have allowed ourselves to be guided both spiritually and poetically by the Attendant Spirit and have allowed our experience to be translated into faith, our travels and travails into aspiration.

Allegory and poetry in *Comus*, then, are matters of setting, character, structure, and theme; they are also a matter of image and word. In all dimensions, the letter killeth, but the spirit giveth life. The operative vitalizing spirit is a function of the Christian capacity for the New Dispensation, but also the audience's or reader's capacity for imaginative poetic participation, for aspiration and enlightenment, for judgment, memory, and translation. Poetry is a or the redemptive energy and process. Comus is the grandson of the sun, a derivative of the sun as it measures the world of time and as it fosters physical life. The Lady is the heir of the "greater Sun" (Nativity Ode, 83), the Logos, the creating and redeeming Word that came to earth, that she and all might have life and have it more abundantly. Sun/son concisely sets forth the contrast of experience and faith and the consequent need for creative Christian translation. Like Christ and mankind, in the words of *Paradise Lost*, the Lady is a "divine similitude." I am not the first to observe that all poems are in an important sense about the making of poetry. I have tried to show that this observation, appropriate to all Milton's poetry, is a particularly apt description of the explicit and implicit action of *Comus*.

University of Massachusetts, Amherst

NOTES

1. *The Veil of Allegory: Some Notes Toward a Theory of Allegorical Rhetoric in th English Renaissance* (Chicago, 1969), p. 55. The summary which follows relies on Murrir especially chapter 3. Angus Fletcher, one of the most provocative students of both *Comu* and allegory, would seem an inevitable source of frequent citation for the following stud) My uses of *transcendent* include a debt to his *The Transcendental Masque: An Essay o Milton's "Comus"* (Ithaca, 1971), but his theories of allegory, in *Allegory: The Theory of Symbolic Mode* (Ithaca, 1964), develop from bases different from Murrin's and my own Further, Fletcher does not consider *Comus* to be allegorical (*The Transcendental Masque* p. 175).

2. *Milton and the Modern Critics* (rpt. Ithaca, 1966), p. 1.

3. "A Mask Presented at Ludlow Castle: The Masque as a Masque," in *The Lyri* *and Dramatic Milton*, ed. Joseph H. Summers (New York, 1965), pp. 48–49.

4. *Images and Themes in Five Poems by Milton* (Cambridge, Mass., 1962), pp. 120 143, 119.

5. All quotations from Milton's poetry and prose are from *John Milton: Complete Poems and Major Prose*, ed. Merritt Y. Hughes (New York, 1957).

6. Robert Graves, *The Greek Myths* (Baltimore, 1966), I, pp. 63–67.

7. *Pagan Mysteries in the Renaissance* (rpt. New York, 1968), p. 122.

8. I quote from the convenient *A Variorum Commentary on the Poems of John Milton*, Vol. II, Part III, *The Minor English Poems*, ed. A. S. P. Woodhouse and Douglas Bush (New York, 1972), p. 786, though the passage is available elsewhere.

9. *The Harmonious Vision: Studies in Milton's Poetry* (Baltimore, 1954), pp. 29, 40, 32.

10. *Milton* (rpt. London, 1956), pp. 67, 70, 68.

11. On what he calls "The Principle of Echo" in *Comus*, see Fletcher, *The Transcendental Masque*, chap. 6, especially pp. 198–209.

12. In *Allegory*, Fletcher follows Ernest Jones's study of *Hamlet* in describing this process as decomposition (taking place when, in the creation of character, "various attributes are invented each endowed with one group of the original attributes"); it occurs, in Fletcher's own words, "when a main character of an allegory generates more than one double for himself, when he is fractionated into a number of other partial characters" (pp. 59, 195). In *Dark Conceit: The Making of Allegory* (New York, 1966), Edwin Honig links the process to dream artifice: "It keeps a realizable purpose alive by dramatizing the dominant sanctions and forms with which the hero must keep in touch. . . . Typifying the procedure is a guiding, usually beneficent intelligence that impels and even shares the hero's consciousness. Sometimes it is that part of divinity present in each man, or it is the corrective effects which reason and imagination can have upon the consciousness" (pp. 78, 197 n.).

13. *The Poems of John Milton*, ed. John Carey and Alastair Fowler (New York, 1968), p. 207. Carey notes also that in Browne's *Inner Temple Masque* (128), "Circe uses moly as a charm to banish sleep from Ulysses" (p. 207). Haemony has been the occasion of much divergent interpretation, including John Steadman's view that it signifies knowledge or divine philosophy ("Milton's Haemony: Etymology and Allegory," *PMLA*, LXXVII [1962], 200–07) and Sears Jayne's similar approach ("The Subject of Milton's Ludlow Mask," in *A Maske at Ludlow: Essays on Milton's Comus*, ed. John S. Diekhoff [Cleveland, 1968], p. 177). Richard Neuse equates Haemony with "the pastoral spirit of humility," in "Metamorphosis and Symbolic Action in *Comus*," rpt. in *Critical Essays on Milton from "ELH"* (Baltimore, 1969), p. 91. Neuse's essay views the masque as Milton's "first publicly avowed

commitment to the career of a poet" (p. 89), but explores poetry in senses quite different from my own. See especially pp. 101–02.

14. See, for example, Carey's *Poems*, p. 206. For an opposing view, see Adams, *Milton and the Modern Critics*, p. 12.

15. On Sabrina's relation to nature, see Neuse, "Metamorphosis," pp. 95–96. Neuse also traces a pattern of harvest festival (Michaelmas) throughout *Comus* (pp. 97–98), though his evidence does not include lines 923–30, which I discuss below.

16. In the Bridgewater manuscript line 243 begins "And hould a Counterpoint," a phrase altered in the margin of the Trinity manuscript to the present reading. Carey notes that line 243 is "the only alexandrine in *Comus*, mimicking the lengthening of heaven's song by echo" (p. 188).

17. "The Argument of Milton's *Comus*," rpt. in *Maske*, ed. Diekhoff, p. 37. Woodhouse compares Milton's use of the Cupid and Psyche myth with Spenser's on pp. 38–40, as does Tillyard on pp. 45–46 of the same volume. See also pp. 56–57. The lines on Adonis and Venus and on Cupid and Psyche are missing from the Bridgewater manuscript, but appear in the Trinity manuscript. In *Poems*, Carey supplies extensive notes on the backgrounds of Adonis and Psyche. In *Pagan Mysteries*, Wind discusses the composite figure of Venus/Virgo in the *Aeneid* (p. 77) and comments on Venus as a goddess of moderation (p. 119). See also chap. 8, especially pp. 138–39. Wind views Psyche's ordeals to regain Amor as stages of mystical initiation (pp. 175–76); he cites Plotinus' reading of Amor and Psyche as follows (p. 59):

That the Good is Yonder, appears by the love which is the soul's natural companion . . . so that both in pictures and in fables Eros and the Psyche make a pair. Because she is of God's race, yet other than God, she cannot but love God. Whilst she is Yonder she knows the Heaven-passion. . . . But when she enters into generation . . . then she likes better another and a less enduring love. . . . Yet learning afterwards to hate the wanton dealings of this place, she journeys again to her father's house, when she has purified herself of earthly contacts, and abides in well-being.

18. *Images and Themes*, p. 143. For additional commentary on the significance of "*virtue*," see Adams, *Milton and the Modern Critics*, pp. 28–29. Adams takes Brooks and Hardy to task for overemphasizing the word's importance.